States of Dispossession

THE ETHNOGRAPHY OF POLITICAL VIOLENCE

Tobias Kelly, Series Editor

A complete list of books in the series is
available from the publisher.

States of Dispossession

Violence and Precarious Coexistence
in Southeast Turkey

Zerrin Özlem Biner

UNIVERSITY OF PENNSYLVANIA PRESS

PHILADELPHIA

Published by
University of Pennsylvania Press
Philadelphia, Pennsylvania 19104–4112
www.upenn.edu/pennpress

Printed in the United States of America on acid-free paper
10 9 8 7 6 5 4 3 2 1

Library of Congress Cataloging-in-Publication Data
Names: Biner, Zerrin Özlem, author.
Title: States of dispossession : violence and precarious coexistence in
    southeast Turkey / Zerrin Özlem Biner.
Other titles: Ethnography of political violence.
Description: 1st edition. | Philadelphia : University of Pennsylvania
    Press, [2020] | Series: Ethnography of political violence | Includes
    bibliographical references and index.
Identifiers: LCCN 2019032795 | ISBN 978-0-8122-5175-3 (hardcover)
Subjects: LCSH: Political violence—Turkey. | Violence—Turkey. |
    Ethnic conflict—Turkey. | Land tenure—Turkey. | War and society—
    Turkey. | Turkey—Social conditions—21st century.
Classification: LCC HN656.5.Z9 V527 2020 | DDC 303.609561—dc23
LC record available at https://lccn.loc.gov/2019032795

For Manuel,
and for Ruya Luanda and Irene Mara
for the freedom to write

CONTENTS

Preface   ix

Introduction   1

Chapter 1. Cementing the Past with the Future:
       The Materiality of Stone and Concrete   33

Chapter 2. Ruined Heritage   62

Chapter 3. Digging with the Jinn   82

Chapter 4. Living as if Indebted   101

Chapter 5. Beneath the Wall Surrounding the Mor Gabriel Monastery   131

Chapter 6. Loss, Compensation, and Debt   149

Epilogue   171

Notes   193

References   203

Index   221

Acknowledgements   231

This book is about the forms of life as experienced, imagined, and produced under the protracted conflict between the PKK (Partiya Karkeren Kurdistane, the Kurdistan Workers' Party) and the Turkish state. The book is bounded by a particular time (2001–2015) and space (southeast Turkey). The time frame is not arbitrary; it corresponds to a moment of suspended temporality. This interval of time-space coincided with the end of the state of emergency[1] (*olağanüstü hal*, abbreviated OHAL in Turkish), intensive military conflict, the instigation of long and short-term cease-fires, and the proliferation of democratization packages and peace talks. During this extraordinary window of time, my aim was to understand the historical and political modes of coexistence practiced by Kurds, Arabs, and Syriacs (*Süryaniler*) as they waited for and attempted to craft the emergence of peace in a border province of southeast Turkey. Specifically, I sought to understand the forms of political subjectivity and the modes of state power at the margins of the Turkish state, margins not only in the sense of geographical location but also in the sense of the borderline flux between normalcy and emergency, continuity and disruption, order and disorder (Das and Poole 2004). The suspended temporality I refer to came to an end. The book closes with fragmented accounts of the violence that resumed in July 2015, the latest phase in the war between the PKK and the Turkish state. The final chapter is composed of what I call after Michael Taussig (1992) "terror's talk"; talk that reveals the dissolution and destruction of hopes, promises, imaginations, expectations, and attempts to establish a good life.

During this period of suspended temporality between the years of 2001 and 2015, I moved between the cities, towns, and villages that lie in the border province of Mardin[2] (Figure 1) and the towns and cities of the regions' diasporic communities in Germany and Sweden. As peace trickled into the region, I followed the traces of absent communities, particularly Syriacs[3], and documented their attempts to prepare for a full-fledged return to their

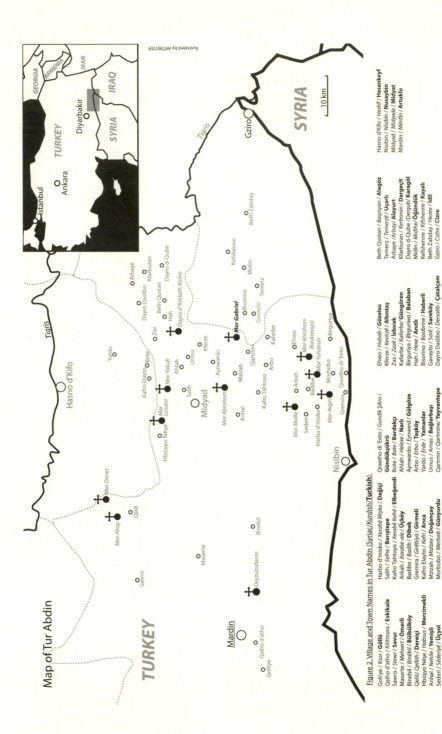

Figure 1. The Tur Abdin region. Map by Miro Kaygalak.

Illustrated by ARTBEITER

Map of Tur Abdin

TURKEY

SYRIA

IRAQ

IRAN

ARMENIA

GEORGIA

İstanbul

Ankara

Diyarbakır

SYRIA

10 km

Mardin

Gollîye

Qalho d'atho

Sawro

Masḗrte

Deyrulzafaran

Binebil

Mor Abay

Qelît

Mor Dimet

Hasno d'Kifo

Yardo

Kafro Elayto

Hbûşyo Nêşe

Mor Lôzor

Mor Yakub

Salîh

Midyad

Mor Abrohom

Arnah

Kafro Tahtoyo

Atbo

Mzizah

Qartmin

Aynwardo

Urmus

Kferze

Hah

Zaz

Beth Qustan

Dayro Daslibo

Kfarburan

Dayro d-Qube

Dayro d'Yoldath Aloho

Bisorino

Gavayto

Temerz

Kafarbe

Arkah

Badıbe

Mor Abrohom
(Kaskonoyo)

Mor Yuhanun

Mor Gabriel

Birguriya

Ehwo

Mor Avgin

Harbo d'misko

Gremira

Qreetho di 'Eeto

Sederî

Mor Malke

Nisibin

Kfarbe

Midin

Kefshenne

Beth Zabday

Gziro

Tigris

Tigris

SYRIA

Figure 2. Village and Town Names in Tur Abdin (Syriac/Kurdish/**Turkish**)

Gollîye / Ksar / **Gölii̇ü**
Qalho d'atho / Kilitmora / **Eskikale**
Sawro / Stewr / **Savur**
Masêrte / Mehsert / **Ömerli**
Binebil / Binêbil / **Bülbülköy**
Qelith / **Dereiçi**
Hbûşyo Nêşe / Habsus / **Mercimekli**
Arnah / Nehle / **Yemişli**
Sederî / Sêderiyê / **Uçyol**

Harbo d'misko / Xerabê Mişka / **Dağiçi**
Salih / Selhe / **Barıştepe**
Kafro Tahtoyo / Xerabê Kefrê / **Elbeğendi**
Arkah / Xarabe-aîe / **Üçköy**
Badıbe / Badıb / **Dibek**
Gremira / Girêbiya / **Girmeli**
Kafro Elayto / Kefrî / **Arıca**
Mzizah / Mizzex / **Doğançay**
Morbobo / Merbab / **Günyurdu**

Qreetho di 'Eeto / Gundik Şikro
Gündükşükrü
Bote / Bate / **Bardakçı**
Ahlah / Helexe / **Narlı**
Aynwardo / Eynwerd / **Gülgöze**
Arbo / Erbo / **Taşköy**
Yardo / Erde / **Yamanlar**
Urmus / Arnas / **Sarıköy**
Qartmin / Qartmine/**Yayvantepe**

Ehwo / Habab / **Güzelsu**
Kferze / Kevizê / **Altıntaş**
Zaz / Zazê / **İzbırak**
Kafarbe / Kafarbe/ **Güngören**
Birguriya / Birguriwa / **Balaban**
Hah / Hexe / **Anıtlı**
Bisorino / Basibrine / **Haberli**
Gavayto / Sarê / **Sarıköy**
Dayro Daslibo / Dersalib / **Çatalçam**

Beth Qustan / Baqisyan / **Alagöz**
Temerz / Temezê / **Uçarlı**
Arbaye / Arbay/ **Alayurt**
Kfarburan / Kerboran / **Dargeçit**
Dayro d-Qube /Derqub/ **Karagöl**
Midin / Midihe/ **Öğündük**
Kefshenne / Kifshenne / **Kayalı**
Beth Zabday / Hezex / **İdil**
Gziro / Cizîre / **Cizre**

Hasno d'Kifo / Heskîf / **Hasankeyf**
Nisibin / Nisibin / **Nusaybin**
Midyad / Midyade/ **Midyat**
Mardin / Mêrdîn / **Artuklu**

villages. I had come to listen to their fears of encountering their old neighbors and needing to coexist with them. Each time I returned to the city of Mardin, another fragment of buried history surfaced. For as the city became the canvas for a stunning array of heritage, tourism, restoration, and art projects, questions lingered about the number and identity of the dead, both past and present. And along with it all came an assortment of other life projects: reparation, restoration, and destruction of the built environment; desire for sudden enrichment; legal and extralegal contests over the confiscation and possession of land; attempts to receive compensation for material loss; and desperate efforts to escape from material and immaterial debts— ideally by sudden enrichment. My concern was to shed light on the complexity of life in the post-emergency period, the aftermath of a fifteen-year-long (1984–1999) intensive military conflict between the PKK and the Turkish Armed Forces.

Violent Peace

The post-emergency period in the Kurdish region took the form of a "violent peace" (Visweswaran 2013) fraught with unilateral cease-fires, peace talks, and their failures. Peace was the abstract and intangible condition between the state and its Kurdish citizens. The declaration of every democratization package preceded the emergence of a new exception (Agamben 1998, 2005) that continually shifted the threshold between legal and illegal, insider and outsider. In this political environment, the post-emergency period witnessed the enactment of the Repentance Laws (Pişmanlik Yasasi) for PKK guerrillas, a symbolic performative return of PKK guerrillas crossing the border and entering Turkey as emblematic of the peace process; the murder of civilians in the village of Bilge (Zangirt in Kurdish) caught in a cross fire among the village guards; the slaughter in the village of Roboskî of thirty-seven villagers in an air strike carried out by the Turkish Air Force.

In the meantime, vast amounts of cash were channeled into reparation, restoration, and infrastructure projects, including heritage-making ventures, archaeological excavations, establishment of new universities, dam and airport construction, the opening of two-lane highways, and massive housing projects in the region. Urban life prospered with cafes, restaurants, hotels, shopping malls, and new gated neighborhoods. Local NGOs run by the provincial governments and municipalities run by the pro-Kurdish parties also thrived.

In the midst of this new generation of locals, there was a boom in lawyers; architects; and civil engineers who returned to start up businesses in their hometowns. In the context of Mardin, this group constituted the core of the middle and upper-middle class, attracting and producing the real cash in the city. They were the main consumers of the amenities of the urban lifestyle. Furthermore, in the post-emergency era, Mardinites were busy devising projects having to do with visual art, documentary filmmaking, oral history collection, handicrafts, and local wine production. The film festivals, the Mardin Bienal (biennial) art exhibitions in the stone buildings, fashion shows in the old madrasas were highlighted on touristic itineraries that wound their way through the city. Residents, visitors and tourists from outside the region continued to produce and consume the artistic, historic, and touristic spaces despite the city's close proximity to war zones in the Kurdish region of Syria and Iraq.

Beginning in 2011, there was a continuous flow of Syrian refugees into the city. In 2014, Yazidis who had escaped the Islamic State of Iraq and Syria (ISIS) were settled in the province's towns and refugee camps. Few locals in Mardin were preoccupied with discussions as to whether the city would still be considered a safe zone after the arrival of the Yazidis or whether they should postpone the Bienal exhibition and send the international artists home. In a few weeks' time, on September 6 and 7, 2014, people were out on the streets in Mardin and elsewhere in the region protesting against the government for having blocked military support for Kurds fighting against ISIS in Kobane, Northern Syria. Over the course of the next three days, fifty people were killed, among them PKK militants, members of the Turkish security forces, civilian passersby, members of the far-right Islamist Free Cause Party (Hür Dava Partisi) and the Nationalist Movement Party (Milliyetçi Hareket Partisi).

All these events took place as milestones in the zone between war and peace. They produced terror's talk that both revealed and concealed the effects of violence while fixing the meaning and covering over the murkiness that emerged from the indistinguishableness between normality and emergency. Despite all this, it was the violent peace that allowed openness, accessibility, and the movement of ideas, practices, and people. It was the violent peace that allowed the performance and production of the political for the possibility of other forms of life.

Over the course of more than a decade, my visits to Mardin were awash in uncanny entanglements of urgency, emergency, humanitarian disaster, and touristic projects. Across that decade, I continued to ask a series of questions. What did multicultural, multireligious life mean in this violent environment? Who was recognized as part of this form of life? More significantly, how do we conceptualize life in a place affected by *unfinished* cycles of violence? What do we make of the divisions and connections that violence creates in spaces of interethnic and interreligious relationship? How do we explore and identify the means through which ruined subjects, places, and ideals become intimately bound up and thereby continuously transform each other?

Public Secrets

In the beginning, 2001 it was, I traveled between Kurdish towns and villages to get a sense of the current situation and, more important, to understand the conditions necessary for long-term ethnographic work in the region. "Long-term" meant little when people were used to receiving visitors for short stays. "Long-term" meant little when they were not sure what might await them the next day. The sudden end of the conflict was suspect. The sudden disappearance of the guerrillas was odd. Where had they disappeared to? Walking down the long main streets of heavily militarized Kurdish villages and towns, it was impossible not to be at once haunted and thrilled by the negative energy released from the silent stares of the local people: the civil police, the head of the village guard (*korucubaşı*), secretly returned guerrilla fighters, newly appointed elementary school teachers, shepherds, butchers, all of them waiting for things to happen.

The atmosphere was different in the city of Mardin, central district of the province. It was the only "mixed" (*karışık*) city in the region, with a population of Muslim Arabs, Kurds, and Christian Syriacs. It was the only mixed city where people would switch between three languages—Arabic, Kurdish, and Turkish—depending upon the socioeconomic setting. It was the only mixed city where people would recognize the identity of others based on their style of dress, neighborhood, language, and name. I was convinced that any ethnographic account of the post-emergency process would be inadequate if it did not include the heterogeneous, contradictory, and intertwined narratives of subjects from different ethnic and religious backgrounds. Accessing the accounts of Arabs and Syriacs would lead to a better understanding of the historical and political contingencies that have shaped the relationships between the citizens and the state at its margins.

In 2001, the city of Mardin was regarded by the Kurds as the city of Arabs. Kurds from the surrounding towns kept their distance, while Mardinite Kurds felt like a minority in the city. This was unrelated to demographic data. There is no evidence to support the belief that Arabs are the majority in Mardin. From the standpoint of the Arabs and Syriacs—who refer to themselves as the city's natives (*yerli*)—the city had not participated in the challenge to state sovereignty; in contrast to the other Kurdish towns, life in Mardin had been tranquil during the conflict. "We witnessed so many things, but we were never part of them" was the perennial claim of the local Arabs, underscoring their submission to the state and their non-involvement in the so-called terror events (*terör olayları*). They were being misrepresented and mistreated on account of Kurdish separatism. They were loyalist because, it was explained to me, they were *conscious* citizens (*bilinçli vatandaşlar*). This consciousness required not only a refusal to ally with separatist groups but also the will to keep the Pandora's box of the city closed and not give its secrets away. This, in turn, was contingent on obedience to the tacit city rule locally known as the three *làà* (*làà* meaning "not" in Arabic): not done, not seen, not heard.

Like their Muslim Arab neighbors, the fifty to sixty families of the Syriac Christian community knew that life conditions in Mardin required them to keep their knowledge of the past within the community and not reveal it publicly. Despite being publicly invisible, they believed themselves to be the original (*orijinal*) inhabitants of the city, knowing not only the place's true history but also the people's true history. They knew what those from other communities seemed to have forgotten about their past.

Rooted in the 1915 massacres—Sayfo (sword in Aramaic) they called it—the Syriac community's implicit knowledge of cosmopolitan life in Mardin hinged on the memory of massacres, conversions, displacements, confiscations, evacuations, and redistributions of the objects and property of their people. Their accounts of 1915 did not include descriptions of the massacre and displacement of Armenians, who were also residents of Mardin at the time.[4] They focused solely on the experience of Syriacs. The presence of five Armenian families who were already mixed with Syriacs through marriage did not deserve mention. In their view, Syriacs alone had borne the brunt of being Christian, for which they had been subjected to atrocities carried out by their Muslim neighbors and endorsed by the Ottoman state.

The Syriacs had been the only Christian community not entitled to the rights afforded to other non-Muslim minority subjects under guarantee of the Lausanne Treaty. The common explanation is that after long negotiations with state authorities, the representatives of the Syriac community dropped their request to be awarded minority status because their aim was not to be treated as a minority, but as Turks. Their submission to the state's will did not therefore guarantee them protection under the law. They were continuously subject to harassment and abuse by their Muslim neighbors, and this in turn accelerated the tide of their emigration to foreign lands. Those who stayed on strategically submitted to Mardin's tacit rule of silence. They remained distanced and reserved in their interactions with the Muslim communities and continued their closed lives clustered around and behind the church walls.

The habitual silence of the city had different connotations for the Kurdish subjects. In their view, this was associated with a particular feature of the city. "This is a city of spies," said a Kurdish man, referring to the events he experienced during the 1990s. Spying and the fear of being spied on has been the order of the day in Mardin since the times when the local Arab elites tended to dominate and exclude the Kurds from the city. In his view, the "mixed" or so-called cosmopolitan structure was the reason for the silent and submissive nature of the city. There never was a collective movement in Mardin as there was no trust among the different religious and ethnic groups. Many of his friends had been arrested, having been informed on by people whom they presumed to be from the other communities of the city. The Kurdish neighbourhoods located on the edge of the city were kept under surveillance and the Kurds were subjected to sudden house searches and arrests during the period of emergency. At the beginning of 2000s, the domain of knowledge in Mardin was that of public secrecy (Taussig 1999); this is the form of memory maintained by the Arabs, Syriacs, and Kurds of the 1915 Armenian genocide, the inter-communitarian relationships in its aftermath, the blood feuds between the Kurdish families, the emergencies of the Kurdish conflict.

Taussig defines public secrecy as knowing what not to know and what not to speak. Public secrecy thus stands for a limit case, an outlier that at the point of limitation serves both to reveal and conceal the violent and rupturing effects these historical and political processes have had on their personal and collective histories (59–77). In the early years of the post-emergency era, public secrecy was a necessity for survival in Mardin. Yet it was not a static form of knowledge; necessity meant that it was constantly changing in relation to events, yielding to the many experiences of death, fear of loss, and conformity to new realities (Biner 2010).

Navigating the Delirio

I struggled to find a framework and methodology that would make sense of the many dimensions of public secrecy and that could at the same time handle the fragmented, elusive, and explosive character of this knowledge.[5] In the early days of my fieldwork I tried to understand how people positioned themselves in relation to "critical events" (Das 1997) they chose to recount in order to explain their personal and family histories. These recounted positions were the subject of fiercely contested exchanges between the different communities in post-emergency Mardin. I was haunted by an impossible yet irresistible drive to establish exactly who had been the doers of the deeds. This sense of public secrecy about the doers occupied everyday conversations, determined survival strategies, and shaped the self-imaginary of Mardin's inhabitants. The real Mardinites (*Mardinliler*), I was constantly told during exchanges with Arabs and Syriacs, were the ones who could distinguish the faces behind the masks because they knew one another's origins. For me, the more I heard the stories, the more elusive and impossible capturing the faces behind the masks became. They grew more blurred and fragmented with every hearing, filtered as they were through the multiple and contradictory interpretations recounted by the inhabitants of Mardin. This was also a defining characteristic of the cosmopolitan makeup of the city, where truth for one community was illusion for the other, the limits of secrecy constantly fluctuating without the secrets ever being fully exposed.

Marie Theresa Hernández (2002) insightfully describes this experience as "delirio," a form of madness created by what has been hidden. In her view, delirio is created "when the reality cannot be placed in a coherent and stable location" (206) and "when repeated moments in history are situated in hidden and inaccessible places" (206). Delirio was in the eye of the Mardinites, who constantly faced a fluctuating reality that could not be easily fixed. For me, delirio seemed an apt metaphor when faced with the challenge of being surrounded by contradictory and repeated stories and the murmurs of countless others that remained untold. Many narratives were made up of fragments that were neither stable nor coherent. They were flowing dialogues made of interruptions, stops, and starts, derived from the implicit connections people drew between themes, memories, and places located as much in the past as in the present. In this regard, I also partook in the regimes of public secrecy as an implied condition for my survival as a researcher.

The feeling of delirio was palpable from my first and longest stay in the city of Mardin between 2001 and 2002. I continued making short visits to the city between 2003 and 2006. The political atmosphere was brightening. Narration of the experience of the Kurdish conflict had become less of a taboo. Memories of the 1915 massacres were being publicly circulated. The Kurds felt less marginalized and were gradually becoming more integrated into the economic, political, and social flows of the city. More Kurds were moving into Mardin as consumers of the urban lifestyle that had developed with the advent of heritage-centered tourism projects and the boom in the construction economy. Syriacs traveling home from the diaspora to visit the villages they had left behind had become more visible in the cities and towns. The possibility of their return was part of the political agenda.

In 2007, following the changing frame of the post-emergency period, I strove to push the limits of public secrecy that had been imposed upon my research. This time, I decided to explore the traces of loss and violence by following the Syriacs who had emigrated several decades before. Return became the new theme marking my ongoing research of violence. I traveled to Sweden to speak with Syriacs about their past experiences of life in Turkey, their migration stories, and the conditions for their return to their home villages in the vicinity of Mardin.

The conversations I had with Syriacs in diaspora were of a different nature altogether. The limits of public secrecy were of a different order. In the absence of the interactions and relations of daily life in the villages, they were able to breathe more freely, able to construct themselves through articulated life experiences in Turkey. Their stories revolved around memories of the Sayfo and its aftermath, and their experiences at the beginning of the military conflict of the 1990s that led to their migration and to the dispossession of their property. Living in Sweden for three months yielded many important contacts and conversations about the political and historical background of coexistence between Kurds and Syriacs. Those narratives allowed me to understand the implicit rules of the tribal order that marked the politics of life and death in the region before and during the 1990s conflict between the Turkish state and the PKK.

In 2008, I traveled back to the Syriac villages surrounding the town of Midyat, sixty kilometers away from the city of Mardin (Figure 2), to follow Syriacs from diasporic communities in their attempts to remake their lives in their home villages amid struggles with the state and their Kurdish neighbors. At the same time, I conducted research with displaced Kurdish villagers who were applying to state institutions for compensation for their material losses. This double research experience with communities who had left and those who had stayed behind deepened my understanding of the complex relationships between places, identities, and senses of belonging, as well as the multiple relationships with the state. Working with Syriacs in diaspora taught me how to think about the category of minority through different legal, political, and affective registers and to ascertain their complex position beyond the obvious categories. At another level, it also deepened my connection to and friendship with my interlocutors as a witness to and participant in their lives across different settings. I followed up on their life projects through a number of short visits to Sweden and Germany between 2010 and 2013.

In 2013, I returned to the city of Mardin again, this time with the prospect of studying the connections between the historical stone houses and the locals. The research was another attempt to return to the public secrets of the city and to locate additional tropes with which to capture the traces of the 1915 dispossession of Armenians and their property. The absence of Armenians in the memories and narratives of loss had been disturbing for me. I collected information concerning the long and complex histories of abandoned, confiscated, and appropriated Armenian property that had been left behind.

In 2013, delving into daily practices surrounding the stone houses, I encountered the digger-tenants who spent their time excavating their own property or the property of others hunting for treasure. Engaging with the practice of digging in my research, I encountered the narratives of the *jinn* (spirits, cinler plurol in Turkish), the spiritual beings said to appear in the stone houses. People were digging up houses that had been demarcated by the state as part of the city's cultural heritage. The jinn were appearing at the excavated sites as guardians of the treasure at stake. Mardinities were able to articulate their emotional and material connection to these stone houses

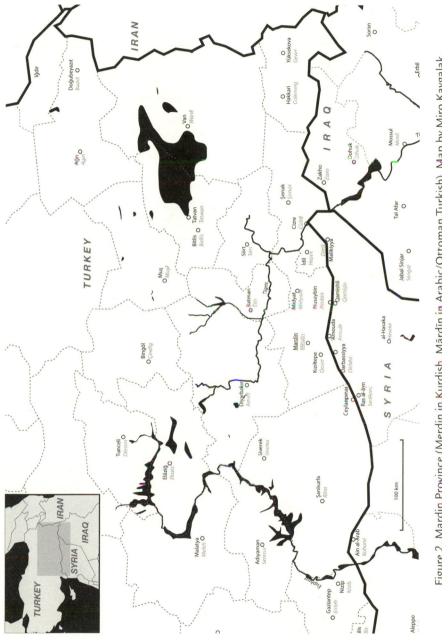

Figure 2. Mardin Province (Merdin in Kurdish, Mārdīn in Arabic/Ottoman Turkish). Map by Miro Kaygalak.

through their attempts to both restore and destroy them as well as through their encounters with the jinn.

In 2015, I made another short trip to the city to visit the Mardin Bienal exhibition. The theme of the exhibition was "Myths," with installations set up in the city's old stone houses, places full of meaning, memory, fear, and hope for many of my interlocutors. That was my last trip before the reacceleration of the conflict between the PKK and the Turkish Armed Forces. In 2017, I managed to return to the city of Mardin for a short visit to get a sense of the place and the people as they were in the wake of major destruction brought on by the last phase of the war that ravaged Kurdish towns and cities.

Throughout this extended period of ethnographic research, my methodology combined participant observation, unstructured and structured interviews, and informal discussions. During the first and longest period of my research in the city of Mardin, I was not allowed to record interviews or take photos. On many of those occasions, the nature of the discussion was such that taking notes was uncomfortable. I therefore reconstructed many of those conversations as retrospective field notes following the encounters. In the later research period, I had the opportunity to record conversations and to take visual images as photos and short films. The possibility of recording was related to context and political contingencies. The increasing visibility of the city of Mardin through the public circulation of images of its urban landscape brought on by tourism- and heritage-centered projects changed the local inhabitants' perception of visibility and normalized visual and aural recordings. By my last visit, it was the excess of violence that had been normalized. The city of Mardin was once again out of the zone of destruction. "Life is quiet in Mardin," reiterated my Arab interlocutors.

My access to knowledge was closely related to the perception and interpretation of my position, which changed significantly throughout the years. My ethnic identity was always the main point of inquiry between me and my interlocutors. Was I Kurdish? Was I Christian? Was I Syriac? Was I from Mardin? Where did my first name, Zerrin, originate? Who was I? Across a timescale of over a decade, I resolutely refused to be identified by any of the familiar categories. Instead, I gave an account of myself through my connections to places and people. No, I was not Kurdish. My grandparents were Kurds from Diyarbakır (Amed) a personal fact I had learned late in life. No, I was not Christian, although I was married to a Chilean man whose presence added another layer to the way I was perceived by my Syriac friends and interlocutors. No, I was not from Mardin. I grew up in İzmir in the western part of Turkey with parents who were originally from the Kurdish region. I was named Zerrin after the mother of my Kurdish grandfather. No, I felt neither Kurdish nor Turkish, and yet I was not a minority, I was often reminded by Syriac friends.

During my time in the city and villages, I stayed with friends and families, at NGOs and association residences, sometimes in hotels. In the first years of my research, my not belonging to any of the regular categories turned me into a spy in the eyes of the Mardinites. I was on occasion asked to leave the houses, the villages, and the city. I left and returned several times. From time to time, I was perceived by my Kurdish friends to be in denial of my essence (öz) as I did not refer to myself as Kurdish despite my "roots" in the region. I was perceived as a secret convert (dönme) by some of my Syriac interlocutors in the city of Mardin; the fact that my father was from Van evoked the suspicion that I might be from an Armenian family forced to convert into Islam. My connection to the United Kingdom and later Germany sometimes provoked those assumptions.

At other times, my insistence on remaining outside the regular categories released the implicit tension that arose from our different experiences and positions as citizens of Turkey. It was that difference that for years made me question my affective, emotional, and political connections, as well as sense of belonging to my habitus of Turkishness. Yet this was not a return to my roots. My returns to the region in effect deracinated me, made me feel ever more distant from the urge to live, and sense of living, within and through identity.

In the meantime, my insistent return to the city and villages changed my position. My outsider stance opened up space for intimate and unexpected conversations with people from different communities. People not only talked about their own lives but also asked about the lives of others. At many points during this long period of punctuated research, I felt myself to be a mediator between *communities*. In Sweden, the terms of belonging and familiarity were different. There, I survived through intimate family connections I discovered late in life, staying with a Syriac Catholic family who had been close friends of cousins of my grandmother in Diyarbakır, a grandmother I have never met. While I remained an outsider, I was a familiar one due to my extended family connections with my hosts.

The use of Turkish as a means of communication had several implications for my research. During my fieldwork, I worked and lived with people who were bilingual and even multilingual. In the city of Mardin, the locals spoke either Kurdish or Arabic or both, together with the official language of Turkish. The Syriacs from the towns and villages around Midyat spoke Turkish and what they call Surayt or Turoyo, a spoken dialect of an eastern neo-Aramaic. The elders also spoke Kurdish and Arabic. Apart from the older generation of Arabic, Syriac and Kurdish women, the majority of the inhabitants spoke Turkish. The use of Turkish led to more difficulties when working with the Syriac communities in diaspora. Syriacs' command of the Turkish language varied according to the speaker's age and the nature of his or her connection to Turkey. The majority of those involved in a personal or collective return project were fluent in Turkish. With my host family in Sweden, the language was not a problem as Turkish was one of their native languages alongside Turoyo, Arabic, and Kurdish. They had a more affective relationship with Turkish as they still have close Turkish and Kurdish friends from their life in Turkey. In the Syriac and Kurdish villages, I asked for the help of my friends or assistants for translation. Even so, in these instances language remained a barrier between us, despite the intimate connections we made and sustained for many years. I accepted that distance without taking its effects for granted and strove to distribute the weight of its inadequacy by exploring and revealing the multiple connections between individuals, communities, and places. Whatever was lost in the travel of ideas, memories, and narratives is of course my own responsibility.

States of Dispossession

INTRODUCTION

November 2001: Bartalı village, Midyat, southeastern Turkey (Figure 2), thirty kilometers from Qamishli, Syria. We are sitting in the house of the *muhtar* (village head). In the 1960s, thirty-two people from this village died while crossing a minefield to smuggle goods to Syria. For hours now, a sociologist friend has been asking the same set of questions of the muhtar, repeating them in different styles of Turkish, in short sentences of Kurdish, in a mixed language of Kurdish and Turkish. Why did so many people die in this village? Was there hostility between the villagers? Who informed on each other? Did they not know about the safer paths in the forbidden zone? What went wrong? The sociologist had a long-standing passion for absorbing the minute details of the lives of citizens living along the border regions of Turkey. I, on the other hand, was a junior friend and young anthropologist, tagging along for the interview in search of a field site where I might study the experience of post-emergency period in the conflict region.

At the time, following the arrest in Nairobi of Abdullah Öcalan, the leader of the Partiya Karkerên Kurdistan (PKK), the military conflict had frozen through a unilateral cease-fire declared by the PKK. This cease-fire would signal the beginning of the end of the decade-and-a-half-long state of emergency imposed over the region by the Turkish state between 1987 and 2002. It was also at this time that the state had begun negotiating its accession into the European Union (EU). As part of these political developments, mobility restrictions were eased in the region, promptly attracting a tidal wave of displaced villagers, human rights activists, policymakers, artists, and EU bureaucrats, as well as journalists who wanted to document what the new era of normalcy and tranquillity looked like on the ground. The jaded sociologist and the young anthropologist were just another pair of souls under a broad umbrella of newcomers. We had landed in the village of Bartalı and had attempted to piece together local histories that were buried under a thick pile of dirt. Why had so many people died? At the time, I failed to understand the relevance of asking why. Had they not simply ventured into a minefield? Why did my friend insist on getting a response other than this self-evident fact?

The muhtar accommodated us with an air of dismissiveness, indifferent to both our questions and our presence. More people joined in the conversation, each responding to the same questions with unrelated fragments from their life or village history. They told us of how they had left the village in the 1990s at the peak of the conflicts between the PKK and the Turkish Armed Forces; how they had escaped to the western part of the country, surviving only by selling cucumbers in the local markets; how the ruins of the early churches were buried at the foundation of the mosque. Hours passed, drinking tea, listening to the stories of newcomers, and reiterating the same line of questioning: Why did they die? Why so many?

It got dark. The curfew was still on, blocking the passage through certain routes at nights. We were stuck, imprisoned in a hostile hospitality, locked into the strangest silence. Then there came the sound of a knock at the door. A moment of relief. A young boy stood up to open it. The soldiers were at the door. They had come to take us to the gendarme station at the entrance of the village. In Bartalı, there were not only Turkish soldiers but also village guards (*korucular*), mostly Kurdish locals recruited by the state to act as local paramilitaries and support the Turkish military against PKK attacks. State employees, these were villagers with a weapon and a regular state salary. The condition of non-evacuation had been dependent on accepting the role of korucu. At first glance, the presence of the korucu was the sign of the complicity of the villagers with the state. But the reality was murkier.

It seems that one of the visitors sitting with us in the house had been the head of the village guard, the korucubaşı. It is he who had informed the local military forces of our unexpected arrival. It was his duty, the muhtar reminded us, offering this as a legitimate excuse for our capture. We were pushed into the military van together with the korucubaşı and four soldiers. A specialized sergeant (*uzman çavuş*) was waiting for us at the gendarme station. What were we doing in this village?

After the ID checks, my friend began crafting a long explanation about the purpose of our visit. We were sociologists doing historical research about old smuggling practices, there to study economic resources and inequalities in the border regions with the aim of contributing to future regional development projects. Development talk was an accepted form of communication about the processes occurring in the region. Development was the remedy for terrorism. The region was undeveloped, underdeveloped, not developed because of the dissidence, resistance, and ignorance of the Kurds. Still, the state would take care of them. This was the state's duty.

As the conversation unfolded, the sergeant found no apparent connections between our curiosities about historical smuggling practices and terrorism, which it was his duty to counter. He was ready to release us. We should be aware, though, he told us, that we were in the middle of the terror zone. There had been a military operation in the village just the previous week. The village was divided between Arabs and Kurds, he explained. Some Kurds had become village guards, fighting against the PKK. Others sheltered PKK guerrillas in their homes. Arabs were switching sides all the time. It was hard to know who was who. We should never have come to this village. For our security, we should stay the night in the station with him and the other soldiers.

My friend declined the offer and asked whether we might return to the house of the muhtar. The sergeant agreed. We were taken back to the same scene of hostile hospitality, the room even more crowded and quieter than before. They had not been expecting us. We had managed to save ourselves from military interrogation, a sign of our intimacy with the bodies of power, a sign of influence that had not previously revealed itself amid our insistent questions.

My friend accepted the offer of a rolled cigarette as the token of the beginning of a new conversation. Before returning to the question of the thirty-two dead people, the muhtar had another request concerning current life projects in the village. The village did not have the infrastructure for running water facilities. They needed jobs with which to earn a living. Perhaps my friend might have suggestions for how to make money with their existing resources. Perhaps she would agree to talk to the provincial governor (*vali*) about their urgent need for water. The vali would listen to her. She had managed to convince the sergeant in the station. My friend talked for hours, explaining to them how to create resources within the village. She stretched her development talk across the village space, from the gendarme station to the house of the muhtar. Her question about the dead was never allowed to return. Its spectre lingered and lurked around the edges of our conversation, answers held tight to the chest by the villagers, who never responded to us. We stayed in the house that night. The next morning, the muhtar told us that we were free to go. We could do whatever we wanted in the village, as long as we did not ask the question of why so many had died. The muhtar's household was busy constructing a new house.

In the afternoon, we left the village. I made my way to the city of Mardin, fifty kilometers away. I had been invited to join a public meeting with United Nations Development Program officers, local NGOs, bureaucrats, and architects from Mardin and Istanbul, including the vali. It was to be a civil society meeting, I was told on the phone by a friend. The main agenda concerned discussion of projects that would help boost Mardin's bid for nomination as a UNESCO World Heritage Site. I was already late for the meeting, trying to prevent my mind from repeating the "terror's talk" (Taussig 1992) of the previous night, talk that had oscillated between a desire for development, a suspicion of the other, and a curiosity for the cause of so many dead.

The vali began his speech by praising the unique and peaceful character of this multicultural city that was home to people of different religions and cultures—Arabs, Turks, Kurds, Jews, Shemsis,[1] Syriac Christians, Yazidis, dead or alive, present or absent. He highlighted the architectural heritage of the city of Mardin as deserving of international protection. Mardin was a distinctive place in Anatolian geography, a jewel in the land of Mesopotamia, an open-air museum. His tone had the real-life incantation of an "affective state" (Stoler 2007), paternalistic and moralistic, entreating Mardinites to be supportive. When it was the mayor's turn to speak, he introduced himself as an ethnic jigsaw puzzle: "My mother is Arabic and my father is Kurdish. So who do you think I am?" He spoke all three local languages, Turkish, Arabic, and Kurdish. The audience responded with sympathetic laughter to his mix of political bravery and cultural generosity. In those days, the use of the Kurdish and Arabic languages was unsafe in Turkey. The mayor's linguistic act was almost circus-like: he was taming these words for the benefit of both local and outside audiences. In his mouth, Mardin became a city of peace and tolerance, faith and stone, a place not tarnished by the surrounding war and the effects of terror. The events—*olaylar* as the conflict was referred to in the 1990s—had taken place on the plain (*ova*) not in the city (*şehir*). As a matter of fact, the trouble was created by Kurds, not Arabs and Syriacs, the conscious citizens (*bilinçli vatandaşlar*).

I did not understand the meaning of all this culture talk. Puzzled by the pretense of a peaceful multicultural life in a small city that had suffered under a state of emergency for over a decade, I also failed to understand the insistent accounts of how the state had protected the city's cultural heritage. I could not then imagine that the development talk that had bridged the worlds of soldiers and villagers in Bartalı would later be replaced by an official desire for a multicultural and multireligious life, an anxiety about ruined cultural heritage, and a rush for the possession of property. Eight years later I would return to Bartalı, this time to talk with the Kurdish villagers about their legal battles with Syriac Christians over the land surrounding the Mor Gabriel Monastery.

States of Dispossession

This book focuses on the violence of the protracted conflict in Southeast Turkey through the lens of dispossession. By definition, the word *dispossession* implies both the act of depriving someone of land, property, and other belongings and the state of such deprivation. In this book, dispossession is used in both modes. Using the term in both the active and passive senses, I refer to practices of dispossession and experiences of being dispossessed. The loss of life, property, and means of livelihood are at the core of the present histories of dispossession. They will be interpreted in connection with imperial and state violence perpetrated through an amalgamation of militarism, neoliberalism, multiculturalism, and tribal order.

To date, social scientists within the fields of Ottoman and contemporary Turkish studies have examined the dispossession of rights and property as a technique for governing territory and those citizens living at its margins. These processes of dispossession have been discussed in relation to the dissolution of the Ottoman Empire and formation and consolidation of the sovereign power of the Turkish state, the construction of the limits of Turkish citizenship and more significantly the implementation of engineering projects that have erased the spaces, bodies, and properties of non-Turkish and non-Muslim citizens. These engineering projects entailed the homogenization of multiethnic and multireligious populations through deportations, exterminations, and displacements (e.g., Dündar 2008; Jongerden 2009; Üngör 2011; Göçek 2014; Kieser et al. 2015; Al-Rustom 2015; Gaunt et al. 2017), through limited recognition of cultural and legal rights of the minority citizens (e.g., Bali 2008; Tambar 2013, 2016; Özgül 2014; Aktar 2014; Iğsız 2015; Ekmekçioğlu 2016), and through confiscation and appropriation of the properties that belong to the non-Muslim communities (e.g., Kurban and Hatemi 2009; Onaran 2010; Üngör and Polatel 2013; Omtzigt et al. 2012; Akçam

and Kurt 2015; Parla and Özgül 2016; Bieberstein 2017). While the consolidation of the Turkish state imposed the process of Turkification of the language, history, and identity, the category of minority (*azınlık*) came to signify
"a process of dispossession—from rights to land, from political status, and
from a sense of belonging" (Tambar 2016:35).

Scholars within the field of Kurdish studies have explored dispossession
in terms of its effects on Kurdish resistance movement within Turkey and its
role in repressive policies that have led to the underdevelopment of the region (e.g., Yadırgı 2017); destruction of urban and rural landscapes and the
displacement of Kurdish villagers (e.g., Jongerden 2007, 2009; Ayata 2011;
Gambetti and Jongerden 2015); resettlement and compensation for damages
and losses (e.g., Ayata and Yükseker 2005; Kurban 2007; Kurban et al. 2007;
Çelik 2013; Biner 2013; 2016; Sert 2017); and transformation of resistance discourses and strategies (e.g., see Bozarslan 2005; Van Bruinessen 2010; Yeğen
2010; Güneş 2012) and gendered and political subjectivities (e.g., see Özgen
2003; Üstündağ 2013; Aras 2013; Neyzi and Darıcı 2015; Darıcı 2013, 2016;
Hakyemez 2017a; Schafers 2017; Düzel 2018). In analyzing the long-term effects of dispossession in Turkey, these studies have contributed critical knowledge concerning the Turkish state's material, legal, and political means of
generating violence and citizens' struggles for political recognition of their
material and immaterial losses. They have provided us with a sensitive, critical, and insightful approach to the political agency that has emerged within
the spaces of the Kurdish conflict.[2]

Yet the conditions of dispossession brought about by political and structural violence are never confined solely to the past or the present as discrete
temporal frames. Nor are they confined solely to the domain of political
struggles and social movements. The logic of dispossession, whether colonial
or neocolonial, capitalist or neoliberal, endures by reproducing forms of presence via structural, political, and everyday violence (Povinelli 2011; Butler
and Athanasiou 2013). These forms of dispossession take different shapes: appropriation of property, occupation, treasure hunting, heritage making, and
debt creation. They also lead to different forms of possession of dead and live
bodies and of land and territories.

Here, dispossession refers not only to the projects of the PKK and the
Turkish state as sovereign bodies that strive for control over territory; it also
denotes the collective practices of multiple local actors involved in dispossession's imagining and bringing into being. The actors that operate in
this collective space—the Turkish government, provincial governors, cada-

stral surveyors, lawyers, treasure hunters, cultural heritage experts, Syriacs in diaspora, monastery foundations, tribal leaders, village guards, the pro-Kurdish party, and the media—all play their part in the organization and transformation of the locales where dispossession takes place. At the same time, the material, emotional, and political effects of dispossession are embedded in multiple realms of ordinary experience (Das 2006; Lambek 2010) where life is mediated and informed by both human and nonhuman actors who coexist in the ruined environment of Mardin. Michael Lambek (2010:2) suggests that ordinary experience implies an ethics that is not explicit but tacit, embedded in "agreement rather than rule, in practice rather than knowledge or belief, and happening without calling undue attention to itself." Ordinary experience embodies the "inevitable cracks and ruptures in the actual and ubiquity of responses to the ever-present limits of criteria and paradoxes of the human condition, hence the attempts in everyday practice and thought to inhabit and persevere in light of uncertainty, suffering, injustice, incompleteness, inconsistency, the unsayable, the unforgivable, the irresolvable, and the limits of voice and reason" (4).

In *States of Dispossession*, I follow on this connection between ethics and the ordinary. By examining the practices and discourses that emerge from the Islamic belief in the *jinn* local memories of unspoken, irresolvable histories, implicit knowledge about the landscape and the built environment, and the continuous struggle with the state to reclaim rights over dispossessed bodies and places, ordinary experience comes into focus. This ethnography is thus my attempt to understand the persistent and intangible effects of dispossession on the transformation of subjectivities (e.g., Verdery and Humphrey 2004; Strang and Busse 2011; Salemink and Ramussen 2016). In it, I call for a conceptual and ethnographic merging of what may at first glance seem like irreconcilable opposites—spirituality and materiality, restoration and destruction, heritage and ruin, labor and waste, and poverty and fantasies of sudden enrichment—situated in the context of protracted conflict. It is the bringing together in one ethnography of these many visible and invisible sites that provides a different interpretation of the ethical and political than those overtly or implicitly employed in much of the scholarship on the protracted conflict in the region (see also Kirişci and Winrow 1997; Özcan 2006; Jongerden and Akkaya 2012; Öktem 2011; Güneş and Zeydanlıoğlu 2013; Tezcür 2014; Yeğen 2016; Tezcür and Gürses 2017; Başer 2018). Without visiting or inhabiting those sites for a time, it is difficult to understand the ways people of differing religious and ethnic backgrounds remember, experience, and live within the remains of violence that is as yet unfinished, enduring still in Southeast Turkey.

The Kurdish Issue

The military conflict between the PKK and the Turkish Armed Forces has endured over the course of the last three decades. Since 1984, the conflict has claimed the lives of more than forty-five thousand civilians, militants, and soldiers, as well as causing thousands of other casualties and disappearances. It has led to the displacement of millions of people and caused the forced evacuation of nearly four thousand villages and towns (Güneş and Zeydanlıoğlu 2013:1).[3] Suspended periodically by various cease-fires, the conflict has been a significant force in shaping many of the ethnic, social, and political enclaves of contemporary Turkey, where contradictory forms of governance have been installed across the Kurdish region. Throughout this period, academic public discourse in Turkey about the conflict has shifted; first it was a problem of "terrorism" and the "Kurdish question," then it became about "underdevelopment" and the "Kurdish conflict." As Kurds began to disturb the limits and possibilities of coexistence under the sovereignty of the Turkish state, the Turkish imagination about the Kurds, the PKK, and the conflict region was transformed.[4]

The political and historical roots of the Kurdish issue originate with the dismantling of the Ottoman Empire and the rise of the nation-state in the nineteenth century. From the late nineteenth century onward, centralization and nationalization policies weakened what were largely semiautonomous Kurdish political structures, leading to a series of massacres of members of non-Muslim communities (Olson 1989; Aydın et al. 2000; Jongerden and Verheij 2012; Özoğlu 2004). In 1915, the Kurds took part in the massacres of Armenians and Syriac Christians (Üngör 2011). This alignment with the Ottoman Empire and the Turkish National Movement during the Turkish War of Independence did not, however, reward the Kurds with an independent territory. The early years of the Turkish Republic witnessed a massive Kurdish response against the assimilation policies instigated by Turkish republican nationalism. The Kurdish uprisings that began in 1925 and continued until 1940 prompted further state violence that ended with massacres, displacement of peoples, and the forced exile of rebels, supporters, and their families (Van Bruinessen 1992; Özoğlu 2004; Yeğen 2007;

Özsoy 2013).[5] The strategy of the Turkish state was not only to deny the presence of Kurds as a separate identity, but to Turkify them through displacement, resettlement, and a ban on the use of their own language (Yeğen 2007; Öktem 2004; Jongerden 2009; Güneş and Zeydanlıoğlu 2013).[6] Official Turkish national identity was constructed through the definition of an ethnic Turkishness that categorically proscribed the country's preexisting multireligious and multilinguistic social fabric. In this context, both non-Muslims and non-Turks were subjected to a politics of exclusion enacted through diverse legal and political reforms, either with the full support of the majority Muslim Turkish population or irrespective of their views.[7]

In 1960, the new constitution and a series of legal reforms provided opportunities to break the silence regarding the situation of the Kurds (Güneş 2012). A surge in Kurdish political and cultural activities and the establishment of Kurdish alliances with leftist organizations recast the Kurdish question from a case of underdevelopment to an issue of nationalism and colonialism (see Gündoğan 2015; Jongerden 2018). This alliance continued to inform political agendas and party platforms until the mid-1970s, when the Kurdish political movement took sudden leave of the Turkish leftist movement (see Jongerden and Akkaya 2012; Güneş 2012). After the 1980 military coup and the imprisonment, torture, execution, and disappearance of much of the Turkish left, the PKK, founded as a Marxist-Leninist national liberation organization, remained as the only grassroots challenge to the Turkish state. At this time, the PKK proclaimed the right to self-determination and adopted a policy of guerrilla warfare with the explicit goal of establishing a unified and independent Kurdistan (see Özcan 2006; Güneş 2012; Jongerden and Akkaya 2012; Bozarslan 2014).

Following the start of the PKK insurgency in 1984, the Turkish state rolled out a series of repressive militaristic and legal strategies. Paramount among them was the declaration of a state of emergency (*olağanüstü hal*, abbreviated in Turkish as OHAL) in thirteen of the seventeen provinces encompassing the Kurdish region, effectively providing the military and state officials with full authority and guaranteed immunity in the case of collateral injury. In 1985, as part of these militaristic strategies, the Turkish state introduced the "Temporary Village Guard System" (Geçici Köy Koruculuğu Sistemi) employing villagers from different Kurdish tribes to gather a paramilitary force of militia members (see Kurban 2007; Ünalan 2007; Balta Paker and Akça 2013; Gurcan 2014). Together, the state's lack of spatial and administrative control of rural areas and the Turkish military's inability to put down the counterinsurgency contributed to the success of the PKK (Jongerden 2007). By the mid-1990s, PKK militants performed duties on par with those of Turkish governors. They had the authority to close shops, collect taxes from business owners, recruit soldiers into guerrilla units, arbitrate blood feuds, and hold trials to punish inappropriate attitudes and resolve family disputes. Over time, the growing political and social authority of the PKK strongly undermined the strategies deployed by the Turkish state (Biner 2013). In 1993, the security forces opted for a strategy designed to quash the PKK by cutting it off from its direct support base. The result was a systematic policy of evacuating Kurdish villages and establishing strict control over PKK territory. Throughout the 1990s, assassinations, anonymous killings, and disappearances were carried out by a diverse ensemble of actors—paramilitaries, village guards, informants, and the heads of some of the large extended families. State violence fueled the power of terror, which grew omnipresent and explosive and led to deaths, fear of loss, and an ongoing mood of paranoia (Aras 2013; Neyzi and Darıcı 2015).[8] In 1999, after the arrest of Öcalan in Nairobi, the PKK declared a unilateral cease-fire and mobilized its guerrilla forces in Iraqi Kurdistan. With the start of Turkey's EU accession process in 1999, the state began lifting the state of emergency in the OHAL areas and took steps toward a partial demilitarization of the region.

Throughout the post-2000 process, the state mobilized new tools for the exercise of power. These can be conceptualized as an amalgam of sovereign modalities of power and modes of governance (Watts 2010; Güneş and Zeydanlıoğlu 2013; Gambetti and Jongerden 2015). Having come to power in 2002, the Justice and Development Party (Adalet ve Kalkınma Partisi, AKP) government cautiously followed in the footsteps of earlier regimes and continued to create development projects to address poverty, education, and unemployment in Kurdish areas. Its goal was to convey the sense that it would keep in step with the prevailing state discourse by providing water, building schools and hospitals, offering literacy and other courses for women, and launching restoration projects to protect the region's cultural heritage (Biner 2013). The maintenance of the status quo politics under AKP governance had a negative effect on the PKK's decision to implement a unilateral cease-fire. In 2004, the PKK broke the cease-fire and declared the renewal of guerrilla warfare (Güneş and Zeydanlıoğlu 2013).

In 2005, then the prime minister, Recep Tayyip Erdoğan, acknowledged that militaristic measures had been unable to resolve the conflict and expressed his willingness to initiate a peace process. Beginning in 2005, the

AKP established various spaces and means of governance that allowed for the enactment of productive but repressive regimes. Its neoliberal policies on security and multiculturalism opened up various channels for the accumulation and distribution of capital among local and international actors. Between 2005 and 2013, these channels were the construction economy, heritage and tourism projects, new universities and NGOs, compensation procedures for displaced villagers, charity packages for the poor, and programs for older and disabled citizens (Yüksel 2011; Yörük and Özsoy 2013). Although local and international NGOs and municipalities run by pro-Kurdish parties were influential actors that governed the economic and political means of daily life, the AKP government used legal and material resources to position its network as the sole provider of all material and immaterial benefits (Küçük and Özselçuk 2015). During this period, the PKK encouraged the legalization and politicization of the Kurdish movement, which still consisted of a combination of guerrilla forces, civic politics, and grassroots activism. The pro-Kurdish parties and the municipalities became the main components of the PKK's civic politics, which also sought to expand political space by establishing NGOs and cultural centers (Gambetti 2005; Watts 2009; Casier et al. 2011; Neyzi and Darıcı 2015).

In the meantime, between 2009 and 2011, the AKP government started a new process, referred to as the Kurdish opening (*Kürt açılımı*), a new round of peace talks with the PKK that became known as the Oslo talks or Oslo process. The process ended when news of the negotiations were leaked through a news agency in Turkey. The end of the Oslo process triggered the PKK's attacks on Turkish military forces. The region again turned into a conflict zone. The Turkish state responded with a new cycle of violence not only through militaristic measures but also repressive legal policies. Over eight thousand Kurdish activists, politicians, and journalists were arrested with claims alleging that they were members of the Turkey Council of KCK (Koma Ciwaken Kurdistan, or Union of Communities in Kurdistan), an organization associated with the PKK (Özkahraman 2017). They were accused of running municipalities under orders from the PKK (see Casier et al. 2011; Bayır 2013b).

In 2013, a new era began with the declaration of a peace process (*barış süreci*) which signaled the start of negotiations between the PKK and the Turkish state. High bureaucrats of the Turkish Intelligence Service and the National Security Council began negotiations with the imprisoned PKK leader, Abdullah Öcalan. In the same period, the Turkish Armed Forces and PKK militants maintained a twenty-seven-month cease-fire; the PKK's plan was to withdraw from the territory of the Turkish state. The peace process led to the transformation of social and political prejudices between the Kurds and the Turks and allowed the reconstruction of Kurdish politics involving political experiments with self-governance and autonomy in multiple spheres (see Jongerden and Akkaya 2013, 2016; Darıcı 2015; Yeğen 2015:9; Hakyemez 2017b). More significantly, what had previously qualified as the sign, space, and symptom of "terror and terrorism" was now considered to be legitimate, legal, and acceptable in the eyes of the government, which in turn engendered popular support for the process. In this process, Erdoğan called upon public intellectuals and prominent figures from Turkish popular culture to serve on the Committee of Wise Persons (Akil İnsanlar Heyeti), giving them the mission of communicating with citizens from all regions of Turkey about the peace process. They were expected to convince the Kurds that the government was genuine in its commitment and to diminish the concerns of Turks regarding national security and unity. Popular support made the peace speakable and imaginable despite the lack of information on the content of the peace talks.[9]

Following the 2014 general elections, the AKP took further steps to lay down the legal ground for the enactment of the peace process. The government first amended the law of the National Intelligence Organization that allowed its agents to negotiate with terrorist organizations and its imprisoned members. More significantly, it enacted a new law, the Law to End Terror and Strengthen Social Integration, which authorized both the military and government officers to take the necessary legal, military, and political steps to achieve the resolution of the conflict. The same period witnessed further exceptions that allowed the release of the imprisoned KCK convicts (Yeğen 2015:9).

At the same time, popular support for the process so consciously nurtured by the AKP was never reinforced by the development of a legal infrastructure to establish peace in actuality.[10] While the AKP provided the legal grounds to legitimize the acts of the state officers authorized to resolve the conflict, no protection or assurance was given to the Kurdish mediators involved in the negotiation process. No change to the constitution was introduced to redefine Turkish and non-Turkish minority identities and legal statuses (see Yeğen 2015; Hakyemez 2017b). While the AKP government asserted disarmament as the condition to commence the negotiations, the PKK declared that a decision to do so could only be made after the two sides reached an agreement on the terms of resolution of the conflict and that disarmament could only be finalized after constitutional changes that would be defined within the negotiation process (Yeğen 2015:10). Such constitutional change on the redefinition of rights never took place. In the absence of such legal recognition, the permissive, emancipated, legitimate space that allowed for the circulation of Öcalan's treatises and publications and the enactment of political practices were made possible through "exceptions." The state refrained from acting against Kurdish guerrillas, militias, and activists, who moved freely between the mountains, villages, towns, and cities, and who for the time being were viewed as the main agents of the peace process. The state waited to act further as the peace process moved along (Hakyemez 2017b).

In the meantime, the start of war in Rojava (*west* in Kurdish, thus Rojavayê Kurdistanê, referring to western Kurdistan) and the emergence of the possibility of an autonomous Kurdish zone in Syria transformed expectations for peace and war. The peace process that had stagnated on the Turkish side was suddenly overshadowed by the war in Rojava, creating multiple future expectations that revolved around the idea of a movement for self-governance (see Üstündağ 2016; Küçük and Özselçuk 2016). The People's Protection Forces (Yekîneyên Parastina Gel, or YPG) and the Women's Protection Forces (Yekîneyên Parastina Jin, or YPJ) managed to control territories in western Kurdistan and northern Syria and became the most effective force against ISIS in alliance with the U.S. Army. Many young people from the region joined the resistance in Kobane, Syria.[11]

The peace talks began to break down in April 2015, just before the Turkish general elections, and came to an abrupt end with the extreme acts of violence that began after the vote in which the AKP lost its majority in parliament for the first time in thirteen years. In ten cities and thirty-nine districts of the Kurdish regions provincial governors (*valiler*) declared round-the-clock and open-ended curfews that lasted for 169 days in total. The conflict moved from the mountains into Kurdish towns and districts as the Turkish Army fought PKK-affiliated Kurdish urban militias in the curfew sites.

The conflict in the Kurdish towns and cities claimed the lives of more than two thousand people, displaced almost half a million people from their home villages and towns in the region, and resulted in the destruction of thousands of houses in the curfew districts.[12] Turkish military operations were followed with political repression that led to the detainment of democratically elected representatives of Kurds, primarily mayors and parliamentarians, and to the imprisonment of thousands of Kurdish activists. The military operations did not take place under a state of emergency and no ruling was passed down from parliament regarding the decisions on the round-the-clock and open-ended curfews.

The failed military coup attempt of July 15, 2016, led to the declaration of a new state of emergency across the country that allowed and justified the detainment of the elected representatives of Kurds and the imprisonment of many Kurdish activists together with thousands of people accused of carrying out or supporting terrorist activities that were at the time associated with the PKK and the Gülen Movement (Gülen Hareketi). The state of emergency has been extended every three months until July 2018. Although this was not a repeat of the events of the 1990s, life in the region entered a dark cycle of violence in which ordinary people were forced to suffer the losses. The window that had enabled peace and reconciliation rapidly shrank, ushering in a new era of discrimination against and hatred for "the Kurd." This came with a refusal to recognize the pain and loss of the Other, which has contributed to growing daily violence in contemporary Turkey that continues as I write.

Violence Continuum

This book sheds light on the complexity of social life in the particular times and spaces of violent peace. That social life is marked with the desires and fears of grappling with the material and immaterial loss of the "violence continuum" (Scheper-Hughes and Bourgois 2003:5) in the conflict zone. region. Nancy Scheper-Hughes and Philippe Bourgois define the violence continuum with reference to the indistinctness between wartime and peacetime violence (2003:20), which includes "all expressions of radical social exclusion, dehumanization, depersonalization, pseudo speciation, and reification that normalize atrocious behaviour and violence toward others" (21). In their view, everyday violence, symbolic violence, and terror as usual reveal the secret connections between violence in war and violence in peace. This recognition in turn uncovers the capacities and intentions of those who become involved in the enactment of mass violence.[13]

Scholarship on the Kurdish issue that has analyzed the legacy of Turkish state violence targeting its Kurdish subject-citizens has articulated the continuum of violence in the analysis of repetition of violent acts throughout recent history—political repression, imprisonments, land confiscation, displacements, military clashes. In the literature concerning Syriacs/ Assyrians scholars have also interpreted current acts of hostility and harassment as a continuation of the Sayfo (e.g., Çetrez et al. 2012; Omtzigt et al. 2012; Gaunt et al. 2017). The continuum of violence lies, then, in the common experience of having been subjected to state violence, from the Sayfo, to the suppression of the Kurdish uprisings in the early years of the Republican regime to the Kurdish conflict of the late twentieth and early twenty-first centuries. (See, e.g., Bozarslan 2005, 2014; Scalbert-Yücel and Le Ray 2006; Jongerden 2009; Van Bruinessen 2010; Güneş 2012).[14]

In this book, I strive to push the violence spectrum beyond the connections between 1915 and 1990. I trace narrative ideas, discourses, and practices of violence that resonate on a spectrum, thereby revealing the continuities between structural, political, and criminal violence that originate in different historical and spatial conditions. I attempt to address "political contradictions" (Visweswaran 2013:19) engendered from long-term violence not only against minorities but also across and within minority communities. Each chapter critically engages with these assumptions and explores the ways in which people construct, destroy, hide, and recraft particular connections and contradictions. Each chapter shows how these contradictions move beyond the historically and politically fixed positions of victims and perpetrators. In this sense, this book is an effort to unfold the category of "violence continuum" by moving beyond the temporal and spatial boundaries of state violence and identity politics.

More precisely, here, in search of the ways in which loss is processed, I go beyond the established prevailing analyses in Kurdish studies whereby political agents speak and are revealed only with reference to the cultural, political, and emotional spaces of the Kurdish resistance movement and its daily activism. In its place, I locate another form of political agency, one generated from the conditions of the state of exception. This political agency acts in invisible, hidden, and fugitive ways and, precisely in so doing, determines and structures the ethics of everyday life (Lambek 2010). The search for a different form of agency does not mean that I neglect to address state violence as constitutive of life in the region. Neither does the search for this alternative agency lead to the actualization of a possible ethics that is critical, inclusive, and politically considerate of the attachments and dependencies that constitute the self (Butler and Athanasiou 2013).

Quite the contrary. By focusing on banal and ordinary attempts at appropriation, dispossession, harassment, legal confinement, and ungrieved death, I encounter another kind of agency that is primarily concerned with survival in the gray zones of violence in the Kurdish region. The Italian Jewish Auschwitz survivor Primo Levi (1989) coined the concept of the "gray zone" to refer to morally ambiguous spaces of betrayal and complicity where people trade their compassion in exchange for the smallest benefit and advantage. In Levi's account, the gray zone was inhabited by "grey and ambiguous persons ready to compromise" with a "desperate, covert and continuous struggle to survive" (41). Levi's gray zone bears resemblances to Michael Taussig's (1984) "space of death." Deriving this concept from a broader analysis of colonial violence, Taussig describes the space of death as "a common pool of signifiers or caption points binding the culture of conqueror with that of conquered" (468). Taussig views such spaces as locales of transformation where terms are inverted and confused in what he calls an "epistemic murk": "through the experience of death, life; through fear, loss of self and conformity to a new reality; or through evil, good" (492). In an analysis of the fearsome stories of colonial rubber traders about Huitoto cannibalism in Colombia, Taussig argues that the most important feature of the kinds of stories and imaginations that are engendered in such spaces is that they create "an uncertain reality out of fiction, a nightmarish reality in which the unstable interplay of truth and illusion becomes a social force of horrendous and phantasmic dimension." This blurring of reality and illusion then "becomes a high-powered tool for domination and a principal medium of political practice" (494).

The Kurdish region is neither a Nazi concentration camp nor a colonial rubber plantation. It involves different forms of life, subjectivities, and spaces that cannot all be described as existing in a relationship of complicity with terror. Yet the Kurdish region is a space of death constitutive of violence on a continuum. As such, it involves unstable interplays of truth and illusion engendered by fear of loss of self and of others. This epistemological instability produces ambiguous spaces of morality that compel people to cleave to their capacity for complicit engagement with an ever-changing reality. In this regard, the chapters of this book are born from an encounter with spaces of death as Taussig describes them and reveal the transformations produced through memory and the experience of loss. Each chapter articulates, too, the forms of conformity and struggle to survive that are constitutive of Levi's gray zones.

Multiple Sovereigns

In this ethnography, the Turkish state appears as an omnipresent and concrete entity. At issue here is how the state, seemingly shaped by neoliberalism, multiculturalism, and militarism and scrutinized by transnational actors, is experienced and imagined as the provider of benefits, care, and violence by citizens from different religious and ethnic backgrounds. I am interested here in how the rational and irrational dimensions of state power as sovereign are enmeshed in local realities and desires so as to possess the people and their territory and to govern the violent localities at its margins.

The state has been an important focus of analysis in Kurdish studies. Mobilizing the dichotomies between ethnicity and nationalism, state and Kurdish society, many scholars have either purposefully or inadvertently reinforced the idea of the state as a unified entity with the aim of integrating or assimilating Kurds into the physical and political territory of the nation-state. In her comprehensive review of the scholarship on state-society dynamics in the Kurdish region, Nicole Watts (2009) highlights the endurance of this distinction in the analytical and political imaginations of scholars and outlines existing alternative approaches for moving beyond it. The endurance of this conventional approach has a historical and political cause, argues Watts: "The dominance of the state-versus-society paradigm is not because we entirely lack alternative information or because we don't know better. . . . Probably the most important reason the model continues is because there is so much empirical evidence to support and perpetuate it" (4). With its unanticipated reiteration throughout the literature, Watts suggests that this binary model does not help us to understand "why so many Kurds in Turkey have not rebelled, how and why the nature of Turkish governance in the southeast has changed over time . . . , why and how Kurdish cultures and dissent survived and changed; and why so many Kurds vote for mainstream Turkish or Islamic parties" (4). In grappling with this problem, Watts notes, there is a growing body of literature that complicates the binary constructions between state and society in the Kurdish region (see, e.g., Aslan 2009; Harris 2009; Casier 2009); moreover, there is a growing literature that has been, for over a decade, examining the grounded practices and experiences associated with statecraft in Turkey (see, e.g., Beller-Hann and Hann 2001; Navaro-Yashin 2002; Alexander 2002; Koğacıoğlu 2008; Babül 2015). Despite all this, Watts's critical and reflexive review remains significant as a solid reminder of a perplexing set of questions. How do we study the state in the violent environment of the Kurdish region without on the one hand dismissing that academic and popular imagination which perpetuates the state-society binary, and on the other hand without taking such references for and of the state for granted? How do we avoid internalization of popular discourses that experience and imagine the state as the main persona affecting different forms of life?

In her influential work on the ethnography of the Turkish state, Yael Navaro-Yashin (2002) engages with the political and analytical sources of this conundrum. In conversation with historical materialists and post-structuralists, Navaro-Yashin deconstructs the distinction between state and civil society, exploring the ways in which the state and political culture are reproduced in 1990s Turkey. In pursuit of alternative tools, Navaro-Yashin suggests, we must not search for the state exclusively in the formal institutional sites of government, public, and social institutions or offices. Instead, she suggests that we search for the state in the "sites of everyday life, where people attempt to produce meaning for themselves by appropriating the political" (135), in the agency of those who benefit from supporting the state and whose actions cannot be easily categorized within the realms of resistance to the state (153), in "the visceral domain," and in the habitual, psychic, and phantasmic effects of political culture on subjects. It is in the uncertainty and fear of political culture that the state produces its effects, captures the bodies of its subjects to the point of haunting them (183).

In a similar vein, Begoña Aretxaga's (2003) work on criminal states warns us to approach the state not only through the "rationality of ordering practices" but also through their "passions of transgression" that sidestep "rational functionality" and operate through the blurring of "the line between the legal and the illegal" (402). In close connection with Taussig's conceptualisation of space of death, Aretxaga argues that the state as the object of fear, disgust, and identification produces "an intimate secrecy in which the fictions of the state about the people it fears gets locked in with the fictions people at the margins have about the state" (401). It is not only the people who imagine the state; the state concocts and enacts its own fantasies upon its people. These fantasies, Aretxaga argues, are not surreal. They are in effect subjective qualities of the state that are embedded in the "the fantasy of statehood, the fantasy of total control, the fantasy of appropriation of the other, the fantasy of heterosexual domesticity" (402).

The works of Taussig, Navaro-Yashin, and Aretxaga have been sources of inspiration for my ethnographic search for the state as it is experienced in Southeast Turkey. Their insistent calls to locate the political beyond the visible and tangible institutions and orders of the state have underlined my analysis. In this connection, I explore the banal and the everyday so as to capture the state's powerful effects together with the agency of people who enact disgust, fear, support, and complicity with the state. The dead invariably occupy the space between the state and its citizens in the region (see Özgen 2003; Özsoy 2010; Üstündag 2013; Neyzi and Darıcı 2015; Biner 2016). Haunting operates across and through numerous temporalities and personas. As the limits of public secrecy constantly shift (Taussig 1999), people transmit and reconstruct their knowledge about the state, which in turn intersects with their personal, familial, and communal histories. In the region, the visceral domain that sustains the endurance of the state has not only been reproduced through the uncertainty and fear of political culture. It is also reproduced through the excess of state practices. This excess of state practices has meant that the state has perennially existed as different personas, exercising its power through the complicit and destructive acts of local citizens. There have been multiple imaginations of the state, multiple actors who have acted as and been perceived as the state.

In this political environment, people have fetishized the state through their long experience of subjection to violence as a victim, perpetrator or witness and through their expectation of care and protection in exchange for obedience and complicity (cf. Taussig 1992; Navaro-Yashin 2002). With this subjective component intact, the state has obliged citizens to keep in touch with it through their response to its interrogative calls, which are made predominantly through state programs: public work on heritage-centered demolition and restoration projects, legal and political measures pertaining to material and immaterial loss compensation, construction economy benefits, property ownership regulations.

In this connection, it is not only the state that has been fetishized by the people; people have also been fetishized by the state. In conflict zones, Aretxaga (2003:402) argues, the state can also be haunted by the fantasized power of the subversive subjects that it wants to control[15] (see Üstündag 2013; Darıcı 2016). State officers, village guards, and security force personnel were also haunted by the power of the subversive Kurds to fight against the state. The power of Kurdish citizens to enrage the state was produced by the very same potent stuff that enables the state to enrage its citizens—the potential of transmutation from friend to stranger, from loyalist to separatist, from citizen to terrorist and back again

Yet these transmutations take place not only during moments of repression against one's enemies. As Aretxaga has also argued, these transmutations are rather "fields in which the state and its enemy are created and recreated," in which communities draw the boundaries between self and other as "fetishes of each other" (2003:402). It is this power to delimit the political field and at the same time blur the boundaries between the legal and illegal that concerns me in my analysis of different forms of life in the region.

In exploring this form of power, I turn to Giorgio Agamben's (1998) work, which has moved the political and theoretical articulation of sovereignty beyond its conventional state-territory connections. Agamben's formulation of sovereignty is based on an intersection of juridical and biopolitical models of power. Drawing on Carl Schmitt's (1985) definition, Agamben (1998:17) defines the sovereign by his (*sic*) power to decide on the state of exception: "For what is at issue in the sovereign exception is, according to Schmitt, the very condition of possibility of juridical rule and, along with it, the very meaning of state authority. Through the state of exception, the sovereign 'creates and guarantees the situation' that the law needs for its own validity." The state of exception in Agamben's understanding emerges as the political realm that is both governed by law and stands beyond the law; in other words, where the distinction between the legal and illegal blurs and constantly disappears and reappears. The sovereign uses its ability to decide on the exception so as to produce the figure of "*homo sacer* (sacred man), who may be killed but not sacrificed" (8). Homo sacer has a "bare life" that is separated from other forms of life that have political and legal rights. In the realm of exception, bare life represents the opposite of the political.

Contemporary anthropological discussions have framed sovereignty—be it in the form of a sovereign state, an authoritarian persona, or a community—as an "unstable and tentative project" that aspires to reproduce itself through "repeated performances of violence and a 'will to rule,' calling attention to the need to contextualize and qualify sovereign power and its "exception" within the political, economic, and legal contingencies from which they emerge (Hansen and Stepputat 2005:3). In similar line of thought, Caroline Humphrey (2008:420) calls attention to the need to reveal "localized forms of sovereignty which nevertheless retain a domain within which control over life and death is operational." Veena Das and Deborah Poole (2004) contribute to this discussion on sovereignty by reflecting on the practices and politics of life along the "territorial or social margins" (3) of the nation-state. They describe margins as not extraterritorial "sites of practice on which law and other state practices are colonized by other forms of regulations that emanate from the pressing needs and demands of populations to secure political and economic survival" (8). In their view, the state of exception does not refer to an event, but to everyday practices of reestablishing the law through violence; it is here that margins are constituted and localized forms of sovereigns enact their power. It is within this form of state of exception that the homo sacer is produced, not through an a priori social life but through a "complex legal process of rendering them as bare life" (13).

In this book, I follow these critical reflections to reveal ways and forms of life produced at the margins of the Turkish state. I situate the Kurdish region as the margins where illegibility, marginality, and sovereignty take place through or outside the state. I use the notion of the state of exception to refer to the time and space that allows a "continual re-founding of law through forms of violence and authority" (Das and Poole 2004:13). This re-founding happens through "localized forms of sovereignty" (Humphrey 2008:420) embodied in the figure of special security forces, provincial governors, public servants, village guards, tribal leaders, and PKK militants. With the sole exception of the last of these, each of these figures enjoys a form of immunity to the law; conferred with the authority to make exceptions to the rules and to assert their own forms of private justice arising from personal histories, subjective experiences of violence, and the level of their identification with the state as an omnipresent entity, these figures are both inside and outside the law.

The intense and compelling effect of such power to govern with and beyond the law has destructive effects not only on the forms of life but also on the subjective experiences of local citizens. In the political context of the violent peace, the law has been a powerful means for the exercise of state power, a tool for legalizing confiscations in land claims, indebting citizens by forcing them to pay for the material losses of the state, and criminalizing people on the grounds of engaging in alleged terrorist activities (Bayır 2013a, b). In 2008–2011, the state went so far as to use the law to initiate high-profile trials against a range of people—high- and low-rank military officers, journalists, jurists—accused of having been involved in a "deep state" clandestine nationalist organization that had allegedly plotted against the government. Some of the defendants who were accused of having been responsible for atrocities and disappearances that took place in the region under the state of emergency of 1987–2002 were judged in separate trials.[16]

This latter point brings me to my final argument about the sovereign power of the state. The potentiality of the exception lies not only in the production of bare life bodies but also in the production of "precarious" lives. Judith Butler (2004, 2010) defines *precariousness* as an essential quality of social life that implies exposure to and dependency on people one knows and people one does not know. Though precariousness stands as a quality intrinsic to life, Butler argues that it may be aggravated under politically induced conditions whereby people are exposed to violence, poverty, and hunger and suffer from the failure or absence of economic and social support. Precariousness in this sense produces another form of dependency whereby people without many options appeal to the state for protection. But, she argues, the state is what they need protection from: "To be protected from violence by the nation-state is to be exposed to the violence wielded by the nation-state, so to rely on the nation-state for protection *from* violence is precisely to exchange one potential violence for another" (2010:26).

During times of violent peace, the neoliberal security-centered policies of the Turkish state were oriented toward alleviating poverty and managing governance of life and death. In the suspended temporality of the conflict, the art of government was not only to create the sense that all citizens were living on a shared ground of precariousness, but also to make them believe that precariousness was a contingent condition that could be overcome first through loyalty to the boundaries of the territorial and political sovereignty of the state, and then through a will and determination to integrate with the political and economic system (Lorey 2015; see also Özselçuk and Küçük 2015). And yet, as the following chapters show, precariousness remains as a permanent state of political existence that marks the nature of the relationship between the Turkish state and the locals at the margins. Even for those citizens with the strongest will and determination to integrate, there would emerge a state of exception in the form of a decision, a personal initiative, a tradition, a rule, or a legal order that would perpetuate dependency on the state and other local sovereigns for economic and political survival.

The Ordinary

In my attempt to analyze these gray zones and spaces of death, I follow the path of anthropologists who have worked to incorporate the everyday local experiences of conflict and violence into broader historical frameworks (e.g. Ismail 2006; Kelly 2008; Lubkemann 2007; Hermez 2012; Allen 2013; Jansen 2014). I delve into the time-space of the ordinary so as to explore how subjects master, domesticate, and settle the resilient and poisonous effects of violence and its aftermaths (Das and Kleinman 2000; Eng and Kazanjian 2003; Das 2006; Thiranagama 2011; Navaro-Yashin 2012). I examine how violence transforms the meaning of loss and value and how people deal with the material and immaterial effects of loss. In search of a description of the ways in which loss is processed, I engage in particular with the work of Veena Das and colleagues. Das and Kleinman (2000:2) do not confine violence to the temporal zone of a particular violent event. Instead they extend their focus to include the processes through which forms of violence are spread, the places where the distinction between violence, conflict, and peaceful resolution is dissolved, and the tasks of daily life that people carry out "in the full recognition that perpetrators, victims and witnesses come from the same social and political space." Das (2006), in turn, theorizes the ordinary as the site of intersection between the event and the everyday. In this way, the ordinary comes to accommodate all forms of engagement between people that are reproduced through the absorption, digestion, and integration of the "poisonous knowledge" that arises from memory of violence. Das's analysis involves hope in that the making of the self is not located in the shadow of the ghostly past, but in the context of inhabiting the everyday and of making concrete relations. The self forms by "descending into the everyday" (2006:74) and finding its "voice both within and outside the genres that become available in the descent" (216).

Das's call for a deep engagement with the ordinary and her search for a voice as the medium of violence's expression form the ethnographic backbone of this study. Yet I diverge from her analysis and interpretation at several levels. First, the protagonists of this ethnography reinhabit the everyday not only to recover life. They may also reinhabit it so as to transform it or so as to continue ruining it with acts of complicity. Multiple functions of the everyday exist in this ethnographic context.

Second, in this book, the ordinary is not limited to the concrete relationships between human beings. The ordinary accommodates and is constitutive of other relationships that involve nonhuman beings and objects and extends to the realm of spirituality and materiality. Material objects and spiritual beings also operate as agents that mediate violence and transform the ordinary. By spiritual beings, I refer to the jinn that are found in Islamic cosmology and that appear in the everyday lives of the subjects in this ethnography. These spiritual beings coexist with human actors as primordial residents that regulate, mediate, and transform other concrete relationships in the city, whether material or immaterial, involving human or other nonhuman actors. The engagement with the jinn, emerges as the descent into other realms of the everyday. And yet the jinn in this ethnography do not exist through its service of "awakening the individual towards its limits" (42) and hence bringing him or her back to inhabiting the ordinary. The conjugation between human and nonhuman does not necessarily generate alternative, hopeful, or critical spaces for the actualization of the individual and her or his self-realization. Despite their mediating effects in prompting talk about justice and the morality of ownership, the spiritual beings can act upon lives with a routine and ordinary violence. Their presence can be destructive, complicit, exploitative, or pragmatic, for they are tangled up in the relationships of materiality that lead to the destruction of space and to debt generation. In this sense, I am not interested only in a vision of the everyday and the ordinary that is organized by the ubiquitous neoliberal militarism of the region but also in the ordinary conceptualized as being disrupted by multiple forces operating in this violent environment. This is the point I return to reflecting on the affective, material, and legal relationships that property generates.

Propertied Subjectivities

Anthropologists have long contributed to the analysis of property regimes, bringing to light through ethnographic analysis the multiple relationships property entails between people, things, and the environment (e.g., Hann 1998; Strathern 1999; Verdery and Humphrey 2004; Benda-Beckmann, Benda-Beckmann, and Wieber 2009). Theorizing ownership as a processual practice, they have demonstrated the effects that the (im)materiality of property and ownership has on individual subjectivity (e.g., Verdery 2003; Strathern and Hirsch 2004; Humphrey and Verdery 2004; Maurer and Schwab 2006; Busse and Strang 2011; Navaro-Yashin 2012; Collins 2015). This book engages with forms of possession and ownership that materialize through acts of appropriation (cf. Hirsch and Strathern 2004; Strang and Busse 2011). Appropriation, in this ethnographic context, operates through diverse actions that range from restoration, registration of the property as cultural asset (kültürel varlık), cadastral survey, and land registration to destruction, treasure hunting, land occupation, and the stealing of agricultural products. In analyzing these practices, my work demonstrates a concern for exploring the transformative relationships between subjectivity and materiality and the ongoing theoretical attempts to denaturalize the relationship between *being* and *having and* politicize the connection between property and concepts of agency. In so doing, my goal in the research has been to unfold the conceit of proper(tied) subjectivity (Butler and Athanasiou 2013:27). With these considerations in mind, this book transforms the tie between property and subjectivity into an object of analysis, thereby revealing the historical, political, and ethical processes (in)visible in the making of the tie.

In addressing these relationships, my approach dwells on expanded meanings of materiality. *Materiality*, in this context, refers not only to the production of commodities and the transaction of the exchange value of goods and labor within the capitalist and neoliberal economic system but also to the physical labor invested in destruction and construction of houses and objects and the effects of the built environment on people. Building on the new materialist turn (Latour 2005; Weizman 2007; Coole and Frost 2010; Bennett 2010), I approach materiality as more than an inert substance in my analysis of dispossession, viewing it as an "active, self-creative, productive, unpredictable" field (Coole and Frost 2010:9) with forces and energies that transgress the distinctions between the human and nonhuman. In this new materialist turn, actor-network theorists refuse to approach material objects as belonging to the realm of human social practices, but rather suggest considering both objects and materials as actors that mediate, regulate, and transform relationships. Bruno Latour (2005:76) proposes an object-centered approach in which he names material things as "non-human actants," ascribing to them agencies independent of their relationships with humans. According to the interpretation of Latour's theory offered by Jane Bennett (2010:9), an actant can be human, nonhuman, or a combination of the two: "An actant is neither an object nor a subject but an 'intervener' . . . , an operator which by virtue of its particular location in an assemblage and the fortuity of being in the right place in the right time makes the difference, makes things happen, becomes the decisive force catalyzing an event." The difference "needs to be flattened, read horizontally as a juxtaposition rather than vertically as a hierarchy of being" (10). The ethical justification for this view is "to distribute value more generously," to provide for an imaginary in which "all bodies are kin in the sense of inextricably enmeshed in a dense network of relations. And in a knotted world of vibrant matter, to harm one section of the web may very well be to harm oneself" (13).

In his important contribution to this discussion, Eduardo Kohn (2015:321) interprets the focus on the distribution of value between humans and nonhumans as an opportunity for anthropology to "become a project of 'cosmic diplomacy.'" Kohn interprets Latour's goals as a move "to recognize and give dignity to multiple modes of existence or ontologies, and to how the beings such modes institute may find a way to dwell together in a common oikos." In this cosmos, "stones, spirits, poetry, and scientific objects can all be described as having unique and valid modes of existence."

Drawing on her work on the postwar environment in Cyprus, Navaro-Yashin also highlights the significance of distributing agency beyond the subject and recognizing objects in politics with a particular focus on energies, forces, and affects "discharged out of these objects themselves" (2012:162). At the same time, Navaro-Yashin criticizes the methodology of the materialist turn, "imagining a flat or horizontal network of assemblages between human and non-human entities, transcendentally and [at] all times, without qualification or interpretation" (163). She invites us to bring "ethnographic sensibility" into play in order to study the relationships between people and objects in their historical and political specificity without "discarding language and subjectivity" (172).

Stef Jansen (2013) provides a more pragmatic critique with an argument grounded in a concern with accountability. While Jansen finds the actor-network theory methodology useful, he also sees problems in the proportional symmetry it proposes between human and nonhuman agency. But he questions the utility of the reconciliatory approach, which attempts to integrate the materialist turn with a people-centered approach. Instead, he formulates the discussion with a question: "Should we start from an *analytical distinction* between human and non-human actants or not?" In his view, "no coherent conceptual framework can simultaneously postulate symmetry *and* asymmetry between agency of things and people" (24). For the methodological and analytical dilemma to be tackled ethnographically, he suggests not collapsing people and things into one category but instead preserving their distinction. An "accountable account . . . would not gain anything from an insistence on the a priori equivalence of the agency of non-human and human actants." Jansen points out the significant insights to be gained by tracing the emergence of the agency of human or things "on different scales as a process over time" (35).

I take these critical readings seriously. Here, I consider the material and spiritual not as background to or as representative of violence, but rather as nonhuman actants that transform regulate, mediate, and act upon the experience of violence. The house, the land, the monastery, and the jinn all play a part in translating and distorting the meaning of interactions, both as part of a wider "heritage assemblage" (Macdonald 2009) and as a symbolic, material, and emotional storehouse of past and present signifiers. In so doing, I give preference to the project of "ethnographic sensibility" rather than of "cosmic diplomacy" and strive to study the relationships between human and non-human in their historical and political contingency.

Stone and concrete are more than artifacts or the passive foundation of the built environment. They are an integral part of politics (see Thrift 2004; Latour 2005; Harvey 2010; Barry 2013). Each of these nonhuman actants relates differently to individuals and communities. While stone houses exert affects on people, the relationships that people construct with their ruined village and land do not have a symmetrical ethnographic valence. The houses exert affective forces on their digger-owners, while the land, the village, and the monastery provide the legal, historical, and emotional connections that people hold on to, reproduce, or refuse in their attempts to transform the world that they are in the process of reinhabiting. The vitality and agency of the matter emerge as the legal and political substances that exert and absorb historical forces and produce different forms of attachment. In tracing these stories of exclusions and inequalities, I do not follow a single methodology in a consistent way. Instead, I follow different routes according to the forms and nature of the relationships between the human and nonhuman as they emerge within this ethnographic context. My main concern is to give voice to and make visible the ordinary practices, affects, and forces that simultaneously produce and violate the networks that constitute daily life. The relationship between having and being remains at the forefront of these explorations.

Cruel Optimism

The subjects of this ethnography show a marked ability to take on several identities while attempting to negotiate their lives with others outside their community and with the state. Their obedience to social requisites and their willingness to integrate with sovereign actors may be traced back to a fear of interrogation, but it ultimately conveys a foundational hope in their own economic and political survival. This subject positioning is therefore a function of their desire for political and economic mobility within the system that governs their lives. Subjects are fully aware of the delicate balance on the threshold of life and death and, at the same time, hold onto the idea that the state should provide them with compensation for all the material and immaterial injuries caused during times officially regarded as the state of emergency. They have been realistic concerning the fragility of the peace process and at the same time optimistic. Borrowing a term from Lauren Berlant (2011), the subjects of this ethnography are "cruelly optimistic."

Berlant describes cruel optimism as "a relation of attachment to compromised conditions of possibility whose realization is discovered either to be impossible, sheer fantasy, or too possible, and toxic" (2011:24). The object of desire might be a project, person, institution, or idea. It is not bound to a single definition. Optimism becomes cruel when the object or scene of desire makes it impossible to achieve the transformation that a person strives to undertake. Optimism becomes cruel because the subject who has those objects of attachment might not survive their loss and hence continues to live in the forms of relationships the person finds at once threatening and affirming. The main conundrum lies in "what happens when the loss of what is not working is more unbearable than the having of it, and vice versa" (27).

Berlant's cruel optimism is useful for understanding the "incitement to inhabit and to track the affective attachment of what we call 'the good life'" (2011:27). The good life that Berlant refers to with reference to the neoliberal contemporary word of Europe and the United States, is also the bad life, one where the conditions of the ordinary are the conditions for the gradual destruction of the subject. It is this contradictory gap between the fantasy of and desire for a good life and the exploitative, destructive conditions of the ordinary life that Berlant points to with this phrase.

Cruel optimism, Berlant argues, attends the practices of "self-interruption, self-suspension and self-abeyance that indicate people's struggle to change, but not traumatically, the terms of value in which their life-making activity has been cast" (2011:27). While the exploitative, destructive, and subject-disenchanting conditions of ordinary life create the cruelty of their subjects' attachments and desires, they also suspend the question of cruelty through the insistence on what Berlant (1997:222) calls "*technologies of patience* that enable subaltern people to seem to consent to, or take responsibility for, their painful contexts" and to "ride the wave of the system of attachment that they are used to . . . or to be held in a relation of reciprocity, reconciliation, or resignation that does not mean defeat by it" (2011:28). Berlant gives a subtle reminder not to see optimism's submission as a diagnosis of error or perversion or an act of revealing the truth. Rather, she suggests seeing optimism "as a scene of negotiated sustenance that makes life bearable as it presents itself ambivalently, unevenly and incoherently" (2011:14).

I take inspiration from Berlant's use of the concept of cruel optimism to understand the construction of the subjects of this ethnography under ongoing neoliberal conditions of exploitation and destruction that operate together with the conditions of militarism and tribal rule. Here, I am also interested in the constructive and destructive effects of the ordinary and in the attachment of my subjects to the reproduction and suspension of the ordinary. I am interested in the cruel aspect of these attachments because, despite their capacity to threaten the subject, they also provide for the subject's continuity. The good life that Lauren Berlant describes as the object of the practices of cruel optimism also emerges as a consensual project between the citizens and the state during the times of violent peace. Some of the ethnography's protagonists reproduce the ordinary in order to digest the enduring effects of their losses. Some reproduce it because of the promise of possessions. Others reinhabit the ordinary in order to release themselves from the relationships of reciprocity, reconciliation, and dependency on the state or other local sovereigns.

My reference to the practices of cruel optimism to describe the agency of these subjects is not an attempt to homogenize dissimilar or unrelated positions and interpret them from the same ethical, moral, or political stance. The daily struggles over the right to ancestral land in the Syriac villages, the legal battles to protect the boundaries of the Syriac monastery, the obsessive hunts to possess haunted treasure stashed in the stone houses, and the three-decade-long struggle for political and cultural rights, autonomy, and independence cannot be treated uniformly. Their roles and locations in the reproduction of habituated and normative life in the violent environment of the Kurdish region remain incommensurate.

My suggestion, however, is that the emphasis on the cruel creates a common denominator with which to understand these different forms of attachments, be they a desire for property, identity, institution, or political project. The protagonists of this ethnography all have cruel attachments that they endure in order to survive. The continuity of these attachments provides the continuity of their sense of "what it means to keep on living and to look forward to being in the world" (Berlant 2011:24). This book discusses practices and discourses that reproduce these crucial attachments to objects, ideas, and projects, revealing those junctures where people confront challenges to their ability to sustain their determination. It explores the conditions under which these attachments "come to make sense or no longer make sense, yet remain powerful as they work against the flourishing of particular and collective beings" (Berlant 2011:13). Each chapter of this book engages with the enduring and recrafted form of state sovereignty, the diverse modes of enacting the exception, the desire for repossession, encounters with nonhumans and humans as witnesses of occupations, and the struggle for recognition of injustice. Each chapter engages with the ordinary from the anchor point of forces, energies, and histories that produce a new rhythm for living a good life. Each chapter engages with stories from different protagonists in which they confront the moral, economic, and political cost of their desire to sustain, repair, and protect their object of attachment.

Mapping States of Dispossession

This book treats the resilient, long-term, resonating effects of violence through historically and ethnographically referenced processes during the suspension of the intensive military conflict between the PKK and the Turkish state during 2001–2015. It studies violence on different scales through multiple mediations. The first chapter focuses on the spatial transformation of the city of Mardin in the post-emergency period, enumerating the fragmented histories and narratives of dispossession, ruination, and cultural heritage in the Old City of Mardin.

The second and third chapters continue to tackle issues of ruination and heritage, this time focusing more on the aspiration for new opportunities. In these chapters, I move away from discussions of current heritage-making projects and delve into the stories of the stone buildings as material and symbolic emblems of heritage in the Old City of Mardin. I record the historical, affective, and economic relationships between these buildings and their long-term owners or occupiers who live, repair, and dig up these houses. The diggers who accompany us in these chapters are not opportunistic outsiders. Instead, they are long-term local residents of the stone buildings who have closely followed the discourses and practices of heritage-making projects rife with rumors about the existence of treasure. While they restore and register their houses as cultural assets with the expectation of the houses increasing in value, they also dig up their houses in order to reach the site of treasure, which is where they think the real source of value lies. Their curiosity and insistence are not independent of the histories of destruction and displacement experienced in the city. Because they are subjects who have witnessed or have been actively involved in the ruination and re-appropriation of these properties, they avoid making causal connections between the histories of ruined heritage and their present desire for treasure.

The subjects and spaces examined in Chapters 4 and 5 occupy different positions within the historical legacy of violence. The narratives are based on histories of dispossession and repossession of land in the towns and villages of the province of Mardin. Syriacs and Kurds are positioned as the descendants of victims, survivors, and perpetrators of the 1915 Sayfo and its aftermath. In these chapters, I flesh out accounts of actions that fall in various places on the continuum of violence. These are incidents that reveal connections between political, state, and structural violence mediated through the renderings of state law and tribal rule over the control of space.

Chapter 4 is based on the personal history of İsa Bey, a Syriac who decided to return to his village of origin and remake his life. The village, Haraziye, had been occupied by Kurdish village guards in 1993 at the peak of the conflict between the PKK and the Turkish Armed Forces. İsa Bey struggled to repossess and revitalize the land belonging to him and his community. He refused to reproduce the traditional protector-protégé relationship that the Syriacs had cultivated with the Kurds, a relationship that had historically exploited and confined Syriacs to the position of perennial debtors. He sought to relate to both the Kurds and the state on the basis of a mutual recognition of rights, responsibilities, and obligations. His transgenerational memory of violence haunted him as he lived out his daily life in the village. Yet it also prompted him to create an ingenious routine based on working the land that generated new forms of relationships with his Kurdish neighbors.

Chapter 5 addresses the political and legal battle that ensued between Syriacs, Kurds, and the state over the dispossession and repossession of the land surrounding the Mor Gabriel Monastery, one of the most prominent shrines of the Syriac Orthodox community. The legal battle unfolded just as the cadastral survey of the land between the monastery and the neighboring Kurdish villagers began. Monastery representatives contested the results of this survey, as well as the mediation of the Kurdish tribal leader in the matter. Their transgression of the tribal order and their refusal to submit to the decision of the cadastral court led to new legal battles, this time between the monastery foundation and the state.

The final thread that weaves together these chapters is the state of indebtedness that serves as the historical mode of relationship between Syriacs, Kurds, and the state. With reference to the memory of the Sayfo and its aftermath, Syriacs protected their properties and sacred shrines on the basis of cash transactions. These transactions came in the form of bribes paid to government officers, gifts given to tribal leaders, and land given to covillagers or neighbors. The narratives in Chapters 4 and 5 chart these relationships as well as others, all of which constitute exceptions in the sense that the victims and perpetrators challenge the rules of submission and transform the modes of possession.

Chapter 6 and the Epilogue take the reader back into different readings of the military conflict between the PKK and the Turkish Armed Forces. In Chapter 6, I reveal another nexus between law, violence, and state that continues to dominate the past, present, and future of Kurdish citizens in Turkey. Using the analysis of two different legal procedures, the Compensation Law (Tazminat Yasası) and recovery of compensation cases (rucu tazminat davaları), I show the ways in which the state uses legal devices to transform reparative justice mechanisms, including the transformation of compensation into debt-producing mechanisms to constitute and force new bonds with Kurdish citizens.

The Epilogue is the account of rupture in the analysis of the violence continuum in the conflict region. It describes the end of the post-emergency period that limited the temporality of this ethnographic research. In so doing, it details the changing frame of the war. Here, I provide partial and fragmented accounts of life and death at a particular time following the return of fighting between the PKK and the Turkish Armed Forces. The Epilogue is drawn from constellations of terror that protagonists of this ethnography—my friends, interlocutors, and I myself—produced when normal life was suspended. This terror's talk conveys a sense of broken voices, interrupted speech, vanished hopes, and injured attachments to promises and possessions. It conveys moments of reflection on the changing meanings and valuation of life, the dead, and debt, and on the new boundaries delimiting (non) recognition and (ungrievable) lives. It conveys fragments of the poisonous knowledge of ruined places and people that arose from this new war, knowledge my friends and interlocutors had not yet learned to work through while living in close proximity to the destroyed places.

CHAPTER 1

Cementing the Past with the Future

The Materiality of Stone and Concrete

In June 2013, I was on my way to the city of Mardin after having spent an intense week in the middle of the Gezi Park protests in downtown Istanbul.[1] The protests had started with environmentalists' efforts to stop developers from cutting down trees to build a new shopping mall in Gezi Park. This was not just an ordinary project of the consumerist neoliberal order. The shopping mall building was designed to reproduce the Old Ottoman Barracks that used to stand on that site. The building not only would replace Gezi Park, but would cover the remains of the Old Armenian Cemetery, Surp Agop, and the church that was seized and confiscated by the state in the 1930s and then razed (Parla and Özgül 2016). Some of the tombstones had been used to create the steps of Gezi Park. Another thirteen Armenian gravestones would be found during the Gezi Park construction process (Bieberstein and Tataryan 2013).

The protest against the destruction of the park sparked a revolt involving thousands of people who occupied the space for weeks. Fanning out into other parks and cities, the Gezi Park protests grew into the first and most significant uprising against the neoliberal conservative order of the AKP and gave way to other imaginaries of public space, coexistence with the other, recognition of the right to the city, and solidarity beyond the politics of identity. People from different political ideologies and backgrounds including students, middle-class professionals, nationalists, Islamists, anarchists, members of non-Muslim and non-Turkish communities, LGBT and feminist networks, workers' unions, and squatter settlement residents stood together against a police force that strove to make this strange, humorous, uncanny

crowd disappear (Yıldırım 2013). Law enforcement's violent response caused
eight deaths and thousands of injuries, yet the crowd did not dissipate. The
protestors continued their occupation against the accumulated effects of the
AKP's conservative, neoliberal rule on their lives, bodies, and spaces. These
effects had materialized through growing authoritarianism that intervenes
in secular life and violates freedom of speech; through neoliberal development projects that destroy nature, seize public spaces, and displace the urban poor; and through state-endorsed projects of democratization and
multiculturalism that constantly change the definition of tolerance and diversity, producing and breaking the limits of recognition for the political existence of Kurds, other non-Turks, and non-Muslims (Navaro-Yashin 2013).[2]
After a legal challenge, an administrative court (idari mahkeme) issued a verdict in the middle of the Gezi protests ordering that the construction project
be halted. In 2015, however, the court reversed its decision and removed the
legal obstacle. In 2016, President Recep Tayyip Erdoğan announced his decision to restart the development project in Gezi Park, emphasizing its importance for the country's history: "If we want to preserve our history, we
must rebuild this historic structure."[3]

The passengers on the Istanbul–Mardin flight I took were a mixed crowd
of Istanbulites, foreign tourists, Syrian refugees, and Mardinites. The walls of
the waiting rooms at the recently refurbished Mardin International Airport
were covered with advertisements for the city's new five-star hotels. I stood
in a parking lot full of hundreds of late-model cars bordering the shiny new
shopping mall, Movapark, that had recently been built just outside the airport. Just a few meters away were the Mesopotamian Plain and the military
posts marking the border with Syria. I was in a touristic place that coexisted
with the (in)visible movements of Syrian refugees and Kurdish guerrillas
who have been traveling back and forth between the war zones of Iraq, Syria,
and Turkey.

I hailed a taxi. My mind was still occupied by flashbacks to Gezi Park. I
felt as if I were still in the middle of conversations about gentrification, pluralism, solidarity, and the invisibility of the Kurds in the protests. I could not
stop myself from sharing my thoughts with the young taxi driver. Most people
were under the impression that the Kurds did not support the protestors.[4]
Maybe they needed to submit to the AKP rule for the sustainability of the
peace process. Maybe after all those years of neglect and disregard, it was too
late to expect that kind of solidarity. The young driver did not answer, other

than to respond, "We need stability and consistency," shutting down the conversation and thus indicating where he stood on the issue.

I recall hearing something similar from my elderly Armenian interlocutor who was originally from Mardin but has been living in Istanbul for four decades. "We need stability," he said, when I visited him at his house during one of my short breaks from Gezi Park. He did not want to talk about the protests. We had known each other for a decade at that point, and I had visited him before and after each of my trips to Mardin. We always discussed the same topic: life in the aftermath of Armenian genocide. No matter what happened outside his window-door frame in the heart of Istanbul, we always talked about the same thing. Even as we listened to the roar of chants on the street, we talked about the same thing. I reminded him that Surp Agop Cemetery remained beneath Gezi Park and mentioned my encounter with young Armenians holding the banners reminding people about it. He refused to listen. For him, these youngsters, this new generation, was against stability. We returned to the same questions: "What happened to us [Armenians]? What happened to my father's house in Mardin? They [current residents] never bought it. They occupied our house. They live in their lie machine [*yalan makinesi*]. They will die in that lie machine. . . . They visited my father the year after we left Mardin. They visited him when he was in the hospital to ask where the treasure was buried in the house. Can you believe that they dared to do that?" At the end of this visit, he gave me a copy of two pages from a book that lists the names of the Armenian families who owned stone mansions before 1915 in Mardin.

What should I do with this list? I rechecked inside my notebook. It was there. Was it a relief? I was not sure. I stayed in my own internal monologue until the young driver interrupted it with a most obvious question: Where was I going? Would I stay in Old Mardin (Eski Mardin), also called Upper Mardin (Yukarı Mardin), or in the New City (Yenişehir)? Yukarı Mardin, I replied. The former referred to the historical and touristic part of the city located on the hill and the latter to the main part that houses residences, businesses, and government agencies. Most parts of Republican Street, the artery that cuts through the Old City, were closed for restoration and demolition projects sponsored by the provincial government (*valilik*). My driver said that he would only be able to drive me to the Republican Square (Cumhuriyet Meydanı) in the Old City. It would not be easy for me to make my way up the rest of the street on foot with my luggage. "You'll see. The street

Figure 3. Republican Street during the historical transformation project in 2013.
The building on the left is one of the well-known stone mansions of the Old City. It
was initially constructed and owned by the Çermes, an Armenian family that left
Mardin in the 1950s. Next to it are two-story buildings evacuated for demolition.

looks like an evacuated village [*boşaltılmış köy*]," he said, evoking a familiar
image from the 1990s of the war between the Turkish Armed Forces and the
PKK. Stability, consistency, and déjà vu, I thought, reading between the lines
of what the driver had said at the beginning of our journey and what was
haunting me and people throughout the country concerning the unforesee-
able effects of the urban renewal projects of the AKP government.[5] It was as
if Turkey was one big (de)construction site (Figure 3).

I got out of the taxi. Piles of rubble were scattered on the narrow pave-
ment in front of me. Some parts of the street were covered with holes that
had been dug to repair the centuries-old sewage and water pipeline system.
Other parts had the shiny look of touristic Middle Eastern cities. They were
full of stone mansions that had been turned into boutique hotels, cafés with
fancy names, and shops brimming with souvenirs. Some of the buildings
stood empty, waiting to be demolished, while others had already been de-

molished and revealed the ruins of other stone houses. The headquarters of Turkcell, the mobile phone company, had been knocked down. Behind it was the half-destroyed building that had been known as the German barracks during World War I. It had originally been the house of an Armenian family, the Atayamans. The half-ruined floor rose above the Mardin Silver House shop, which had belonged to the Chaldean Catholic Church Foundation. Next to it was the old Bağkur Building, a social security organization for the self-employed and artisans. It had been demolished too. The remaining part of the building had been turned into a temporary coffeehouse. The house of my Armenian interlocutor was a few meters from the rubble.. Having been restored, it looked clean and emptier than ever. A few meters away there was the former police station, now a five-star hotel owned and run by the city's former mayor. Next to it was the old post office building, which had been restored by the local university and was being used as part of the Tourism Faculty. The teahouse with the view of the Mesopotamian Plain was one of the few untouched properties on the street. It wasn't covered with rubble or stones. The street ended in a fork marked by placards directing visitors to the City Museum (Kent Müzesi) or Mimarbaşı (head architect) Sarkis Lole Street, named a few years ago after the Armenian architect Sarkis Lole.[6] There was also a sign bearing the logo of the local government apologizing for the inconvenience and indicating that this was all part of the "Historical Transformation Project" (Tarihi Dönüşüm Projesi).[7]

Initiated by the local government in 2009, the Historical Transformation Project was promoted as the first step in the most comprehensive urban renewal (kentsel dönüşüm) project to be developed in Mardin. It promised the full demolition of 570 concrete buildings, the partial demolition of 860 buildings in the Old City and its outskirts, and the construction of new apartment buildings in the New City.[8] Populated by Kurdish locals, the outlying areas were designated as vulnerable to natural disasters. The majority of the houses were unregulated or unauthorized and were subject to removal or gentrification. The residents of these neighborhoods were to be moved to the houses built by Turkey's Housing Development Association (Toplu Konut İdaresi, or TOKI). These new TOKI houses (TOKI evleri) would be built in these outlying neighborhoods or in the New City. The local government would pay the rent for the first two years. The cost of the new TOKI house would be subtracted from the value of the owner's current house, and the remainder would be given to residents as credit so that they could pay off their mortgages. This was standard procedure for the urban poor in the TOKI

MARDiN 1920'LER   EREN parfümeri tel:2126361

Figure 4. Mardin in the 1920s. These images of Old Mardin were circulated and sold in different places, including photo, stationery, and perfume shops on Republican Street.

housing system. In Mardin, the urban renewal project was in the planning phase. According to the public relations officer from the Ministry of Urban Planning and Environment, nobody knew whether the local government would ever make it happen. However, the Historical Transformation Project was the new reality of the Old City. It had been taking place every day beneath and above Mardin since 2009. The project's main goal was to demolish the concrete structures on Republican Street and reveal the stone façade of the Old City, which was reckoned to belong to pre-republican times when one-quarter of the city residents were Armenian (Figure 4).[9]

With the return to its "original" structure, the city would be ready to be nominated as a UNESCO World Heritage Site. It would search its past for its future, as its motto suggested. The state technocrats were in a rush. The rubble would have to be cleared and the demolition of the remaining concrete buildings on Republican Street would have to be completed along with the repair of the infrastructure. This was a requirement for the release of an estimated 7.5 million euros that had been promised by the EU to provide technical support for the restoration of the Old City and increase its tourism capacity. More important, it was a requirement that the UNESCO application be submitted in 2014, one year before the centenary of the 1915 Armenian genocide. The state was in a rush to return to the imagined authentic form of the city in order to attain international recognition and capital.

The Historical Transformation Project was not the first heritage project to be implemented in Mardin. The promotion of Mardin as a showcase of historical and cultural heritage began before the AKP era. The nomination of archaeological and historical sites as UNESCO World Heritage Sites has been the Turkish state's main strategy for expressing its political and economic aspirations in its engagement with the EU. Following the accession process into the EU, the state selected and nominated sixteen sites for inclusion as UNESCO World Heritage Sites in 1999 (Atakuman 2010:120). The Ministry of Culture nominated the city of Mardin to be a UNESCO World Heritage Site in 2001 and initiated various projects designed to rehabilitate and renovate its built environment. The city was presented as an open air museum for the region with a long-standing presence of diverse cultures, religions, ethnicities, and monuments (Biner 2007). The application was submitted in 2002. In 2003, the AKP government withdrew it, asserting that it had done so in order to avoid its rejection. Over the next ten years, the AKP government used heritage and construction-centered policies to reassert the expression of its neoliberal rule in the country, reclaiming its political and economic territory in the conflict region and reestablishing its credibility in the eyes of transnational actors. Meanwhile, heritage consciousness flourished within pro-Kurdish political circles in opposition to the destructive and denialist politics of the government. The struggle over the recognition of the tangible and intangible heritage that belonged to the Kurdish culture, people, and territory has been the significant mean of reclaiming the political in the region (cf. Aykan 2015; Schafers 2015; Torne 2015).

In Mardin, the practices and discourses of heritage-centered projects did not revolve around the struggle between the government and pro-Kurdish party activists. Although the conflict framed the discursive limits of multiculturalism, the presence of Arabs and Syriacs has shaped the definition and imagination of the "historical" and the "cultural" within the multicultural domain. The cultural has been promoted as if it existed above and beyond the political, as the political has been associated with the Kurdish political movement. The boundaries between the ethnic and the cultural, between the nationalist and the multicultural have constantly shifted under the AKP rule of "neoliberal multiculturalism" (Hale 2005). Arabs and Syriacs and later even Kurdish locals in the city of Mardin agreed to live in the fantasy of this (in) distinction. While this fantasy allowed the Arabs and Syriacs to hold themselves away from the explosive domain of the Kurds, it gave the Kurds enough space to integrate into the acceptable domain of the neoliberal multicultural order. Though the boundaries of the distinction constantly fluctuated, heritage talk never disappeared from the horizon of future possibilities. It remained set in stone as a potential project. The Historical Transformation Project emerged from this space of potential development as yet another material expression of heritage-centered economies in the process of violent peace.

Anthropologists discuss heritage as a "thing" in and of itself, or as a "political idiom" that can be employed to support or oppose the political and economic aspirations of the neoliberal order of states.[10] From different perspectives, they have shown the ways in which these strategies can coexist and take place within hegemonic practices and discourses of heritage (e.g., Collins 2008; Brumann 2009; Herzfeld 2010; Franquesa 2013). In this connection, they have also explored how heritage has established its own domain-obscuring relationships with other social, economic, and political realms of life. In his comprehensive engagement with the academic and public discourses about heritage, Jaume Franquesa aptly argues this point, noting that "heritage is not a neutral category open to endless manipulation," but rather an "ideologically loaded notion operating in interlocking social fields fraught with power differentials and inequalities tending to reinforce these power dynamics" (2013:347). Franquesa adds, "Heritage should not be used as an analytical category but must be approached outside of its own web of practices and discourses" (347).

In his work on the politics of heritage in northeastern Brazil, John Collins (2008:283) makes a similar point, defining heritage as an exception "generating a certain amnesia to its emergence." Collins draws analogies between heritage planning and Agamben's notion of the state of emergency. Both heritage planning and claims about exception, Collins argues, "stamp out knowledge of their historical situatedness through simplification and re-codification within claims to essence that are in fact reflections of the very conditions that spurred the emergency or the claim to exception" (289). I follow these important methodological suggestions.

In Mardin, too, heritage-making projects are implemented to conceal the traces of histories of exceptions and transform the ruined Old City into a space of "exception" as a potential World Heritage Site. Here, I use heritage to reveal different forms of exceptions and to explore the relations between the legal, political, historical, and spiritual spheres that underlie locals' relationships with the built environment, the state, and the ethnic and religious other. My account of heritage goes against the nostalgic gaze of local notables and outsiders' Orientalist gaze to reposition the city in the broader structure of care and protection within the underdeveloped and authentic geography of Turkish Mesopotamia. I contextualize Mardin as a violent place created through the confiscations, appropriations, and unequal distribution of resources in compliance. I insist on asking: What made a city that has been subjected to the repressive measures of the Ottoman and republican regimes and that has accommodated the traces of this violation a site of cultural heritage? What techniques were used to stabilize the effects of ruination?

Ann Stoler's (2013a) work on ruination introduces an anthropological and historical sensibility to the study of relationships between colonial pasts and postcolonial presents. Stoler refuses to take these relationships as self-evident and calls attention to following the persistent and tangible effects of the imperial formations in the ruined landscapes and ruination of people's lives. In her view, to think with ruins is not to highlight the material products of the imperial formations as "remnants of a defunct regime," but to engage with their "re-appropriations, neglect, and strategic and active positioning within the politics of [the] present," to reveal "the protracted quality of decimation in people's lives" (2013b:11). Stoler defines *ruin* "as a violent verb that unites apparently disparate moments, places and objects" and puts her focus more on ruination "as an active, ongoing process that allocates imperial debris differentially" (2013b:7). "Ruination is a political project," argues Stoler, that "lays waste to certain peoples, relations, and things that accumulate in specific places" (11). Yet it is not a linear process. It actually evokes three senses of "being an act of ruining, condition of being ruined and a cause of it" (11). All these senses could overlap but they are not the same. "Each has its temporality," she asserts. "Each identifies different durations and moments of exposure to a range of violence that may be immediate or delayed, invisible or visible, prolonged or instant, diffuse or direct" (11). In breaking the linear imagination, Stoler pushes her argument further against the literature of victimhood and violence and postulates that ruination should not be approached as a project of constructing the history of trauma or redemption, but rather we should recognize that these are "unfinished histories, not of a victimised past but of consequential histories of differential futures" (11).

Inspired by Ann Stoler's work on ruination, I interpret the history of dispossession in Mardin as a resilient account of ruination from the Ottoman
Empire to the republican regime. The massacres, displacements, resettle-
ments, and appropriations that accompany those histories of violence have
left tangible and intangible, abrupt and yet persistent traces on landscapes,
objects, and people. At the same time, I argue that Stoler's call to view ruination as a process must be qualified. While her approach prevents the narrow identification of ruins with objects and sites from the past and invites us
to look at the persistent traces and connections that these ruins produce, we
run the risk of forgetting that these processes emerge from engagements with
objects that produce social, legal, and political relationships that are constitutive of ruination. In this ethnography, I study ruination not only through
"uneven temporal sedimentations" (Stoler 2013b:2) but also through different forms of materialities and their effects on people. Here, *ruin* refers to stone
buildings such as houses, sacred shrines, and other monuments. I engage with
these ruins as objects that evoke fear, desire, and obsession, as sites of destruction, construction, and haunted histories, and as cultural property that produces exchange and historical value. As such, the ruined stone buildings
emerge as the "mediators" of unfinished histories of dispossession. At the
same time, in this ethnography, the analysis of ruination is not limited to the
destruction and restoration of stone buildings as "monumental leftovers"
(Stoler 2013b:9). Ruination manifests itself in other areas of life produced
through the construction economy as the most aggressive material expression of neoliberal policies in the region. Drawing on this connection, I discuss heritage-making projects in juxtaposition with the construction boom
as active political projects of ruination in the city of Mardin. I explore these
relationships through the entanglements of different materialities. Stone and
concrete emerge as metaphors and materials that embody different tenses and
temporalities of ruination. They materialize and represent different forms of
state power that have opened up new territories of common interest as well
as new imaginaries of the self and other, past and future (cf. Harvey 2010;
Fehervary 2009; Abourahme 2014; Rubaii 2016). In the following chapters
(Chapter 2 and 3), I engage with the affective registers of these materials as
articulated, experienced, and felt by the residents of the Old City.

In the next section, I present a fragmented narrative of the history of
dispossession in Mardin. The narrative addresses double valences of ruination: the destruction and transformation of the built environment as it relates to stone and concrete and the displacement and replacement of different

ethnic and religious communities in the city. In this narrative, I produce a portrait of Mardin, its residents, postemergency discourses of heritage and construction economies, and the AKP version of neoliberal multiculturalism that encompasses all these components.

Multiple Layers of Ruination

As one Mardinite (Mardinli) said, "This city has always been a witness, but could never have been a homeland [vatan] for anyone." Beneath a historical castle, standing atop a hill covered with gigantic stone houses, each posed like a fortress surrounded by high walls, the Old City of Mardin looks like one body with many eyes gazing out upon the Mesopotamian Plain toward Syria. The city marks the crossroads of Syria, Iraq, and central parts of Turkey, controlling the routes from Diyarbakır to Mosul in the east and from the Plain of Harran to Aleppo in the west. In the social and historical imagination of the Mardinites, the castle has endured as a symbolic and material entity that embodies the historical and political character of the city. As the foundational territory, the castle(s)[11] appeared in the multiple narratives that chronicled the city's name and revealed the tensions that exist between different ethnic and religious communities over the historical representation of Mardin. According to Syriac authors, the city's name has its origins in the Aramaic words *Merdi* or *Merdin*, with the respective meanings of "castle" and "castles" (Dolapönü 1971; Akyüz 1998). According to Armenian historians, it originates from the Armenian word *Mardi*, meaning "martyr" or "warrior," and refers to the Armenians who sheltered in Mardin in the aftermath of the conflicts between Persians and Byzantines in 351 (Çerme 2000). According to a legend often told by the Arabs, its name comes from the story of love and hostility between Muslim and Christian communities. Mardin was a castle city governed by a Christian king who had a daughter named after the city. A Muslim emperor fell in love with Mardin, the daughter of the king, and occupied the city for his love of God and Mardin. He won the subsequent battle and succeeded in possessing both "Mardins." The legend came to be the symbol of the fusion of divine and human love, as exemplified by the glorious heroism of the Muslim emperor, who subsequently occupied and converted the castle to Islam.

Until the seventh century, Mardin remained under the control of Christian tribes despite the on-going attacks by the Persians and the Byzantines.

The trajectory of the conflict changed after the spread of Arabic influence in the region. The Arab occupation did rapidly lead to the conversion of most of the Christian population into Islam, the resettlement of Arabic tribes into the territory, and the taxation of the remaining Christian population. Against this backdrop, the oppositional position of the Syriac and Nestorian Christian communities against the Byzantine church pushed the local Christians to side with the Arabs. This alignment allowed the Christians, particularly Nestorians and Syriacs, to practice their religion and to accumulate capital through their integration into the economic and political system of the Arab imperial regimes (Aydın et al. 2000:71–76). At the beginning of the twelfth century, the region was taken under the control of the Turkish principality of Artuqid. Mardin became the capital city of the principality. Mardin Castle was transformed into an urban dwelling through the construction of stone houses, madrasas, and mosques. The historical architecture of the Old City was shaped between the twelfth and fifteenth centuries under the rule of the Artuqid principality. The stone-based built environment evolved through the continuous production of masonry and architectural decoration by Muslim and Christian masters (Açıkyıldız-Şengül 2012). In the sixteenth century, the Ottomans took over the city and changed its administrative status. Mardin became a province of Baghdad and later of Diyarbakır (Aydın et al. 2000:111–21). Located at the crossroads, the city of Mardin was the hub of different local sovereigns who included Kurdish and Arab tribal leaders, high-ranking military officers, and state bureaucrats. It was also a significant transit point for merchants involved in the local and translocal commerce of slaves, animals, agricultural products, and other goods. The population was composed of Kurds, Arabs, Turks, Syriacs, Armenians, Nestorians, Chaldeans, Jews, and Shemsis.[12] Until the nineteenth century, half of the city's population consisted of non-Muslim locals, Armenians and Syriacs who were dominant in the sectors of trade, agriculture, manufacture, and artisanry, mastering jewelry and masonry (Abdalla 2013:135).[13]

Under the Ottoman regime, the city witnessed protracted tensions between the Kurdish and Arab tribes struggling to consolidate their power in the city (Aydın et al. 2000:167–90). These tensions intensified significantly during the nineteenth century. The modernization and centralization reforms of the Ottoman state prompted violent struggles between the recently appointed Ottoman pashas and local tribal sovereigns (196).

The Tanzimat (reorganization) reforms promulgated between 1839 and 1876 granted rights to non-Muslim subjects, shifting the balance of the social and political hierarchies between the Muslim and non-Muslim subjects (Aydın et al. 2000:196). The same period witnessed the organization of missionary activities in the region. As a cosmopolitan city, Mardin gained a new function as one of the main hubs of the Catholic Capuchin mission and American Protestant mission, which became highly influential in the social, religious, and political realms of life by providing health and education services and employment in the city (Özcoşar 2005; Macar 2013; Naby 2013). They established their operations near the Syriac and Armenian churches and in other neighborhoods. These political and social transformations had significant impacts on the relationship between Muslim and non-Muslim communities. Specifically, some of the Kurdish tribal leaders emerged from the local conflicts with increased power and autonomy and played a role in provoking public uproar and uprisings against the non-Muslim population, who were accused of being traitors because of their economic and political links with European powers (Aydın et al. 2000:243; Üngör and Polatel 2013:20–22).

The architectural development of the city was suspended due to the chaotic atmosphere and economic stagnation in the sixteenth and seventeenth centuries. At the beginning of the eighteenth century, during a short period of stability, local elite families constructed new houses. In the nineteenth century the Ottoman administration built government buildings such as offices, municipal buildings, military barracks, and a prison. The same period also witnessed the proliferation of church construction as Christians were allowed to erect new religious buildings as a result of the Reform Edict of 1856. During the last years of the nineteenth century, the most prominent examples of stone masonry were built. The owners included Muslim and Christian tradesmen, artisans, tribal leaders and aristocratic families who were elected as members of the councils to govern the city (Açıkyıldız-Şengül 2012). The stone mansions built in this period for the governors were regarded as the material expression of state power (Aydın et al. 2000:233).

The 1912 Balkan Wars were the first manifestation of the drastic changes that led to the forced displacement of Armenians to designated locations within the territory of the empire (Dündar 2001). The outbreak of World War I precipitated the massive displacement and extermination of the Armenians and the sudden departure of the Syriacs. Because the main road between the northern Kurdish provinces of Van, Erzurum, and Bitlis and the cities of Syria led through Mardin, thousands of deportees were gathered in and subsequently pushed through the city.[14] In 1915, more than half of the

Christian population in Mardin was forcefully disappeared.[15] While crowds of Armenian men were deported[16] (Ternon 2013:265–293), the women and children who remained were soon forced to leave their houses following the mass deportations (Abdalla 2013:137). Only those who converted to Islam or pretended to belong to the Syriac community managed to survive. Some were abducted and sold to prominent local families who were also involved in looting the properties. The majority of the disappeared came from the Armenian Catholic community. With the sultan's amnesty, the Syriac Ortho-dox community was held exempt from deportation (Gaunt 2013:19; Aydın et al. 2000:336). The same amnesty later saved Syriac Catholics and Chal-deans in the city (Ternon 2013:292), though it did not apply to Syriacs living in the rural hinterland

The perpetrators, witnesses, and survivors referred to the 1915 massacres as Nakabat ("disaster" in Arabic), Ferman ("order" in Arabic), Qase ("mas-sacre" in Aramaic), and Sayfo (the term abbreviates *shato d'sayfo*, "the year of the sword," in a western dialect of Aramaic) (Gaunt 2013:14). While elder Kurds and Arabs used Ferman, the Syriacs adapted Sayfo and circulated it in the region and diaspora to refer to the massacres of their community in 1915 (see Chapter 4).

The 1915 massacres and their aftermath led to a long period of destruc-tion and dispossession of material heritage in Mardin. The properties of the Armenian community were not only destroyed or looted but also dispos-sessed through legal orders enacted by the Ottoman authorities that allowed for their confiscation and liquidation (Gaunt 2013; Ternon 2013; Çetinoğlu 2013; Üngör and Polatel 2013:42–43). The new Turkish state adopted this leg-acy through the enactment of the laws of *emval-i metruke* (abandoned prop-erties), which legitimized the dispossession of the properties of the Ottoman citizens who left and did not return before the publication of the Lausanne Treaty in 1923. Under these laws, which were revised and adopted according to the political and economic needs of the new Turkish state in 1928, as Üngör and Polatel (2013:55–56) aptly explain, "the immobile properties that were allocated to the immigrants or liquidated by the Treasury according to the laws of the abandoned properties would not be given to their original owners. Rather their values (decided by the 15 April 1925 law) were paid by the Min-istry of Finance." Furthermore, they note, "the title deed to these abandoned properties could be given to the non-exchange people, immigrants, refugees, members of tribes, and victims of fire" (55–56).[17] The last category of "vic-tims of fire" would have also involved the families of the assassinated ex-leaders of the Committee of Union and Progress (İttihat ve Terakki Partisi), the government party that ordered the extermination and deportation of the Armenians. In 1926, the new Turkish government recognized those assassinated ex-leaders as martyrs (55–56), the assassinations being blamed on Armenian hit men. According to a law enacted in the same year, the families of these assassinated leaders "were given immovable properties from the Armenian abandoned properties which were worth 20,000 Turkish lire" (56). They would be given the deeds "with the stipulation that they were not allowed to sell these properties within ten years" (56). The laws on abandoned properties were abolished in 1986. The Turkish state continued to liquidate the abandoned properties, as Üngör and Polatel report, "in effect [for] 73 years" (57). In 2001, the "General Directorate of Land Registry and Cadastre (Tapu ve Kadastro Genel Müdürlüğü) enacted and published a new order stating that abandoned properties could not be passed down to any individual, but to the state. Neither the real owners nor their heirs would be able to make any claim on the properties" (58). The abandoned properties of the Armenians, in short, were regarded as not inheritable.

Following the establishment of the new republic, Mardin was designated as the province bordering Syria. Its administrative offices were moved to the Old City of Mardin, which served as the seat of administrative government for all of the Kurdish towns and villages that had been politically and historically significant during the Ottoman era (Aydın et al. 2000:364–365). In 1925, Kurdish uprisings against the new regime prompted new measures that generally targeted the Muslim (non-Turkish) population of the region, and Mardin in particular. Many members of Mardin's influential Arab and Kurdish extended families were exiled, while some leaders of Kurdish tribal families were executed as a result of verdicts of the tribunals of independence (istiklal mahkemeleri)[18] (366–367). Some of the accused fled to Syria or Iraq to avoid execution and returned to the city after the general amnesty of 1928. However, the Syriacs and the Armenians who fled between 1915 and 1919 were excluded from the general amnesty under a law that banned citizenship for subjects who had not participated in the war for independence and, having left Turkey, had returned only after 24 July 1923 (Çapatay 2003). In this emerging spatial and political context, the Turkish state empowered Arab notable families and gave them new positions and roles in the bureaucratic system. They were entrusted with promoting and implementing the reforms of the new regime and surveying their efficacy in the public and private spheres (Aydın et al. 2000:375–387).

After 1915, Syriac and Armenian churches and monasteries were appropriated by the military, used as barracks, hospitals, and prisons, and then occupied by Muslim locals. The buildings of the Syriac Catholic Patriarchy, the Armenian Church of Surp Hosep and Surp Kosevk, and the Syriac Orthodox of Deyrulzafaran Monastery were appropriated in the early months of the new republic (Abdalla 2013:139).[19] Properties belonging to Armenian families were allocated to local families—Kurds, Arabs, and Syriacs—who participated in the extermination of their neighbors, or to immigrant Muslim populations, such as the Chechens. In the same process, Armenian women and children were sold through auctions in public and made part of the transaction of property (Çetinoğlu 2013:18–27). The laws enacted during the first two decades of the republic encouraged locals to employ individual techniques of appropriation and to use the law to legitimize their acts and claim official ownership of Armenian properties. According to the narratives of the Armenian locals who left Mardin before the 1950s, the Muslims acted as calumniators, falsely claiming that they had seen Armenian owners in another country, since this statement would change the status of property to abandoned property. Others accused owners of owing them money and pressed charges against them, asking the court to grant ownership of the property to cover the debts.[20] These (il)legal transactions prompted the emigration of the majority of the Armenian families who had managed to remain in, or return to, the city after 1915. In the end there were only five Armenian families left in Mardin and these continued their lives in the city, through mixed marriages with Syriacs and recognized as such by Muslim locals.

Property continued to change ownership over the next three decades due to migration movements in the region and throughout Turkey. In the 1950s, notable Arab families started to leave the city for educational and economic reasons. The Syriacs started migrating in the 1940s and escaped to Qamishli, Syria, which was already a place for Syriac and Armenian survivors and protagonists of the Kurdish uprisings and blood feuds (see Altuğ 2013). During the same period, Kurds and Mhallamis (Mahalmiler in Turkish)[21] from nearby villages and towns migrated to Mardin. Confiscated Armenian properties changed hands again during this period. The state auctioned off the houses that it had used as military stations, hospitals, and schools. Affluent local Arab and Syriac families who were the first occupier-owners of these houses sold the properties before they left the city. They were purchased by wealthy Kurdish families who had just migrated to the city as well as the remaining

Arab and Syriac families. Kurdish and Mhallami migrants without means rented or occupied rooms in the stone houses, some of which belonged to Armenian and Syriac church foundations.

During the post-1950 period, stone buildings were destroyed and concrete structures invaded the urban landscape. Apart from the legal and political measures that regulated the politics of dispossession, starting in the 1930s, the Turkish state established institutions and built concrete buildings as the infrastructure of the new statecraft in Mardin. The city was rebuilt through the gradual demolition of stone buildings, particularly the ones associated with the Christian legacy, such as the buildings of the Catholic missionaries, in which case the alleged goal was expanding the road on Republican Street. Armenian and Syriac cemeteries in that area were also destroyed. They remained under the new constructions or were transferred and distributed to other existing Christian cemeteries in the city. Well-off Kurdish families, landowners, traders, and old-time smugglers began to use concrete to extend their stone houses by building additions or new floors. Families without means who settled in single rooms of the stone houses used concrete to build walls separating their space from that of the neighbors with whom they shared a courtyard. The erection of the statue of Mustafa Kemal Atatürk, founder of the republic, and the opening of the Republican Square at the site of what had been the Capuchin monastery, school buildings, and the cemetery of the Syriac Catholic Church are the most visible examples of the officially endorsed spatial transformation in the 1960s (Küçük 2013). In parallel, following Turkey's entry into NATO in the 1950s, the border zones began to be heavily militarized. In 1953, the Mardin castle was earmarked as a base to house NATO radar to monitor territory all the way from Russia to Egypt. Consequently, the castle was turned into a military zone, cordoned off with barbed wire, separated from its surroundings, and closed to the public.

The migration of Syriacs and Arabs continued throughout the 1960s and 1970s. Kurds and Mhallamis continued to fill the void that the emigrants left behind. Mhallamis who had previously worked as the servants of affluent Arab and Kurdish families and lived in the vicinity of their stone mansions occupied and appropriated the properties of the recently migrated families in the Old City. Kurds who arrived during this period settled in two different parts of the city. Some moved into stone houses at the bottom of the Old City and others built one- or two-floor concrete houses outside the visible boundaries of the Old City that fall within the cemetery area in the south or at the east end. These new settlements outside the Old City in the cemetery zone turned into new neighborhoods that were mainly occupied by Kurdish villagers. A road built in the 1970s that circumvented the southern border of the Old City to connect it to its hinterland gained an additional function in those years. Known as the New Road (Yeni Yol), this passage was the border between the Old City and the new neighborhoods, and it functioned as the battlefield between Kurdish and Mhallami youngsters and families.

In 1979, the Old City was declared a protected historical area (sit alanı) and three hundred of the stone buildings were registered as cultural assets (kültürel varlık) (Aydın et al. 2000:374), Following the 1980s military coup and neoliberal-oriented government policies, all of the illegal housing built without permits was legalized (Karaman 2013:722). This gave way to heavy concretization of the built environment in the city, regardless of its special status as a protected historical area. Another spatial development that emerged in the 1980s was the expansion of the city to the east and west. The land on the west end had been set aside for housing for state and military officers. The land on the east end of the city was opened for the construction of apartment buildings, effectively turning it into the city's main residential area. It would come to be known as the New City.

The conflict between the Turkish Armed Forces and the PKK had a significant impact on the social, political, and spatial structure of the city. Mardin was, on the one hand, was a sanctuary for the families of the military officers and the state authorities. On the other hand, it was one of the settlement areas for Kurdish families who had been forced to leave their villages under emergency conditions. In the process and because of their support for the PKK, some of the already established Kurdish families were subjected to constant interrogation and acts of repression by the state. In order to avoid being caught in the cross fire, Syriacs precipitously left the city. The displaced Kurdish villagers either filled the vacuum of locals in the Old City or settled in the neighborhoods outside it. The Arab and Syriac locals stigmatized these places as terörist mahallesi (terrorist neighborhoods). In the eyes of the Kurdish locals living in these neighborhoods, the Old City was a foreign land. They would only go there to visit the market and public offices or send their children to school. Otherwise, they would avoid it and continue life in their own segregated corners.

In the Old City, with the flight of the Syriac and Arab families, control of the territory passed to the Mhallamis and Kurds, the long-term occupants who had migrated to Mardin in the 1950s. They managed to control ruined and abandoned spaces of the Old City such as houses, shops, church buildings, parks, and teahouses. Mhallamis owed their authority to the cash that they accumulated through occupation of the properties and bribery that they received from the Syriac families as a protection fee, as well as the network established with state employees. Kurdish families owned their immunity to their aggressiveness, which had helped them to protect the boundaries of their territory from both Mhallamis and other Arabs. In 2000, when the intense military conflict came to a temporary end, Mardin was a spatially and socially segregated place. It was split between the rising apartment blocks of the New City, the ruined stone houses in the Old City, and the one-floor half-completed concrete settlements on the outskirts. While the neighborhoods outside the Old City were set aside as the areas of the Kurds, the Old City itself was a zone of abandonment and neglect. It was inhabited by a mixed population of Arabs, Mhallamis, Kurds, and Syriac families; the majority of the latter kept within their residences on properties that belonged to Syriac Orthodox and Catholic foundations.

Mardin Post-2000

In 2001, the Turkish Ministry of Culture nominated the Old City for a UNESCO World Heritage Site candidacy as part of the postemergency rehabilitation projects. The end of the conflict attracted new visitors, culturally sensitive tourists, and national and international experts who aimed to implement various projects to rehabilitate the city in a way that would enhance Mardin's bid to become a World Heritage Site. The discourse on Mardin's possible status as a World Heritage Site changed how both insiders and outsiders viewed this space. The national media portrayed Mardin as a remote and mystical city of the "Turkish Orient" with a unique architectural heritage, a kind of Babylon that allowed its multireligious and multilingual communities to peacefully coexist (Biner 2007). Stone was the main component of the landscape that was thrust into the spotlight.

After 1999, Mardin gained widespread visibility through imagery of stone architecture circulated as part of documentaries and photo exhibitions.[22] Promoted as *taşın ve inancın şehri* (city of stone and faith), Mardin was represented through the juxtaposed images of the minaret and the cross and bell of the church. Stone was portrayed as the essential fabric of the background context framing people, objects, and places. These images ranged from an old man rolling tobacco in front of a half-demolished stone building covered with a Turkish flag to children passing through the gigantic wooden gate of a stone house or peering from behind the bars of a window with stone carving. They also included conscripted soldiers having their Mardin souvenir photo taken in traditional Arab dress with the stone façade of Mardin as the background.

In the middle of the decade 2000–2010, the city's stone architecture was a popular backdrop for films and TV series based on stories of blood feuds, honor crimes, and unnamed wars between soldiers, tribal leaders, guerrillas, or terrorists depending on the politics of the representation of the moment. Within a very short period, stone houses became the scenes of love, death, and revenge associated with authenticity, tradition, and violence as the essential qualities of life in the East. This created an illusion of familiarity. The Old City was the point of entry to this imagined land of the East, providing artistic, cultural, and authentic space that outsiders could consume without touching, smelling, or seeing the rest of the scarred landscape fraught with scattered images of sudden enrichment, deepened poverty, and exclusion that emerge as the constitutive parts of the everyday politics of neoliberalism in this conflict-ridden environment.

As a matter of fact, the state discourse of multiculturalism in 2000–2010 avoided the political presence of ethnic identities. Despite the strong emphasis placed on the cultural plurality of the city, Kurdishness and Arabness were not necessarily part of the culture talk in Mardin. While the Armenians were absent from this discursive space, Syriacs were portrayed as the local Christians. They were evoked through representations of religious practices or descriptions of their return to ancient lands after their long stay in European countries. They were painted as authentic yet unknown subjects waiting to be rediscovered. The Arab elites who were actively participating in the promotion of the city and the design of related projects were complying with the official state discourse's disavowal of the city's ethnic politics and mimicking the slippages between the culture and ethnicity (Karaca 2009; Schafers 2015). On the other hand, the Kurdish locals who were closely following the process were seriously disturbed by this conscious dismissal. In their view, the popular image of Mardin as a peaceful city was an illusion that had been officially crafted with the complicity of the Arabs and Syriacs to cover up the violence and poverty in the city (Biner 2007).

Mardin's World Heritage Site application was submitted to UNESCO in early 2003. A few months later, officials explained that the application had been withdrawn because they had been unable to submit all the required documents and had received a negative evaluation from the International Council on Monuments and Sites that operated as the advisory board of the World Heritage Committee. The report from the council confirmed the historical value of the city but did not support the application for two main reasons. First, although Mardin was described as the center of Syriac culture and the capital of the Artiquids, the Deyrulzafaran Monastery and the Kasımıye Maadrasa were not listed on the map of the Old City. Second, the Old City was in serious decay. Mardin Castle was still marked as a military zone. The city walls were eroding. The stone buildings were destroyed or badly damaged (Biner 2007).

Heritage-Construction-Tourism: Business for All

Despite the withdrawal of the application, the AKP-supported provincial governments and municipalities continued pushing the projects further in an effort to promote the city's cultural heritage. In the AKP era, the discourses and practices of cultural heritage gradually changed. Drawing on the reinvented tradition of multiculturalism of the Ottoman Turkish past, the new official ideology was based on the principle of "tolerance of difference" to justify and legitimize neoliberal and cultural policies (Iğsız 2015:327).[23] The reinterpretation of tolerance once again shifted the slippery distinction between ethnicity and culture and lifted the implicit ban on the public visibility of the Kurds in the cultural sphere (see Karaca 2009, 2011; Schafers 2015). The local governments encouraged the economic and cultural initiatives of all actors regardless of their ethnicity as long as their projects served to make Mardin a brand synonymous with tolerance and pluralism without threatening the sovereignty of the Turkish state (Karaca 2011). Individual projects would be supported through state or international funding, and organizers would be encouraged to collaborate with the global cultural and economic elites. Access to opportunities marked the official limits of cultural recognition in Mardin. In this period, neither cultural nor political capital fell under the hegemony of elite Arab local families. Syriac Christians were welcome to contribute to the exhibition of material culture at city museums or at the Bienal art exhibitions. Token Armenian Mardinites would be invited to international conferences on Mardin's urban history and their challenge to the official discourse of multiculturalism would be tolerated. The locals living inside or outside Mardin would be integrated into the cultural and heritage economy as long as they attempted to participate in the AKP government network and comply with the government's capital-oriented pragmatism.

Due to a lack of infrastructure for the export-led economy and structural economic inequality, most of the cities in the region have become part of the heritage and construction economy and employed the cultural and economic strategies of the localized version of neoliberalism. As Ayşe Seda Yüksel (2011:442) has aptly described, the cultural appropriation of space through heritage-focused projects was accompanied by a spatial expansion and segregation in which "the housing market and land speculation have become strategic means for articulating to global markets." Regardless of the EU-encouraged and -funded "cultural diversity turn" and the transnational character of the Kurdish movement, "construction, construction-related activities and the housing sector form a lifejacket for many firms in the urban economy," argues Yüksel (442).

In 2004, the AKP enacted the new Municipality Law (Law No. 5393), which granted municipalities the authority to implement urban transformation projects in risky areas with the partnership of TOKI (the Housing Development Administration). This government institution gradually became the strongest real estate developer in the country, "the sole agency to regulate the zoning and sale of almost all state-owned land" (Yüksel 2011:441). The speculative economy that revolved around the housing and land market has become an important source of wealth for the property owners who benefited from the boom of the construction economy.

TOKI planned three megaprojects in the region: the regeneration of the Sur neighborhood in Diyarbakır, the rebuilding of the Hasankeyf in Batman, and the Mardin Houses project in Mardin (Yüksel 2011).The Mardin Houses Project did not take place in the Kurdish neighborhoods, but in the New City. During 2000–2010, the New City became filled with concrete apartment blocks without any proper planning for infrastructure. This led to both unlimited construction of concrete buildings and opportunities for sudden wealth. Any landowner could get permission to build. The rules were flexible. Bribery was common practice between landowners, builders, and the public officials who worked in the urban planning offices of the local municipality. The floor area ratio was open to shifts depending on the relationship between the real estate developers and the urban planning officers. One could get permission to increase the number of floors and apartments in the building even if that number violated the terms set out in the municipality's urban planning regulations. This would generate more cash for the landowners and builders as well as the officials who granted the unofficial permit for the addition of each extra floor as part of the bribery economy.

Regardless of his family, class, or ethnic background, any landowner with a potential building permit could be the next neo-rich Mardinite owing his present prosperity to the flexibility of the construction sector. The landowner would sign a contract with a builder, who might or might not be a technically expert person. In the exchange of the land, the landowner would get half of the apartments that were to be built on the property. According to the builders, engineers, and architects, it was impossible to stay out of this system because there would always be someone tempting them to break the law and build more. There were absolutely no bureaucratic obstacles. Two thousand Turkish liras[24] would buy the permit to build two extra floors. That was just the beginning of the cash flow. With the high demand for housing, prices would go up and provide the builder and owner an enormous amount of cash. The capital would be reinvested in the purchase of more land or the construction of more buildings. The landowner-Kurds from nearby towns, the middle- and upper-middle-class professional Kurds with the desire for a consumptive social and urban life, the Mardinites who live abroad, and wealthy Syrian refugees were all looking to buy property in the New City. The construction companies would present the model of the new apartments in the shopping mall, Movapark. The apartments would be in different sizes and prices with the promise of security guards, car parks, children's parks, and interior swimming pools. They were in gated and enclosed spaces that would provide the residents with all the facilities they would need. The prices would range between 150,000 and 400,000 Turkish liras (Figure 5).[25]

Concrete was the main material of expression for the AKP-ruled neoliberalism that created the vicious cycle between cash, land, and apartment blocks that literally destroyed every empty area in the city. The city was growing wildly and in all directions, in a rush for cash because no one had any certainty about the future. The peace process could collapse at any time and these conditions for sudden enrichment and access to resources and benefits could vanish. The construction boom and excess concretization of the New City had material repercussions in the Old City. While space-oriented policies led to new accumulation strategies through spatial intervention in urban spaces, the daily imaginary was fraught with discourses and practices surrounding the change and exchange of the built environment: selling a house, buying a house, getting money for the restoration, waiting for demolition of the concrete structures built as extension of the stone buildings.

Figure 5. People looking at the models of the luxury apartments promoted in Movapark, a shopping mall, 2013. Photo by Yektanurşin Duyan.

During this process, half of the houses in Mardin were declared cultural assets. While a few stone houses still stand in a repaired state and are occupied by the old locals of the city, others have been transformed into museums, hotels, or cafés. The majority of those declared cultural assets have become ruins alongside the temples, madrasas, or church buildings restored for historical tourism. They have been standing as abandoned sites in the Old City, providing cheap accommodations for the urban poor and most recently for the latest Syrian refugees who cannot afford expensive apartments in the new part of the city.

The cultural turn that magnified the ethnic and spatial texture of the city created new entanglements between the state, local actors, and transnational institutions such as the EU and UNESCO that were involved with the regulation and management of historical sites as the gatekeepers and main funders of cultural heritage projects (Çağlar 2007). These projects were not independent from the new political process called Kurdish opening (Kürt açılımı) that the AKP introduced in 2009, promising to open up new spaces through the recognition of rights for ethnic and religious minorities. The ambiguous nature of the opening allowed the state to apply arbitrary sanctions and rules regarding cultural, artistic, legal, and political practices.

It was within this political context that the provincial government initiated the Historical Transformation Project in the Old City. The provincial government's plan was to implement a robust demolition and restoration project that would guarantee further EU funding for the heritage and tourism projects. More important, it would lay the groundwork for resubmission of the UNESCO application. Old Mardin would be an unpopulated open air museum, an attraction for foreign tourists, an excavation site for diggers, a place of return for Christians that would offer them an opportunity to return and reappropriate their property.

In Mardin, the limits of the Historical Transformation Project were expressed in the personal acts of the provincial governor (vali) who was running the project with the authority to make exceptions and who dismissed all the opinions and critical intervention of civil society stakeholders who wanted to be involved in the process. The valis' affective and political position as the representatives of the sovereign state was still prevalent in the postemergency period. Even though their authority to make the exception was expected to expire with the end of the state of emergency, they were still acting as the official persona of the sovereign with the power to decide on the exception and considered as such. This was even more visible and tangible in the city of Mardin as the mayors were often elected among the candidates from the AKP. During the local elections of 2014, the Mardinites for the first time voted for a candidate from the pro-Kurdish party. A well-known political persona, Ahmet Türk became the mayor of the province of Mardin. That did not change the dynamic of the process as the project continued to operate as the trademark of the provincial governorship. The vali that initiated the project was not in the post any longer. The next vali continued with the same mission. Yet, the Mardinites—both the local officers working as part of this project and the locals who benefited and witnessed—still had the vivid memory of the vali who initiated, named, and funded the project. The project was narrated through his stubborn, vehement persona.

I provide a detailed analysis of the rumors, speculations, and practices that emerged from the enactment of the Historical Transformation Project in the next chapter. First, though, I explain the way in which transformation was expressed in the built environment of the Old City. This will take us back

to two main premises asserted at the beginning of the chapter. The first refers to the heritage-making practices that stand out as an exception "generating a certain amnesia to its conditions of emergence" (Collins 2008:283).
Here, we observe this process through the sovereign performance of the vali
that acts to transform the appearance of the Old City. The second premise
refers to the analysis of relations between concrete and stone that reveals the
mapping of ruination as a historical and political project in Mardin.

The Historical Transformation Project

"Be careful not to confuse the two projects. You should separate the Historical Transformation Project from the urban transformation project. In fact,
Mardin does not currently have an urban transformation project. What is
currently taking place is the Historical Transformation project, which was
initiated as a result of the personal and political aspirations of the vali in 2009.
To be honest with you, it was his individual project at the beginning. He
wanted to demolish all of the concrete additions and buildings on Republican Street and conduct an architectural survey of the stone houses in the market area." The project administrator clarified the purpose of the project as
we sat in his fancy office in one of the state-owned renovated stone buildings. In between sentences, the project administrator would pick up the phone
to answer a call from yet another property owner who wanted her/him to
explain how to obtain compensation or apply for restoration funding if her
or his house was registered as a heritage property. He was tense as he tried to
find different yet noncontradictory ways of explaining the project to different actors. "Demolition of 110 concrete buildings was set as the condition
for the EU to fund the heritage- and tourism-centered project," he said. "The
vali did everything he could to fulfill the promise. He brought in all sorts of
money to complete the process."

The demolition process didn't cause any conflicts, but it turned out to be
very costly for the provincial government as all the evacuees were paid regardless of whether they actually held the deed to the property. According
to the project administrator, what was executed was not an official act of confiscation. "We didn't use our legal rights to vacate these houses. We waited
to receive the residents' consent. We wanted to satisfy their expectations," he
said when asked to explain the government's position vis-à-vis the evacuees.
The word *satisfy* was carefully chosen to convey the meaning behind the pol-

itics of the demolition and evacuation. The act involved a consensus between the vali and the residents.

The vali formed a Reconciliation Committee composed of technical experts and bureaucrats who were in change of establishing the values of the properties and negotiating compensation with the owners. In the view of most of the members, there was no standardization or enforcement. The priority was to reach an agreement between the provincial government and the residents without either taking legal action. The parties were to reach an official deal with flexible terms that would be respectful of local sentiments and serve the political aspirations of the vali, who desperately wanted to complete the initiative. The priority was to make a deal without any conflict.

According to the rumors that were circulated daily by the technocrats who were critical of the process, the value of a property was not determined on the basis of its size, but based on the "size of the people," referring to the residents' economic and social status within the community. Big men got more than the rest. The vali paid a lot of money to local notables to make them vacate their homes. Playing the role of arbitrator, the vali drew on different economic resources to absorb the cost of relocating major local players and regain full control of the Old City. Again, there was no visible tension, enforcement, or opposition in the public sphere. Only a few opponents went to court because they were not satisfied with their compensation. In all, 110 concrete structures purchased or constructed by Kurds, Arabs, and Mhallamis in the 1950s and rebuilt throughout the 1970s and 1980s were demolished as a result of the swift action of the vali with the consent of the Monuments Council (Anıtlar Kurulu) under the scrutiny of EU institutions.

The demolition of the concrete was followed by the restoration of the stone structures. Under the Historical Transformation Project, the provincial government funded the restoration of some of the public spaces and buildings, including shrines, monumental buildings, and the tunnels (*abbaras*) that connected neighborhoods. Efforts also were made to improve infrastructure in that area. The local architects were critical of the vali's dismissive attitude. He hired private contractors from outside Mardin who did not know much about the distinctive architectural and historical fabric of the Old City. They dug alleys using industrial excavation machines that cut into the historical urban fabric and destroyed the spatial balance of the built environment. The alleys were full of garbage because the donkeys—the traditional garbage collectors of the Old City—could not enter sites with holes. The areas were soon populated by rats. The vibrations caused by the machines compromised the foundations of the houses. The method that the private companies employed was not appropriate for the distinctive fabric of the historical stone architecture. It was too speedy and intrusive, and its use reflected a lack of knowledge of the nature of the material used in the homes' interiors and exteriors. Restoration was undertaken in a similar way. In fact, architects and engineers would call what was done in Mardin "renovation" rather than "restoration." The general approach involved removing concrete additions from the stone buildings and filling in the cracks between the stones with special cement. In some cases, the façades of run-down, ruined, or concrete buildings were covered with stone in order to give the area a clean look. This method was far from being restoration, which involves recovering the original appearance of an object or space. It also went against the grain of conservation because it violated the maximum lifespan of the stone. The cement that contractors used to fill in the cracks between the stones not only erased the marks between the stones from different periods but also damaged the stone itself. The method turned what was meant to be an act of restoration into destruction, thus making demolition the main component of the Historical Transformation Project.

The goal of renovation and demolition as they occurred in Mardin was to cleanse the stone buildings of concrete as the marker of dirt, ignorance, destruction, violence, and occupation and to cover it up with stone as the authentic, original, and native material of the original landscape. According to the nonlocal experts who worked on the project, what was referred as technical was actually political in Mardin. The vali and bureaucrats used demolition and restoration to conceal the political aims, and the residents of the Old City submitted to their rule. As one of the engineers aptly put it, "The vali wanted to finish all of these restoration projects so that the city could be chosen to be a UNESCO World Heritage Site. The state desperately wants this recognition so that it could make the whole world believe that despite the absence of the Armenians, the state is in charge of protecting their heritage."

The provincial government recognized the Old City of Mardin as a ruin to be assessed, restored, and preserved in a manner that met UNESCO's World Heritage Site program criteria. The bureaucrats confused the absence of people with ruined heritage and treated the restoration of the material legacy of Armenians as a technical project involving the cultural salvaging of certain historical buildings. The vali created an exceptional technopolitical space to erase the marks and control the process of ruination as proof of preservation of cultural heritage that can be documented in the context of the

UNESCO application. They sought to craft a clean, fixed image of the past without allowing the ruins to evoke the memory of destruction and dispossession. The restored ruin was now free of all traces of the movements, appearances, and disappearances of local communities. In this context, stone has become the revitalized and reauthenticated material of the Old City, while concrete has become the main material of the New City, which represents the mass housing projects of the government, abundance of cash, a new class of nouveau riche Mardinites, and a desire for consumption of a new urban life style.

In this chapter, I have traced the connections that exist between exception(s) and heritage making in the Old City of Mardin. My emphasis on exception refers to the traces of "uneven temporal sedimentations" (Stoler 2013b:2) produced with(in) the foundational violence of the sovereign state as well as in its aftermath. In this historical and political context, heritage emerged as exceptional through state-sponsored projects that removed the ruined buildings from their impoverished contexts; through the decisions and actions of the valis; through the ideology of neoliberal multiculturalism, which offered rights to the selected minority citizens in the conflict region. However, not all of these ruins receive the political and economic attention of the state. While some of them become part of the abstracted and homogenized space of heritage, others are left to waste and further decay (cf. Abu-El Haj 2001; Breglia 2006; Collins 2013; Gordillo 2014; Çaylı 2016). The following chapters explore how the locals deal with these ruined buildings, the material remnants of past atrocities, a commodity of the present as an object with a heritage quality. What kind of relationships do they form with the political, material, and affective registers of these ruins? How were they affected by these concurrent processes of demolition, restoration, surveying, and registration of historical stone buildings as properties of cultural heritage?

Ruined Heritage

Although heritage has always been a tricky area of potential conflict over the possession of remnants of violent pasts, it has the power to generate new relationships that find their expression in struggles over the right to access resources and the creation of new connections between people, objects, space, and the environment (see, e.g., Ferry 2005; Bunten 2008; Collins 2008; Herzfeld 2010; Cesari 2010; Franquesa 2013). In Mardin, heritage was never seen as an "exceptional object" imagined as separate disentangled from the political economy of everyday life (cf. Collins 2008:292). While the Armenians who had left the city decades earlier would regard the stone houses as objects of loss and pain (Biner 2007, 2010), local Arab notables and Syriacs viewed them as objects of cultural and economic capital. The Kurdish elites and newly wealthy Kurds from the city and the region regarded them as a new economic opportunity. Many people, particularly the urban poor regardless of their ethnicity, feel privileged and integrated into the value system of the national and global markets when they own, rent, or occupy one of the stone houses.

The commodification and restoration of the stone buildings transformed individuals' self-image as well as their perception of the built environment. Mardinites came to realize that stone was the original material of Old Mardin and the authentic source of the economic value of the houses and the distinctive quality of the city for local and foreign tourists. They recalled knowledge of stone, cement, and concrete and shared casual conversations with visitors about the quality and value of the stone, comparing it with concrete.

Stone would hold in heat and keep the house cool in summer and warm in winter. Stone would not fully absorb layers of paint. Over time, it would change color and adapt its texture to the changing conditions of the environment and climate. Stone was resistant to physical destruction such as demolition and burning yet sensitive to the vibrations produced by crashes or friction. One can put dozens of camels on top of a stone house, but one should never crack a walnut inside one. Stone would hide things, be they sacred or mundane, and it would also release things, such as smells or dust as the evidence of their previous lives. The stone house was vulnerable to disturbances by material and spiritual entities, and yet had potential economic value as the only resource of future expectations in life.

Day after day, Old City residents heard and circulated rumors about stone houses that had been sold at gigantic prices. The well-known Tokmaklı house that originally belonged to an Armenian family was sold to a Kurdish businessman from another city in the region for 5 million Turkish liras (around U.S. $2.6 million in 2013). No one knew who he was. The Cona family was asking U.S. $400,000 for their ruined stone house, which also had belonged to an Armenian family. Another Kurdish family from the Jewish neighborhood was selling their house for 900,000 Turkish liras There was rarely justification for expectations that one would be paid these exorbitant prices. The stone houses were not the main focus of state-funded restoration initiatives. The majority of the houses registered as cultural assets were neglected while mosques, madrasas, and other stone buildings owned by the state were restored for historical tourism (Figure 6).

In regard to the terms of ownership, the owners of cultural assets had the right to sell their property but were not allowed to make any repairs, renovations, or restorations without securing the approval of the Ministry of Culture. Owners of cultural assets could apply for grants from the Ministry of Culture that they were expected to use to plan restoration projects, but the grants often fell short of covering the full cost of the work. Moreover, the stone houses would never fetch their list prices, which were based on the housing market in the New City. Real estate agents and archaeologists recalled negotiations in which the initial price would be 800,000 Turkish liras and the parties would end up at 100,000. Despite this, the urban poor would sell their properties or shares to investors who would turn them into stone mansion hotels.

These restrictions did not stop the proliferation of daydreams, discourses, and practices around the houses as the material and symbolic emblems of heritage. Since the Historical Transformation Project began in 2009, the majority of the residents have rushed to register their houses as cultural assets, expecting this official status to increase their market value or make them

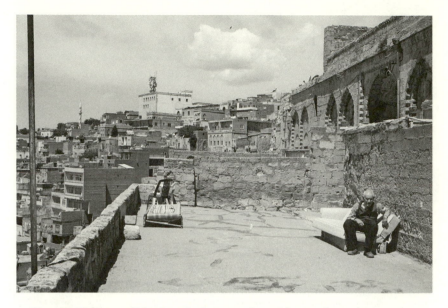

Figure 6. Old tenant living in a single room of a well-known formerly Armenian-owned stone house in the city of Mardin. Photo by Yektanurşin Duyan.

eligible for state grants for restoration. For a local restoration architect, the focus of restoration and registration for the Mardinites was profit. The majority of the occupants of the stone houses in Mardin did not know how to use them. They appropriated these houses or bought them from their owners, and built walls to divide them into different parts. They painted or covered the stone with cement. They ruined the stone ornaments. They did not take care of the houses. Those who managed to restore their houses believed that the visibility of the stone would increase the value of the house. Their restorative work was similar to that of the team of experts working for the Historical Transformation Project. It involved clearing cement or concrete from the stone walls or other parts of the structures of the house. Yet they were curious. Why were these ruined houses now valuable? Who were the new buyers? Was it the stone or the treasure they used to believe in that made these buildings visible and valuable in the public eye? For the occupants, the "real" value of these ruined houses was located inside or beneath the stone. Perhaps it was the combination of the visible and invisible that made the stone houses a cultural asset? People were digging up their houses to search for the invisible and unknown (Figure 7).

Figure 7. The ground floor of an old stone house. The walls are covered with cement as part of the restoration work undertaken by the family. Photo by Yektanurşin Duyan.

Digging was a practice of curiosity, greed, hope, and obsession. As the diggers of this ethnography explain, once they opened a hole, it would be difficult to close. For many of the subjects of this ethnography, digging turned into a life long practice or a project where they continued their search across time and space, some tuning their ears to the circulating rumors on the signs and symbols about the site of the treasure and others grabbing tools that would range from the spoon or the simplest detector to the technologically most sophisticated scanning computers, bringing the priest or imam for the interpretation of the signs. Digging was an evocative and pervasive practice.

Digging is not a recent phenomenon in Mardin. Digging is an ongoing form of ruination, in the city of Mardin and in other parts of Turkey. In Turkey's internal colonized geographies it is a significant component of the looting economy enmeshed with foundational violence (cf. Navaro-Yashin 2012; Bieberstein 2017). What has changed recently, however, is the frequency and visibility of treasure-hunting practices. Digging for treasure is no longer a secret activity hidden from the gaze of neighbors, the community, and the state. People boldly talk about digging for treasure, publicly revealing both their desire for sudden wealth and their curiosity about history. Daily life is filled with overnight enrichment narratives about people who are imagined to have found treasure, received permission to build on agricultural land, transformed their stone houses into hotels, or received state funding for restoration. The publicity and speculative value of houses inspire fantasies about the treasures buried inside them. Eyewitnesses spread stories about pots of golden coins found during building and refurbishment activities in cities, towns, and villages. This triggers more rumors, and they motivate many people to search for objects with value: coins, doors, lamps, door handles, pots. The stories embody the surreal experience of finding an item with exchange value and gaining recognition through its market value.

Diggers are not only the poor, unemployed, or underprivileged. They included painters, plumbers, construction workers, housewives, teachers, and both old-money and newly wealthy Mardinites who have acquired old stone mansions and turned them into luxury hotels. Recently, the influx of Syrian refugees has revitalized the market. New mediums of Syrian origins are sought after because they are able to read the codes and symbols of treasure maps and grapple with the power of the jinn which are regarded as the guardians of treasure. People perceive the flow of cultural and economic capital into the Old City as further proof of what they have believed for many years: that previous residents left buried treasure behind, the sacred belongings of Christians and Jews that underpin the economic value of these houses. This imagined source of wealth creates a new network of actors that includes restoration workers, sheikhs, magicians, cin experts, estate agents, and lenders who facilitate searching for and retrieving the treasure. The ruined heritage generates capital for all actors. In the Old City, the line between restoration, reparation, and digging has became blurred.

Anthropologists and other scholars have discussed the ways in which ruinous places and spaces create a unique experience of temporality and form. They animate senses and sensibilities that produce forces and energies affecting the agency of the subjects as they produce and live within these environments (see e.g. Edensor 2005; Dawdy 2010; Stoler 2013a; Navaro-Yashin 2012; Gordillo 2014; Laszczkowski 2015). These disjointed and formless states inspire fragmented narratives with multiple temporalities that produce "recollections which flow into each other and diverge, resonate backwards and

forwards, splice the personal and collective" (Edensor 2005:126). In her study
of the postwar environment in Cyprus, Yael Navaro-Yashin highlights the
significance of studying ruination, with reference to both "material remains
or artefacts of destruction and violation" and "the subjectivities and residual
effects that linger, like a hangover, in the aftermath of violence" (2012:162).
Drawing on the literature of the affective turn and nonrepresentational theory, her argument suggests that materiality can exert a force on human beings that is perceived and articulated by human beings yet evokes realms
beyond the human imagination (161). Navaro-Yashin describes this as an affect that "refers broadly to an emotive domain but its scope goes beyond that
of human subjectivity or of the self" (167). In this line of thought, *affects* refer to intensities and energies that emerge and get produced through the encounters between human and nonhumans at the intersections between
materiality and subjectivity (Thrift 2008:222). Affects are "a kind of contact
zone where the over determinations of circulations, events, conditions, technologies of power literally takes place" (Stewart 2007:3). Affect is "the nondiscursive sensation that an environment generates" (Navaro-Yashin
2012:168). At the same time, affects are transmitted through language, ideology, and subjectivity (see Massumi 2002; Navaro-Yashin 2012) and "bodies, dreams, dramas and social worldings of all kind" (Stewart 2007:3). These
transmissions of affect in the form of energies or forces, argues Navaro-
Yashin, emerge within particular historical and political contexts, inviting
their study not only as examples of entangled relationships between human
and nonhuman within ontological systems but also as objects of "political
and legal substance" (2012:178) that transmit politics and law into the intimate spaces of personal lives (179).

In this ethnography, I use this affective materiality approach to rethink
the multiple forms of relationships that people build with these ruined buildings as part of the "heritage assemblage" (Macdonald 2009). People's relationships with these ruined buildings are produced through daily engagement
with their materiality, which involves the energies of the building material
such as stone and cement, the labor invested in their construction and destruction, and the encounter with the jinn (Chapter 3). The affect of these engagements and encounters emerges from persistent histories of state
violence, conflicts between communities, and hidden memories of "critical
events" (Das 1997). The affect produces a desire for recognition, an anxiety
about the future, and an obsession with sudden enrichment. The ruined stone
buildings have agency as legal, political, and historical objects that produce

particular attachments, belongings, and practices. People develop various forms of inhabitation and use of these houses, as tenants, owners, or occupiers. The meaning of owning or appropriating a stone house that is registered as a cultural asset brings legal and historical responsibilities that people recognize, disavow, or feel burdened with. The ruined environment moves senses and sensibilities and evokes knowledge that connects the visible and invisible, the surface and the subterranean, as well as humans and nonhuman beings. In the next two chapters, the protagonists will take us through these cracks, holes, and tunnels while unfolding different forms of relationships of ownership and possession. My goal in this discussion is not to demystify the truth about the dispossession and ruination of these buildings as material remnants of loss. Rather, following the insightful approach of Kathleen Stewart, my aim is to tell something about the "ordinary affects" of living in and with them. Stewart describes the ordinary as a "shifting assemblage of practices and practical knowledge, a scene of both liveness and exhaustion, a dream of escape or of the simple life" (2007:1). In her view, ordinary affects "happen in impulses, sensations, expectations, daydreams, encounters and habits of relating, in strategies and their failures, in forms of persuasion, contagion, and compulsion, in modes of attention, attachment, and agency, and in publics and social worlds of all kinds that catch people up in something that feels like something" (2). Here, I analyze the practice of digging through "ordinary affects" as engendered in the spaces of encounters between human and human and between human and nonhuman, including the built environment and spiritual beings. Digging produces affects that relate to forces of relationships, such as apparition, dreaming, hoarding, and attachments, fantasies that haunt persons, places, and things. My focus in these chapters is the relational interaction between the material and virtual, which draws my attention to what Nigel Thrift describes as "fugitive work" that is "the little, the messy and the jerry-rigged as a part of politics and not just incidental to it" (2008:197). Digging is the fugitive work that allows me to trace relationships of possession and processes of ruination in this conflict-ridden environment. The ethnographic narratives that I present below reveal the destabilizing force of digging as an act of ruination and dispossession and open up the ground to think through processes in which the diggers constitute their moral agency.

In her essay "Cruel Optimism," Lauren Berlant (2010) defines optimism as the underlying condition of all attachments. The conditions of ordinary life, in Berlant's argument, also constitute the conditions of exploitation, destruction, disenchantment of the subject, but the very same conditions create specific implications and ways of suffering that suspend the question of cruelty (97). To understand cruel optimism, Berlant suggests thinking about "episodes of suspension" of "the reproduction of habituated or normative life" (97). These suspensions, Berlant argues, lead to revelations about the promises that accumulated as "people's object of desire, stage moments of exuberance in the impasse near normal, and provide tools for suggesting why these exuberant attachments keep ticking not like the time bomb they might be but like a white noise machine that provides assurance that what seems like static really is, after all, a rhythm people can enter into while they are dithering" (97).

As I discuss in further detail in Chapter 3, the act of digging can be interpreted as another episode of "cruel optimism" whereby people project their desire for survival and sudden enrichment into the obsession with finding the treasure as if the search for the unknown, hidden, or the absent somehow suspends the current conditions of poverty and structural inequalities, as well as the past atrocities that oppressed, displaced, or terrified the previous owners of the houses. To paraphrase Berlant's description of hoarding, digging creates both explosive yet white-noise-like comfort that constitutes the rhythm of living in these stone houses, insulating its digger-owners while accommodating connections and promises. My concern here is with the singularities of certain narratives through which people identify their attachment with the house: attachments that, as Berlant insightfully points out, are "made of promises and not possessions at all" (2010:112).

In the sections that follow, I introduce two narratives. The first is that of a young couple who have invested all of their material resources in the restoration and exploration of their stone house, which is their sole inheritance. They repair, restore, and dig up their house. They have spent their entire adult lives trying to find the resources necessary to erase the marks of the ruination while contributing to the destruction of the building through their search for treasure. The second narrative focuses on an elderly Kurdish man who occupied the premises of an ancient Armenian church, named Surp Kevork in the Old City. He transformed it from a scarred, abandoned, excavated site of massacres into a home for his extended family. He spent forty years repossessing the place, repairing the buildings, dividing them into new households for the various members of his family, and fighting against representatives of the Armenian Catholic Foundation and other intruders while waiting for the vali to order him to evacuate. Both narratives open up complementary and comparative spaces in which to explore different experiences of possession in the midst of ruined heritage. They reveal personal narratives of ruination as experienced and imagined by the people who remained in the city.

"We Revealed the Genetics of These Houses"

Veysi Bey was regarded as the most passionate, obsessive, and experienced digger in the province.. As much as he was a digger, he was also a local historian, an archaeologist, and a flaneur. Veysi Bey might be spotted in different parts of the city waiting to meet curious visitors of various kinds. He might be seen walking through the narrow alleys of the Old City or sitting in the dark shadow of a tree watching passersby or at the reception of a five star hotel. I was introduced to him by one of his friends who was also a digger. For days we walked together and talked as we inspected exquisite and hidden details of stone houses. He confided in me about the tunnel system that reportedly connects the Old City to the Mardin Castle, recalled the previous owners of the stone houses, and discussed the presence of the jinn. For Veysi Bey the Real Mardin (*Gerçek Mardin*) was underground, twenty-four meters below the surface, a place that according to him was filled with cemeteries. And, I would learn, in pursuing treasure an inevitable encounter—that could take place above and below the city, both inside houses and inside excavation pits—involved meeting the jinn. Veysi Bey will accompany us through the narratives of the next two chapters

"The first time I started digging, it was for money," he told me. "Then I started excavating out of curiosity. One searches for something but one comes to find something else. Now, I am digging to find myself. The material aspect has turned into a spiritual one." Veysi Bey, who comes from a local Arab family, has been digging all over Turkey and the Middle East for the past thirty years. He lived in the Old City as a wanderer, builder, and treasure hunter. He was married and had two children, who were born in stone houses and raised in thirteen different ones in Mardin. He never owned property and always rented stone houses. He taught himself about these gigantic structures and mastered their interior and exterior details, including their carvings, the shape of their windows, their hiding places, the layout and size of their rooms, and the connections of each to other houses, other parts of the neighborhood, and the city. Veysi Bey also knew each house's history. He kept his own log of appropriation, confiscation, and dispossession of these properties, one that seemingly traced their biographies back to their first owners. However, he never shared the full details of any building we entered together.

Veysi Bey had been a witness and a perpetrator of ruination for decades. The time of "violent peace" had not shifted the limits of public secrecy for him. The growing popularity of Mardin as the emblem of cultural heritage also had not altered his motivations to dig. He had, moreover, his own ethics as a digger: he would never dig into a sacred shrine, a church, or a mosque. He would not dig for wealthy people who were simply curious about what could be found "behind" or "below." He had once even called off excavations when he felt that the expectations of treasure were about to divide the family that owned the property.

His admiration for the historical and his desire for possession always coexisted in his sense of what defines heritage. Veysi Bey was locally respected: people would trust his knowledge of place and his interpretations of signs and symbols. He, in turn, would channel people's sense of trust to accommodate his ethical principles as a digger: he would stoke curiosity and promise to show people the sites with potential treasure yet, in parallel, push them not to sell their houses, especially to people who did not live in Mardin. For him, the global attention paid to Mardin as a World Heritage Site was a sign of a new wave of occupation and dispossession of the city brought about by the valis (who were collaborating with the holders of international capital). External anonymous buyers, in his view, would buy the houses from locals and empty out the city.

Veysi Bey's local attachment to and knowledge of the place led him to resist practices that locally constituted forms of neoliberal order. For him, however, there was no contradiction between this stance and his collaboration with multiple networks of people who invested in treasure hunting. These collaborations, on the other hand, did not provide him with capital and he was constantly in debt, needing to borrow money from friends to rent tools for excavation. Cash was an impossible fantasy that both was fueled and would be rewarded by the promise of treasure. Since he could never afford to buy a house in the Old City (or, for that matter, the New City), he had opted to help their ruination, eager to dispossess buried belongings in lieu of becoming a stone house owner. And when embarked in a new excavation project, all of a sudden he would become unreachable. His phone would be turned off and no one would see him for many days.

This was not one of "his" houses in the sense that he did not excavate this house on his own. That was what I assumed. Veysi Bey never gave me the full story behind his engagement or attachment to the house. "They worked so hard to repair it," he said, when we arrived at the small entrance. The walls of the house had been painted bright green, a sign of extreme care. Sonay, the lady of the house, gently pushed us inside, out of the clutches of the heat wave. "Come inside! It is cool in here." The house was indeed cool. It was also dark, with a beam of light coming through the door and reaching the high ceilings before hitting the stone walls. It was full of objects: flowers, furniture of different sizes, including big armchairs with embroidered pillows, a bureau with a mirror, a dinner table with chairs, and a child's bunk bed, all in one room. The main room opened onto two other rooms and a bathroom. One of the rooms was a little cave excavated into the rock. The other was a spacious bedroom decorated with shining purple linen. There was not a single empty spot in the room except for the space near the high ceiling. Light was reflected by shining objects: crystal lamps, candleholders, mirrors, and a big TV. "I am like my mother. I am excessively attached to my house, my belongings. That is what I do with my earnings. I buy furniture and objects for the house," said Sonay while we looked for a place to sit.

The house, I would soon learn, was originally owned by a Syriac family and then passed on to a Muslim family. Sonay's father-in-law had bought it: "He paid for this house," Sonay's husband, Cemal, said. They were making clear that it was not an occupied property: they were legitimate owners of the house. A disclaimer. I appeared not to pay attention to this, opting to let the story float away. Property talk has never been easy with diggers, tenants, and owners. Back in the 1960s, I was told, Cemal's father had extended their one-room stone house by building additional floors out of concrete, where he settled his elder sons. Thus they were now owners of a four-story building—one stone structure and three concrete floors—in the middle of the Old City: another palimpsest bearing witness to the history of ruination of Mardin. In the 1990s, after completing his military service, Cemal had returned to Mardin and moved into the stone part of the family house. By then his parents had passed away and the place was like a ghost house.

Soon after his return, Cemal married Sonay. Sonay's mother was from a local Arab family. Her father was Kurdish from a nearby village. She had spent all of her childhood in the mixed neighborhood of Syriacs and Kurds. She was used to living in stone houses. But this house was different. She explained, "I felt shocked the first time I saw this place. It was like a cave. My family did not own a house. We rented and lived in many houses. Somehow, though, they were cleaner and more spacious than this one. For the past eighteen years, I have been cleaning and repairing this house. I have now accepted my fate." Sonay started repairing her new house as soon as she moved in as a young bride. First they had built a bathroom. Next, they repaired the kitchen. She had actively participated in the construction work: "I prepared the mortar for the worker. My hands bled." Then they bought the room next to their house with Cemal's four brothers. They connected two rooms. "Yet we did not have enough money to put in a door, so instead we put up a curtain as a divider. Then we built in windows. Later on we put in a door and separated the rooms."

The next step was to remove the cement from the walls and the ceiling and then paint the surfaces with plaster. "It looked so beautiful when we finished it," Sonay said. "It was like we were surrounded by mirrors. I saw my reflection in the ice blue colored walls." The wall remained intact only for three months. As Sonay put it, "The stone walls rejected the paint. They vomited it. I would leave the house clean, tidy, with shining objects and then find everything buried under chips of paint that fell off the walls. I felt miserable. A relative suggested that we remove the paint from the stone walls and restore the house. I started visiting hotels and observing what others were doing." Cemal and Sonay eventually invested all their money and labor into the construction and restoration of their stone house and transformed a one-room house into a two-room house with a bathroom and kitchen. They studied architecture, researched traditional techniques and formulas to change the texture of walls and floors, explored the connections between the inner and outside, above and beneath the house: "I heard this from a Christian neighbor. First, they boil animal heads in a pot and they release thick-layered fat that then becomes fluid, like water. They leave it to cool down and then use it to polish the floor. And for the tiles and wall, one can mix this liquid with the yolk of the egg and the white cement. This mixture gets stronger through time and sticks to the stone for much longer."

Cemal had done all sorts of different things to survive and look after his family. He had worked as a porter, a grave digger, and a builder. His main area of expertise was plumbing. He was interested in architecture and the mechanisms of wells and water tunnels. He pointed at the well camouflaged in the corner of the main room. "This well has four eyes, meaning four sections. When I climbed down, I saw four rounded stones that were used to close up these sections. The question of who had opened them in the first place and who had closed them hung in the air. I am brave enough to go into these tunnels. I have done it before, and I can do it again. I am not scared of the snakes, monsters or whatever. I know how one feels when one gets ten metres underground. One gets scared of one's own voice, one's own echo. You shout 'Cemal' and ten 'Cemals' come back to you. But I learned not to be scared through experience, through my work." The experience of walking beneath the city had an effect on his perception of the textures, surfaces, and movements of his surroundings. He was sensitive to changes involving things and people. He would stop and smell the atmosphere when he noticed signs of a crowd between the alleys. No potentially valuable object on the street would escape his attention. Cemal's senses were open to physical and social changes. He knew how to draw connections between the visible and the invisible.

Cemal recalled, "One morning when we were restoring the house, I was washing the floor in this room and I noticed that at a certain point, the water changed direction." After observing it for few minutes, Cemal got curious and called a few people whom he trusted. They explored the texture of the floor, dug up the room, and found two marble graves, six marble boxes measuring thirty-five centimeters by thirty centimeters, and pistols lying next to them. Cemal repeated the description of what he saw. Each time he gave me more information about the size of the boxes and the tombs. "Give me a piece of paper," he said. "I cannot read or write, but I do not forget what I see." He drew it. It was right there, a few meters under where we were sitting. "We got scared and we did not want to open them." They closed up the hole. A few years later, he decided to give a second try. "I was not the only one who knew that there were tombs underneath this house." There had been other people that previously had offered him to dig up his house. Even the vali had once come with a crowd escorting him. "They entered the house, we greeted them, they measured the walls, did something on the computers. They had not told us who they were. We noticed that he was the vali only after his driver called him on his way out 'Vali Bey.' We never understood why he did not tell us who he was nor why he visited our house."

As he talked about the houses, heritage, and the vali, Cemal felt obliged to express his thoughts about the popular image of Mardin as a multicultural city. He was confused and not at all confident about the official idioms used to articulate the alleged harmony of coexistence. While he repeatedly referred to the multicultural and multilingual character of the city, he felt troubled about naming his ethnic identity. "I am an Arab, I mean, I am an Arabic speaker. I am also a Turk, I mean, a Turkish citizen. There are all sorts of people living here: Arab, Kurd, Turk, Christian, Caucasian. We all live together." To prove that he was knowledgeable, he would rush outside, and point to the homes of Christian families he knew in the city, then return to the house, touching the stone walls of the living room that were cleared of cement, invoking the stone as evidence of their yearning for an authentic existence.

Thinking about his identity, Cemal recalled complicated memories from his military service in the 1990s, when his marksmanship skills were immediately associated with him being from Mardin. All his comrades thought that he was a Kurd and thus a terrorist. Returning to his current position, he reiterated that as mağaralar (caves referring to stone houses) had been declared kültürel miras (cultural heritage), the people living in those caves came to be regarded as kültürlü (cultured) and medeni (civilized). As property owners, they received respect and admiration from outsiders, visitors, Turks. For Cemal, they should have always received admiration and respect for spending a lifetime taking care of these caves: they had continued living in these houses even when they were rotting due to humidity. They had slept with the smell of moistened cement. Cemal described the burden of possessing these houses over and over again, pointing to the niches in the room.

"We call this, I mean, in Arabic, it is *taka*. But you [outsiders] call them *niş* in Turkish. We repaired them all," he said and then moved to the back room of the house. The dark-green-colored, cemented, noncleared, wet walls were the material evidence of previous living arrangements. "*Gerçek bu* (This is the truth)," said Cemal. They were now using this room as a cellar to store their refrigerator and other unwanted items that would not fit into the newly revamped house. The truth was hidden inside the cracks of the cemented, humid walls, invisible to the eye of the outsider-visitor but still visible to Sonay and Cemal as a reminder of their daily struggle to survive financially with their two children. According to Cemal, people had only started digging up their houses a few decades before, "People did not have this fantasy before. How could they?" said Cemal. Twenty-five people would share a single room, and they did not have the luxury of digging up the only place where they could eat and sleep. In addition, this implicit knowledge was exclusively held by Christians. Thus Christians and Muslims dug up the houses together, and they shared whatever they found. "The other day, I heard that they dug up a house and found sculptures worth thousands of liras. I have not seen them myself, but I heard it from others." Cemal believed that Muslims no longer needed Christians to decide where to dig. If they dig up their house, they do so because someone has pointed out their house (as a place of treasure) or because they got curious while they were repairing it. "They see the first tunnel, and then they want to go further and deeper in order to find something. They cast a net and no one knows whether they will catch a mackerel or a dolphin." Once one started digging, said Cemal, it was difficult to stop. He knew it well: after his first encounter with the tombs, he wanted to open up the same place again, this time with a team that included a sheikh. Veysi Bey was on the team, too. In the midst of the excavation, they had felt a sudden movement: the house had started to shake. Veysi Bey, who had gone to his place to take a short nap, dreamed of the shaking and ran back to Cemal's house to tell him to close up the site. Cemal was not convinced, but he still followed the advice and closed it up. As you might expect, his desire for the unknown and the feared and his ability to imagine it have by no means dried up.

With the stone being visible, Cemal and Sonay made themselves visible, and yet not fully. They knew that the house was the entrance into an unknown and hidden place underneath the city. The spatial and historical knowledge of what lies beneath kept up their optimism: the house was the only source of cultural and economic capital that they could possess in their whole life. The scarcity of resources, the uncertainty of the future, and the desire for enrichment together made their attachments to the house and its promises cruel. Through reparations and digging they had buried their income to destroy the house.

Uncle Ragıp's Home: The Red Church

Veysi Bey had been there more than a few times. It was once a very popular site for treasure hunters. They dug in the garden, inside the church, under the tombstones in the walls, and in the basement under the rooms of the monks and nuns. Every inch of the site had been explored. Veysi Bey looked reluctant when I asked him to accompany me. He said that whatever might have been left there would have by now already been removed. In addition, he was not on friendly terms with the resident-occupiers. The presence of Veysi Bey would trigger their curiosity and make them anxious because they believe that even his shadow could pull other treasure hunters. The premises were empty, derelict, invisible from outside. There was no placard or sign to show the way. The locals knew it as Kırmızı Kilise (Red Church). Following Veysi Bey, I tried to memorize the path, repeating the directions to myself, watching my step so that I would not make a wrong turn:

> Go past the old Republican Cinema. Keep on walking until you reach the Tatlıdede Hotel. Continue on to the Jewish Fountain [Yahudiye Çeşmesi]. Don't hesitate—just keep walking through the alley. Stop at the gigantic rotted out metal door. It is usually left half-open. Don't knock. Just walk in and follow the path straight to the courtyard. On the left, you will see the main building of the Armenian church. The church door is locked with a big chain, but there is a small gap that allows the curious to peek through. If you peer between the chain and the door, you will see the tidy or untidy emptiness that ends after few minutes. Outside the church building, notice the Armenian scripts toward the edge of the wall as well as the stone carved with the same scripts surrounded by dark gray cement. You will have no more than ten minutes on your own. The loud voice of whom I will call here Uncle Ragıp or the whispery flat voice of his nephew Ercan will catch up with you, firmly yet casually asking why you have come.

Founded in 420, Surp Kevork was the first Armenian church of Mardin. It was also regarded as one of the first shrines in the city of Mardin. During the nineteenth century the church was used as the home of the Armenian Catholic archbishop. In 1915, its residents had been killed. The church was subsequently evacuated, occupied by the military, and transformed into a gathering place for Armenian orphans from different cities and towns. It was returned to the Armenian Catholic Foundation in 1949 but never used as a church again. In 1979, Surp Kevork was registered as a cultural asset. After 2000, it had started attracting the attention of architects, who made detailed plans of the premises and denounced how the church and other buildings had been subjected to destruction during the military occupation between 1915 and 1919, as well as during subsequent renovation and restoration by Armenian Mardinites in 2002 (Alkan Reis 2012:35–36).

Uncle Ragıp had been living within the premises of Surp Kevok with his extended family for forty years. He was Kurdish and was originally from the nearby village of Mansuriye (Yalimköy in Turkish). As a child, he would come to Surp Kevork with his father to sell wood to the soldiers who had occupied the church and used it as the gendarme station. "My father would go inside to deliver wood and receive his payment. I was not allowed to enter, but I watched it all from the entrance. The officer would sit under that fig tree, where I sleep now," said Uncle Ragıp, recalling his first memories of the place. When Uncle Ragıp decided to migrate from his village to Mardin in the 1970s, he followed in the footsteps of his uncle, who had taken over one of the rooms at Surp Kevork. The place had already been completely dug up when he settled in.

Uncle Ragıp continued to explore the space. He cleared out the area in front of the church, removing all the remains that he found. He had also encountered six Christian families living in the property but did not remember if they were Armenian. He may not have wanted to remember. In the imaginary of the older Mardinites, there were Christians, Kurds, and Arabs in Mardin but often no ethnic signifier was used to qualify Christians. For Uncle Ragıp, too, it did not matter whether the Christian residents were Armenians or Syriacs. What mattered was that they left soon after he settled in Surp Kevork with his family.

Uncle Ragıp spent years trying to turn the place into home for his family. "There was no door when we moved in," he said. "I found this one in another neighborhood. I brought it here and fixed it." The door kept out drug dealers, treasure hunters, beggars, thieves, and animals. Uncle Ragıp removed unwanted visitors from his new territory and closed the gigantic metal door behind them. He turned the field that he cleared from the remains into a garden, planting dozens of fruit trees, hauling water from a fountain far from the church. He fixed the biggest room and moved into it with his family. The other rooms were used by his uncle and cousins once they married. The church grounds and the adjacent houses that belonged to the church foundation were occupied by still other relatives. There were no strangers, foreigners, or outsiders living in their territory. Dozens of people were married and had their children there and their relatives died in these rooms.

Uncle Ragıp owed his untouchability to his pro-state position. "First God, then the state" was his motto. His mother tongue was Kurdish, but he had learned fluent Arabic early on in his life through his interactions with the Mardinites in the Old City. However, he disavowed any connection to Kurdishness: "We are not Kurdish. We are all Turkish. We are all citizens of Turkey." Uncle Ragıp would follow the orders of the vali, even if he was asked to evacuate the Surp Kevork. "We could never resist the orders of Vali Pasha. We await his orders." The uncertainty of their status as occupants became more intense once the city of Mardin was selected for candidacy to be a World Heritage Site.

Over the past fifteen years, he and his family hosted many architects, some of whom stayed for months to survey the site. They also hosted Armenian and non-Armenian visitors from all over the world. Various officials came to show the site to international visitors and delegates from UNESCO. During this time, they waited in expectation to be told to evacuate Surp Kevork. For Uncle Ragıp, the church was the property of the state, not the Armenians. Though he acted as a tenant and paid some rent to the Armenian Catholic Church Foundation for the first years after he moved in, he had never agreed to their request to evacuate the place. His aggression enjoyed the implicit support of valis, who encouraged Uncle Ragıp to hold on the property. He did not see his position as an act of dispossession or occupation. "Nobody has hammered a single nail here," said Uncle Ragıp. As a family, they felt they had saved the place from destruction and invasion by humans and nonhumans and prevented its destruction by repairing and taking care of its buildings. He thus believed that the state should compensate them for their losses and needs and provide an apartment for them in the New City. His daughter and daughters-in-law of the family were secretly enthusiastic about the idea of moving to the New City.

Uncle Ragıp's village, Mansuriye, was now regarded as a small-sized town and became home to luxurious multistoried apartments. The current mayor of Mansuriye was alleged to have granted construction permits in exchange for variable fees. Being given a house from their village was another impossible dream. For years, they had been forced by their father to live in the middle of the ruins without any infrastructure. They did the minimum to maintain the structure as they gave birth to and raised their children in these rooms, courtyard, and the garden with the stone wall that held the remains of Armenian priests. They refurbished the rooms, rearranged them, built new kitchens and bathrooms, painted the walls until the paint fell off, and caught dozens of scorpions. They knew that they would not be able to move to the New City. Moreover, Uncle Ragıp would not leave his garden behind. It was a space that he had created and looked after for decades. He owned the trees. They were his property. The garden was the breathing space between the locked up church building, the semiforbidden cave area, and the silent tombstones of the Armenian priests. It was also the space of coming together with outsiders whose presence in front of the church building was a source of uneasiness. The garden would camouflage the family from the gaze of others, sheltering them from curious questions about the ownership of the place. In response to insistent questions about the absence of the Armenians, Uncle Ragıp would issue his standard invitation: "Eat the fruit of the garden. It does not belong to one person. It is everyone's. And everyone comes from the same Adam and Eve."

Over the past ten years, the number of Armenian and other visitors has increased. Surp Kevork is no longer a dark spot left under the occupation and protection of Uncle Ragıp, who knew that his position as occupier-protector was more precarious than ever. His hopes have been maintained by the ambivalent position of the state concerning the recognition of the material and immaterial losses that occurred in 1915 and its aftermath. While the local government funded the restoration of mosques, madrasas, and other religious and historical sites representing Islamic-Turkish culture and allowed the restoration of Syriac Christian shrines to be undertaken with the economic support of communities in Istanbul or the diaspora, Surp Kevork remained an undesirable ruin. It sat outside the processes of establishing heritage and attracting tourists to the Old City. It was not reopened as a shrine to be used as a setting for films or exhibits. It was not restored as the material evidence of Armenian heritage in the city. Rather, the site was treated by architects, heritage experts, and Armenian visitors as a remnant whose future existence depended on a series of negotiations between the valis (as the representatives of the Turkish state), the EU, and UNESCO bureaucrats, along with international tourism experts and a few representatives of the Armenian Mardinite community who were consulted on the recognition of the material and immaterial heritage of the Armenians in the city.

In 2013, Surp Kevork was chosen as one of the "seven most endangered" heritage sites under a joint program sponsored by the European Investment Fund Institute and Europa Nostra, a federation working with the network of civil society organisations that work for protecting the cultural and natural heritage in Europe. With a special emphasis on Europe, the federation promotes its work as a citizen movement. Each year Europa Nostra identifies the seven most endangered landmarks in the European Union in an effort to mobilize local, national, and transnational actors to take action to protect the sites by providing financial resources, drafting business plans, and increasing awareness. Against the background of deliberate state negligence, the members of the Armenian Catholic Foundation in Mardin sought international protection while trying to avoid direct confrontation with the provincial government. Their application was accepted and they managed to secure "most endangered" status for Surp Kevork, themselves, and their silent demand for recognition.

In 2015, the members of the Turkish branch of Europa Nostra launched a campaign to collect donations for the restoration of Surp Kevork, which was expected to cost 6 million Turkish liras. The Armenian Catholic Foundation in Mardin asserted it would not be able to cover the cost. The Ministry of Culture and Directorate General of Foundations (Vakıflar Genel Müdürlüğü) refused to respond to the Armenian Catholic Foundation in Mardin and Europa Nostra. As the Historical Transformation Project proceeded in accordance with the personal aspirations of the vali and financial contributions from various budgets with the promise of significant funding from the EU and the submission of an application to UNESCO in 2015, the centenary of the Armenian genocide, Surp Kevork remained a ruin, a registered cultural asset, a selected "endangered" heritage site.

The new status of the church as an endangered heritage site did not change the life of the church or that of Uncle Ragıp's family. Uncle Ragıp had occupied Surp Kevork for decades with the knowledge that the church was a zone of exception. It was a site of resentment and disregard that held ungraspable moments of the massacres and its aftermath in juxtaposition with Uncle Ragıp's four-decade family history. In the heart of the Old City, Uncle Ragıp made Surp Kevork his home through occupation of the ruined property of the Armenians, a ruin that nobody wanted to take over. Uncle Ragıp protected his home in solidarity with the vali at all times. The last time I visited, there was still no placard or sign identifying it as Surp Kevork. There was, however, a new warning posted for hesitant explorers: a big green R painted on the outside wall, Uncle Ragıp's first initial.

CHAPTER 3

Digging with the Jinn

"Do not sell it," Veysi Bey said. "Do not let people sneak into the house to restore it. Do not touch it," he repeated insistently while walking inside the courtyard. "I have not figured out the essence of this one yet." Located in the old Jewish neighborhood, which consists of Jewish and dominantly Armenian houses and shrines, the house in question was considered as a unique example of the Jewish architecture of the city. "This was the meeting place of the Hakhams," said Veysi Bey. The present owners of the house, who had met Veysi Bey earlier, were showing him around the rooms. Veysi Bey looked around and pointed to sculptures on the walls and floors. "These lions . . . you can't see these lions [in this position] in other houses. When I was last here with the Israeli archaeologists and historians, they had this spot marked on their map." The owner of the house, an elderly Kurdish man, reassured him: "We have not touched the lions. Actually I do not know exactly what they are, they do not look like lions to me. I think they are sheep. Someone offered us 24,000 Turkish liras[1] for them but we did not sell. The Jews, with apologies, put them in the place of God. They love them. But it is me who peeled off the cement, brushed it with vinegar. It is me who washes them with shampoo."

Looking at the sculpture, Zelda Hanım, the elderly wife of the house owner, said, "today, I should wash them again." As the present owner, the Kurdish woman was eager to remove the signs of abandonment and disrepair: "Jews left this place because of the war. Later on, tens of families lived in this house. These men [the previous owners] sold the house very cheap and left Mardin because they were involved in a blood feud. We paid a lot for this house." The house had been a wreck when they had first moved in. The previous owners had been digging inside the house and continued even after they had sold it (although Zelda and her husband had received the title deed, initially they were not allowed to enter it). "There was a 2.5 meter hole in the room," she said. After a short pause, she continued: "We also dug inside the house, but only once." They dug with a machine and found rubbish. "I was scared, we were scared of getting into trouble," Zelda Hanım said, unsure about how to explain what she meant by trouble. She paused again. It had to do with the old houses. She continued:

> We, Kurds, are not scared of these old houses; if need be, we can even live in caves. Still, these are historical houses. Maybe there is a cemetery underneath the house. So maybe we cannot sleep under that tree: maybe, there is a shrine belonging to Muslims or Christians; maybe they are the ones who are waking us up. A while ago I killed a snake in the house. Sometimes, the children also see a snake, they run after it but the snake disappears. . . . I really don't know. The house is historical. By historical, I mean, maybe there is a cemetery, a tomb underneath, something, though not necessarily something dangerous. Sometimes, people claim that the previous owners dropped hot water on this floor and burnt the jinn. In fact, all sorts of strange things happen in this world. Thank God, we are happy in this house.

Zelda Hanım's repeated references to the house as historical invite us to reflect about what is meant by this very statement. For Mardinites, what is that makes a house "historical"? Is it the cemetery, the tomb, the presence of the jinn, treasure? Is it an internal feature of the house or is it the things that are held by it? Zelda Hanım believes that a treasure exists within the house, but that it is protected by a spell. As she explains, one needs to sacrifice a significant person (or at least let out some blood) in order to break the protecting spell. She continues: "I do not want to dig. Even if we find the treasure, could we ever spend it? Would it be *halal* [sanctioned in Islam] to do so? Maybe it is *haram* [forbidden]. We don't want to be involved; we are scared, and we are believers. We pray and we read the Quran."

In this chapter, I explore the ways in which people search for and situate the "historical" between the realms of the material and the spiritual. Pursuing this understanding requires broadening the concept of history beyond written and oral narratives of events, extending it to other modes of telling that involve imaginary and invisible sources (see Lambek 1993; Naveeda 2006; Mittermaier 2012; Taneja 2012). The expression of this ethereal realm in Mardin frequently involves tangential mention of or discussions about the jinn, which are a widespread presence in the Islamic world. Robert Lebling (2011), who provides a detailed historical account of the matter, refers to two different bodies of knowledge on their genealogy: Mesopotamian folktales incorporating legends about demons and spirits, and Greek and Roman philosophers who discuss the part that "demons" play as intermediaries between humans and deities. The belief in the jinn, Lebling argues, persisted in the Arab East through Roman and Byzantine times and continued through the emergence of Islam, which—via Qur'anic revelation and via the personal experiences and narratives of the Prophet Muhammad integrated these spirit beings into its body of knowledge (16). The Quran mentions the jinn in sura (chapter) 72, which describes them as life forms different from humans, neither angels nor devils. They are said to be made of a smokeless fire invisible to the eye of man (see Naveeda 2006; Taneja 2013).

A number of scholarly accounts explore how the jinn embody complex arrangements of memory, subjectivity, violence, mental illness, inequality, and religious difference (see Crapanzano 1980; Rothenberg 2004; Pandolfo 2000; Naveeda 2006; Taneja 2013). The common thread of these analyses is that jinn stories provide a language that allows one to give voice to senses of loss and to sentiments of being troubled. They open up a space through which we can think and speak about the coexistence of humans and spiritual beings in the past, present, and future.

In her work on dream narratives in Egypt, Amira Mittermaier (2012) warns against dismissing dream stories because of a secular understanding of history. She draws attention to the need to understand how dream stories can alter what "history" itself means; how they can "undo secular assumptions about time, history, subjectivity, and community" (394). She suggests that "dream stories, like ghost stories, elsewhere, appeal to justice in ways that cannot be fully captured by empiricist and secular modes of history-telling" (414). In her view, this is a significant political act that operates quite irrespective of the actual fulfilment of the dream's promises in this or the other world.

In the context of this ethnography, too, jinn stories offer an alternative mode of storytelling. In Mardin, these stories are distributed across different historical periods, such that they transgress the linear temporality—pre-Islamic, Ottoman, and republican periods—of the official historiography of the nation-state. As they are told and circulate, they imbricate multiple actors and amalgamate religious, secular, and official versions of histories of destruction that involve human and nonhuman beings. Although jinn stories do not embody a critical account of the history of property confiscation or challenge existing religious- and ethnic-based hierarchies, they open up an experiential and discursive space that provides for encounters between those who have left and those who remained. For this reason, they have enormous significance within the social, political, and economic life of the people of Mardin.

The Jinn in Mardin

Who are the jinn? How do we interpret their presence at excavated sites if we go beyond the tropes and symbols of the local cosmology? What do jinn stories reveal during the search for the unknown? In Mardin, the jinn are regarded as special beings created by God whose origin predates Islam. My interlocutors refer to Gırnavuz, a neolithic archaeological settlement fifty kilometers from the city of Mardin, as the jinn capital. Their Muslim identity and the city's proximity to the ancient settlement are mentioned as two important factors that explain the presence and power of the jinn in daily life. The jinn are said to live in dark and damp places such as basements, cemeteries, street corners, and baths. They can appear in different forms, including scorpions, snakes, birds, cows, humans, or half animal, half humans. The relationship between the jinn and humans can take different forms, ranging from love to hatred to protection, and from warfare to punishment (cf. Crapnzano 1980; Rothenberg 2004; Naveeda 2006).

The jinn can have destructive and disruptive effects in the form of haunting and possession.[2] People are used to their haunting effects. They speak of the jinn's ability to move things in and around the house, to make sounds or become visible in different shapes and forms, and to leave marks on the bodies of humans. Possession is distinct from haunting. It refers to the capacity of the spirits or the jinn to enter and seize bodily and mental control of the individual. Possession shows itself through trance states, epilepsy-like attacks, sudden fainting, and loss of consciousness. The breach of moral values, the dismissal of religious obligations, and the weakening of physical strength can make a person an easy target for the jinn.[3] Punishment and revenge are also reasons for possession. In addition, the jinn may choose to possess the human out of attraction and passion. Many choose to live in women's bodies.

There are also sudden and unexpected moments that might cause jinn possession. Burning the jinn or their children with hot water while washing is one very common element of narratives of such unexpected encounters. The jinn can also be motivated to possess bodies out of mischief, envy, or the evil intentions of one person toward another. People often go to healers or sheikhs who act as intermediaries between the jinn and the possessed in order to tackle the destructive effects of possession. These intermediaries—who might also be possessed—communicate with the jinn to convince them to release possessed bodies or attempt to burn the occupants in order diminish their effects. Some of the intermediaries avoid harming the cins because they are afraid that the jinn will seek revenge against them. In some cases, they facilitate a transformation of the jinn from being badly to well intentioned.

The jinn are important agents associated with treasure hunting practices, especially since they might be guardians of treasure left by former dwellers on behalf of their owners. Also, unrelated to any commitment to act as guardians, the jinn may occupy places where treasure is located. Either way, treasure needs to be released from jinn protection or possession. In order to do so, people often invite sheiks to either communicate directly with them or to manipulate those jinn who are good-natured into possessing the bodies and minds of children and teenagers. This possession, which manifests itself as trance states, allows the sheik to order the possessed child to look for the treasure. During this process, the children often encounter a guardian jinnī in the form of a snake. While the possessed child is in a trance, the child will report on what he or she sees and hears, particularly talk by or conversations with the guardian jinnī. Such a trance reportedly lasts between two and three hours, ending when the sheikh releases the child from the possessing jinnī, after the guardian jinn have released the treasure. The jinn, it will be seen, cannot be reduced to the supernatural in Islamic theology or pre-Islamic beliefs. Their spectral reality is deeply entangled with rumors about treasure and often associated with speculation about the value of houses.

The jinn narratives evoke social relationships linked to the political economy of treasure hunting practices that involve material transactions between diggers, the owners of the houses or the land, illicit traders, and spiritual people such as sheikhs and hodjas (*hoca* singular in Turkish) who are regarded as capable of decoding the signs and symbols needed to find the treasure and to communicate with the jinn in order to release the treasure from their custody. Children acting as intermediaries are selected by the community of treasure hunters, who are the main funders of this material, technical, and spiritually conceived operation. Children are believed to be immune to the destructive effects of the jinn. Their families often agree to requests of treasure hunters to employ them for economic reasons.

Diggers often borrow significant amounts of money at high interest rates to pay their technical and spiritual teams. This creates a new vicious cycle in which the diggers live in permanent debt and want to dig more so that they can find the treasure and pay off the debt, which increases daily. As they dig more holes, they encounter all sorts of jinn that do not allow the object to be removed from the house. They pay the sheikh to convince the jinn. They see the jinn as the cause of their failure to possess the treasure, and yet they do not give up. The presence of the jinn gives them hope even as it evokes the misery of their failure to find treasure and of their growing debt. This creates a paradoxical situation in which diggers feel conscious of debt yet not in debt due to their desire to acquire the belongings of the absent other. However, they fall into debt by being part of a clandestine economy that operates in the interstices of religious sensibilities and desires for sudden wealth.

Getting into the Depth of the Matter

Hüseyin had known Veysi Bey long enough to understand that he would not stop digging. Hüseyin had always been fascinated by the passion and patience of Veysi Bey, and this had had an impact on his own involvement in treasure hunting. However, he felt he was more pragmatic than Veysi Bey. Hüseyin was familiar with secrets and rumors about treasures oozing out in different conversation as well as the possibility they raised of sudden enrichment. For years, he had owned a place outside Mardin where he ran a cockfight arena during the day and a gambling den during the night. He was a man making and holding connections and networks of different kinds that allowed him to be in touch with smugglers, illegal traders, healers, prostitutes, priests, imams, and treasure hunters. People would seek him not necessarily for his knowledge of the physical space, but for his knowledge of people and his relationship of trust with Christian healers and fortune-tellers, for whom he would occasionally work. He was an expert in earning and losing fast. Still, in his view, finding treasure was a matter of fate (kısmet): one would find it if this had been so written.

"A friend, an outsider, not a Mardinite, has found me," he told me. "There was a rumor about treasures in Mardin. 'They pointed out your house,' he said. 'My house, where in my house?'" Hüseyin did not want to miss out so he decided to help the visitor, who then brought all manner of people and tools to dig up Hüseyin's house. Prominently these include the hodja and young teenager to be hypnotized, and the diggers. The hodja hypnotized the child and gave him orders to find the treasure. The child, lying on the floor of the house, visualized hunting for the treasure. Hüseyin narrated the dialogue he recalled in the present tense, as if he was witnessing the conversation at that very moment:

> *Hodja:* Enter into the room.
> *Hypnotized child:* I cannot, it is too dark.
> *Hodja:* You will. Recite the name of God. . . . What do you see out
>   there?
> *Child:* There is a hole here. Light shines through it.
> *Hodja:* What does the light beam point to?
> *Child:* The first beam lands on a bowl with four squares, the second
>   beam on a buried pot. There is also a small pot closed with a
>   wooden cork.

Hüseyin recalls getting more and more excited, especially about the small pot.

> *Hodja:* Open the buried pot.
> *Child:* It is very tight. I can't open it.
> *Hodja:* Say Bismillahirrahmanirrahim [with the name of God, the
>   merciful]. Say it loudly. . . . What happened?
> *Child:* Half of the pot is full of gold.

Hüseyin reminded me that the hypnotized child was lying down in front of him and the hodja. He was talking as if he was experiencing the encounter physically. He was holding on to that pot and was trying to bring it back.

> *Child:* Hodja, my arm has slept.
> *Hodja:* Why?
> *Child:* I am pulling the pot to bring it up, but there is someone on
>   the other side, pulling it in the other direction.

The child talked about this for one and a half hours, reported Hüseyin, who asked the hodja:

Hüseyin: Who is on the other side?
Hodja: These are the ones protecting the treasure, the ones with the
    spell. They want something in exchange [for] the treasure.
Hüseyin: What can we give them? We are the ones who are starving.
    If we had something to give would we bother searching for
    treasure?
Hodja: [to the child]: Who is s(he)? What is their faith?

Hüseyin recalled the child said it was a she and that she was Christian.
The hodja instructed the child about what to say and the child conveyed the
hodja's words to the Christian female presence. After that she changed her
mind and decided she would let them have the treasure without demanding
anything in exchange. But then two more spiritual beings arrived, a male and
a female. The child reported that the female was a Muslim and wanted to let
him have the treasure. However, the male did not and told the female: "why
have we waited here for so long . . . just to give it away?" Then an argument
between them had started and the female had left. The hodja had then instructed the child to run after her, which he did until he caught up with her.
But at that point the male figure ran away. The child then ran after him too.
He then reported that the escapee had stopped, turned around, and started
laughing at him.

Hüseyin: Hodja, so what do we do next?
Hodja: We do nothing. This needs to stop here.

Hüseyin recounted how the hodja had then blessed a glass of water by re-
citing sacred verses and beckoned the child to drink it. The child had then
woken up and no longer reported seeing visions of any kind. Hüseyin felt confused and frustrated. He had asked the child about what had happened with
those three beings, the two females and the male. The child responded, "There
is a lady living beneath your house. She made a beautiful garden. She is here
to protect this house and its members." The child had then given a full description of the garden, pointing out the location of the door and the direction of flowing water. Shortly thereafter he had left.

After these events Hüseyin continued living with the effects of this encounter. Although he felt cheated, the idea that there might be a room beneath the house tormented him: he knew that there was a small chance that
he could find treasure. Two weeks after the first excavation in the house,

Hüseyin had a dream. "I had to kill this worm inside me, not to be rich, not to find the gold, but to satisfy my curiosity," he said. Hüseyin felt the urge to restart the digging. He could no longer avoid it and made use of his own social links to get opinions from different peoples, including imams and Christian healers. To each he described the site where he planned to dig in great detail, and justified this choice by appealing to dream interpretations, illusions, holy insights, rumors, and more mundane aspects of the built environment. He had decided to dig at the entrance of the house, where iron bars had been carefully set in stone. Hüseyin interpreted the geometrical harmony between the metal and the stone as a sign pointing to something hidden. He calculated the distance between this point and the imaginary room that the hypnotized child had described underneath the house and which later another imam had confirmed.

"I dug, dug and dug," he said. "I dug through the stone and that led to the soil and I dug through the soil that led to the stone. It was the same thing again and again. I opened up a hole nearly two meters deep inside the house. Neighbors and friends visited and saw me digging. The doors to the kitchen and two rooms surrounded the hole. We stayed inside a triangle. I placed a plank as a makeshift bridge over the hole. That is how we walked inside the house." After a while, Hüseyin's children started helping him out, especially when he went out to work. Hüseyin could not recall exactly how long he dug inside his house. At some point he had backfilled the first pit and, with the help of one of his friends, opened a second one inside another room: "We dug, took out soil, and hit another stone. We got excited, my heart started beating fast. My friend pulled up the stone. We saw a space, an empty space. It had been opened previously. We found bones, pots, and other things without value. I mean, they have value, but of course, only historical value."

Hüseyin would not give up and called another hodja for further investigation. "The hodja burned up charcoal there and claimed that it was all empty," he recalled. "I got annoyed. Everyone claims something different. Everyone lies. That does not mean the place is empty, no, it is not. I have witnessed many things. There was a very poor man in our neighborhood. All of a sudden, he bought a car, land, house, he opened up a shop. But [for one to be as lucky] it needs be written in your fate. If it is not written for you, then it is all a lie."

There can be little doubt that treasure hunting was more than a pastime for Hüseyin: evidently it had serious spiritual and material significance. Although he had been seduced by the circulating rumors, he narrated his experience as an intersection of coincidences that had been shaped by spiritual and religious causes, such that his soul had never been left in peace. While he eventually stopped digging up his house, he never lost his curiosity for what he perceived as real history. For Hüseyin, treasure hunting had become a search for the traces of previous lives. While walking the streets and alleyways of Mardin, he would look at the stones making up an old wall and point out the odd one out. His skill in engaging with the texture of the walls satisfied him. It was a proof of his belonging to and knowing the city.

But who were the first owners of these houses? How did they live here? Who were they? Muslims, Christians, Jews? How would they worship? As Hüseyin put it to me, "I am getting into the depth of this matter. I sometimes sit in the house and just daydream." He was not sure he could ever resolve the matter: "There are many claims about the people who lived in this city. Some say that the city was once ruled by a king, others by a sultan, and yet others by an agha (ağa). Everyone, here, just makes it up as they go along," he added, as we parted ways outside his house.

"You Cannot Remove the Treasure if You Are Not the Real Owner of the House"

Yaşar Bey's family and their house were objects of curiosity in the Old City. They were often regarded as diggers of their own place. Yaşar Bey, an engineer in his early fifties, was one of the inheritors of the house. His parents were from a landed Kurdish family. He returned to Mardin recently to, in his own words, "take care of their ruined property." Yaşar and Veysi Bey were old acquaintances. Veysi Bey had lived in one of the floors of the house for three years until he was kicked out: "these houses are durable and strong yet sensitive to the vibration. You cannot even break a walnut in these houses. I did not know then," Veysi Bey had said by way of explanation. He had been forced to leave with his two young children after being caught chopping wood in the courtyard.

"They have dug up everywhere, when we were away. They burnt the house, they dug it up, and they filled all these rooms with the soil that came out of these holes. There is a rumor that there is something hidden in this house. They even believe that we have taken it out, which is absolutely untrue. Even if we had tried, we would not have been able to. Even the best technology would not break the magic spell. Jinn would not let us do it." Yaşar Bey was pointing out the holes in the ground floor of the three-story mansion.

Veysi Bey was looking at the stone carvings and figures on the arches in a mixture of admiration, adoration, and resentment. Yaşar Bey, instead, tended to talk about his knowledge of the house through the medium of wells, basements, excavated holes, and dark corners of the house. According to him, this was a haunted house full of jinn who would move furniture and bring food and other objects.

Yaşar Bey had spent sixteen years of his life with a hodja to learn the science of dealing with the effects of the jinn, as well as to save his sister from their capture. "They were everywhere, before, and now they only live in the basement," he said, while walking with us on the ground floor of the house. "I saw the same scorpion three or four years ago, and my brother saw the same one yesterday entering into this hole. I looked for it, and could not find [it]. I broke down the brick, still could not see it. It was gone." Veysi Bey added to his excitement: "I would have helped you to get into the hole. I am scared of the scorpions and snakes. And this is an old house which God protects." Veysi Bey now changed the topic (and the tone of his voice) and asked me, "now, could I learn what are you doing here?"

I explained the purpose of my research. No further questions were asked. He muttered "this is not a house to roam around," and walked away to the next room. The ruined state of the house was not alienating or frustrating to him. This is what happened in any abandoned house. It required enormous money to restore it. We followed the light of the torch that Veysi Bey was holding in his hand. He walked us into the rooms that earlier had been used as classrooms. The house had originally belonged to an Armenian family that disappeared in 1915. The mansion was later turned into an elementary school and was used as such until 1958, when the Directorate of National Real Estate (Milli Emlak Müdürlüğü) sold the house to Yaşar Bey's family. "The vali called me the other day," Yaşar Bey said. "I thought, he wants to convince me to demolish the cement parts of the building. Before he asked, I told him that I would not. But he had something else in mind. He said, 'I want to buy this house, how much do you want?' My house is not [for] sale. Two years ago, they offered 3 million dollars, and my brother asked for 5 million and we could not make a deal."

The rooms were divided into small units with wooden planks and the niches were filled with plaster and turned into walls. They were walls with holes that had been opened up by treasure hunters. "First we lived on this floor, then we moved upstairs," Yaşar Bey said. Different people had constructed each floor at different times. Pointing out the drawings of the stars on the inner side of the window frames, he said, "This part was constructed by the Jews. Their architectural style is plain." Veysi Bey looked at the piles of stones left aside. "They fell off the wall because of humidity," Yaşar Bey explained. "They are all carved. Do you see the carvings? . . . And here," he continued, "there are two boxes inside each other. Can you see the gate at the very bottom? I went through that door. It was broken, so I wondered whether someone dug further down." Yaşar Bey had gone down through the hole and found a clean shiny place, full of light, "like a *hamam* [Turkish bath]." A year later, he climbed down the same hole again but this time saw something totally different. It was dark and dirty.

Veysi Bey: How come?
Yaşar Bey: Magic
Veysi Bey: Yes, it should be that.
Yaşar Bey: I know it is. There is magic in this house.
Veysi Bey: I remember seeing an animal in this courtyard. I thought
    it was a cow, but it was not.
Yaşar Bey: Were you awake or sleep?
Veysi Bey: It was not a dream. Do you remember the cows and sheep
    carried to the butcher through the path behind the house? I
    think it was one of the animals that had escaped from the herd.
    I heard its voice and then looked at its face. I wish I had not
    looked at it. I still remember, right now I could still draw this
    face, its nose. It was terrible.
Yaşar Bey: Did you hear its voice? Did you hear its roar?
Veysi Bey: Yes, but not only me. All the neighbors heard that.

Listening to this conversation between Veysi Bey and Yaşar Bey, I was puzzled. They seemed to know what they were talking about but were not naming it. I asked: "What does this all mean?" My voice was high pitched and more impatient than usual as I wanted to avoid hearing a one-word answer in the usual style: jinn. Performing my most secular, urban, and alien self, I asked them to explain to me their presences in the house. Why was the house haunted? Why were they here? Was it because the house was built on the top of the cemetery? Or was there a tomb underneath, as other people kept on repeating? Was there a link between the jinn and the cemeteries?

    Yaşar Bey did not engage with my panic. He was the first house owner I had met who was being open and vocal about his personal experience about the jinn. His narratives were not based on others' (or his own) treasure hunting experiences. Yaşar Bey was a full believer in the jinn and, having abandoned his profession altogether, had devoted his life to learning the mysterious ways that permitted tackling the effects they had on people's lives. He was neither a victim nor a witness. He was calling them by their name, "jinn," not using the euphemism "three-lettered ones" that locals would often use to refer to the jinn. "They can't take away what God has granted me," he said. "I do not obey them. I learned how to fight them." The house was full of jinn, he reiterated. "They used to be everywhere. Now, they are only in the basement."

Yaşar Bey did not imagine the house could exist independently and separated from the jinn. They were permanent dwellers of this, his mansion. I repeated my question about the connection between the cemetery, the house, and the jinn. Well, he said, "Gırnavuz is the homeland of the jinn. This is also mentioned in the Quran. Do I remember correctly?" He turned to Veysi Bey for confirmation.

Veysi Bey: The jinn of Nusaybin and the jinn of Gırnavuz visited the Prophet and gave him a letter. They heard him reading the Quran loudly.

Yaşar Bey: And then they converted to Islam.

Veysi Bey: Yes, and they also occupied our city.

Yaşar Bey: Yes, all the old houses, the dark places, the barns, they are full of them.

Veysi Bey: They also settled into quiet places.

Yaşar Bey: They can take any form and shape. If they want to scare, they take on the appearance of a monster.

Veysi Bey: And sometimes they appear in the form of a human being but their feet point backwards.

Yaşar Bey: Yes, that is true. Opposite sides.

Veysi Bey: Their eyes are catlike, big.

Yaşar Bey: Shaped like baklava [triangular]. Ours are round and theirs are triangular.

Veysi Bey: I did see that too.

Yaşar Bey: The color of the eyes is red.

Veysi Bey: They are harmless as long as one keeps away from them. If they touch, though, it becomes maddening. Look, these figures are very beautiful.

Veysi Bey had changed the topic, moving his attention to another detail: the wooden carvings under the window frames. "Jewish architecture," he said. Yaşar Bey was still in the dark, thinking of the jinn. He called us from the other side of the room: "Look, they dug up here too, look at the pits." Our gaze was shifting between the colorful carvings hidden under the window to the pits on the floor. The shift in conversation from the jinn of the house to the carvings to the pits was all in the same tone, with similar smooth transitions. Yaşar Bey went out of the room and joined Veysi Bey in revisiting old corners of the house. "And these two floors," pointing the torch upward, he murmured, "were constructed by the Christians. Look at the stones carefully. The stones will tell you the difference," he added. "The Jews had a plain style whereas the Christians knew how to process and carve on the stone." He then came and inspected the pits on the floor and the holes on the wall once again. The house had a life of its own and Yaşar Bey was moving between and through marks to remember it.

"Do you want to see the bats?" Yaşar Bey asked in one room. "Our house is occupied by the bats too. Take a photo if you want, be careful with the flash, do not focus on them and do not scare them." Veysi Bey entered the room. The bats were hiding in the ceiling. Nostalgically he chose to look at another place, drawing out attention to signs of beauty. Looking at the floor, Veysi Bey noticed the fireplace:

Veysi Bey: Imagine the dishes cooked on this stove.
Yaşar Bey: Can you take a close-up photo of the bats?
Veysi Bey: Imagine the songs sung around this stove in Kurdish,
    Turkish, Armenian, Hebrew, and Turkish.
Yaşar Bey: The visual skills of these bats are very weak. But they feel
    anything that will get close to them.
Veysi Bey: Were the Armenian owners of this house sent to exile?
    Were they all killed or [has] anyone remained alive from this
    family?

This was the first time I heard Veysi Bey making explicit references to the 1915 massacres and displacements in Mardin. Yaşar Bey nodded: "they were all sent to exile, and the state confiscated their property." In his view, not all of them had been killed: some had been protected and hidden by Muslim families. The tribal Kurdish families that had arrived in the 1950s had then bought the prominent houses that originally had belonged to Armenian families, either from the state or from their first or second owners. They had been the first ones to build two- or three-story apartment blocks on top of the stone houses. According to Yaşar's father, Armenians had been sent into exile because they wanted to create their own state, so they were traitors. Even despite this, his family had sheltered many Armenians in their own house, including neighbors and close friends. "No one would dare to take them from our house," he said. Yaşar Bey's grandparents were one of the big landowning Kurdish families: "Our family is fearless." They were scared of neither humans nor nonhumans, meaning the jinn, as he had said earlier.

"My grandmother was Armenian too," Yaşar Bey continued, revealing another part of his family history. "She was from an affluent family of Diyarbakır; she would buy her clothes in Paris, and was educated by private tutors." Yaşar Bey's grandfather, he explained, used to go to Diyarbakır every month and, one time, he noticed a big crowd waiting outside the city walls. "My grandfather and his brother heard from others that these Christians will be sent to exile in Palestine and no one knows what will happen to them next, so my grandfather grabbed a young girl of thirteen to fourteen years old (himself being sixteen at the time) and brought her back to Mardin. We are a big and rooted family in Mardin, with a history of twelve hundred years." His grandfather married the Armenian girl when she turned eighteen and her name was changed from Rosa to Zekiye. Rosa's sisters were abducted by another family in Mardin. "They were beaten up and used as servants in the house. My grandfather sent his two men to the house of those girls and they were helped so that they could flee to Syria; they then stayed at the house of the priest before being sent to the USA. They are my great aunts, I have their photo. But we have never met." Yaşar Bey's imagined connection to his Armenian roots did not end there. As a family, he claimed, they had always been the protectors of victims, especially Christian ones. They would protect them from harassment, robbery, and abduction. "Justice means telling the truth," he said. "When you claim justice, it should be there for all regardless of ethnicity, race, language." "Does such a thing exist?" asked Veysi Bey promptly. "Maybe not," responded Yaşar Bey.

Yaşar Bey is also an explorer, like Veysi Bey. He has a deep knowledge of the city, including its different entrances and exits, the converted mosques and churches, and the treasure sites surrounding the churches and monasteries. His imagination of the space is not independent of the jinn. By his account, there are jinn that have been living for sixteen hundred to seventeen hundred years. The jinn, he added, can be used by humans for their purposes.

"In the early days in Mardin, we used to capture the jinn. If you stick a needle into their shoulder, they cannot escape until the needle is removed. They
stay in the family as slaves and servants and do whatever one wishes." In his
view, the jinn could belong to any religion, Muslim, Jewish, or Christian, or
be nonbelievers. "There are all kinds of jinn, like there are all kinds of people.
And there are jinn who capture other jinn and [are] using them as slaves,
servants. Once here, in this house, I saved the good jinn from the bad ones,"
said Yaşar Bey. "I saved the Muslim jinn from the Christian and Jewish ones.
Two of the Muslim jinn were females and one of them was badly tortured. I
recited a prayer, and some of them got burnt and others escaped. I saved the
Muslim jinni, she lived with us for six months and then she died." Yaşar Bey
had connections with significant hodjas who knew how to deliver the jinn to
humans for their own good purposes. "I talked to [one such] hodja the other
day. He told me on the phone, he found two new sites without any spell. He
is waiting to hear from the diggers."

Yaşar Bey also recalled a story that had happened about then: "a few days
ago, three Christian Mardinites from Canada were standing in front of one
of the museum buildings, which used to be their house." Yaşar Bey saw them
from afar and asked what they were waiting for. The visitors told him that
they wanted to see their house, but they were not allowed to since the house
had now been turned into the office of the head of the museum. Yaşar Bey
got furious, found the gatekeepers, and said, "These people are the real owners
of this place. They lost their house by force. I will take them inside for a walk.
If you do not let me in, I will break in and get inside myself." Yaşar Bey walked
the visitors inside the museum. "One of them told me that they had stuff buried here. I said, let your stuff remain there. I told them that I know the spell,
yet no one could possibly break it and take the treasure away." Yaşar Bey suggested they see a lawyer and file a claim for their house.

> *Yaşar Bey:* They can reclaim their house in court, there are now new
>   laws.
> *Veysi Bey:* No, they cannot.
> *Yaşar Bey:* Look, if they want to get my house, they should pay for it,
>   but if the occupier is the state, then they can make a claim by
>   showing their title deed and proving that it was taken from
>   them by force.
> *Veysi Bey:* If the state signed any ratification about this property
>   issue, then they can reclaim it.

Yaşar Bey: Mark [one of the visitors] really liked me and wanted to
show me the place where the pot is hidden. He said there are
two pots of gold in the house. I told him not to. If I dig it now, I
cannot remove it. This is true. Mark also knows that. The real
owner could dig it and take it, but I cannot, even if I see it, I
cannot touch it. I can see all the crocodiles, snakes, but if I
open it, then I know that they [jinn] will come and get the
treasure before me and . . .

Veysi Bey: Then, they will escape to another house.

The Limits of Optimism

In her work on treasure hunters in a Kurdish town, Muş, in eastern Turkey,
Alice von Bieberstein (2017:186) has demonstrated how the recognition of the
Armenian genocide and of the Armenian heritage in the area, promoted as
part of the Kurdish movement's ideology expressing solidarity with other oppressed groups, dissolves as soon as the search for treasure begins. Bieberstein argues that material relationships that revolve around treasure hunting take over a political consciousness about past violence and help produce
public secrecy and complicity among locals who would conceal the identity
of the owner of the treasure. In contrast, in Mardin the Armenian genocide
is often not spoken of through the dispossession of property. The multiethnic character of the city, moreover, helps to avoid the need to name and recognize the ethnicity of past house owners, even when exceptional encounters
with the jinn take place. And yet, as in the case of Bieberstein's research, complicity and obsession structure feelings that mark the relationship between
diggers and the object of their search.

Digging is one of the few practices that transgresses the social, political,
and economic enclaves defined by Kurds, Arabs, and Syriacs. Digging creates a community of diggers that exists inside and outside the city. The desire to dig coexists with the appreciation of cultural heritage along with, but
independent of, expectations for peace and reconciliation in the region. However, it is also potentially toxic for locals. People dig until they run out of
money. They dig until they dismantle and ruin their houses. They backfill
pits and dig again until they encounter the jinn holding the lid of the pot.
Their optimism initially makes them believe that they can convince the jinn
to release their treasure. As these beings resist, however, they recognize the

jinn as legitimate guardians: their desire for a good life then becomes conflated with religious sensibilities, fractured memories of the past, and their
sense of justice for the absent other. They maintain their attachments to the
object of desire, the hidden treasure, but live it through experiences of haunting and possession. This desire for returning is where cruelty lies. People
return to the scene of promises regardless of potentially threatening encounters with the jinn, who live in the cracks and holes of the house. But people
continue to dig. They continue to borrow money to excavate, to break the
spell, to release the jinn. The ruination of these houses as heritage continues
under this "cruel optimism."

The jinn are not invisible or unknown to the digger but important ele-
ments of daily life. The jinn are never imagined as belonging to a particular
era. Nor are they imagined as the representatives of the dead or repressed.
Rather, they are imagined as familiar mediators between the living and the
dead, the present and the absent, blurring the distinction between past, present, and future. It is this that allows for an encounter between those who
have left and become dispossessed and those who have remained and come
to possess, between Yaşar and Mark. In this juxtaposition, the jinn emerge
as external arbiters that remind people of the permissible limits that should
govern their desire to possess. At the same time, cin narratives allow people
to question origins and foundations and rethink the notion of what is right
and just. They lead to the imagination that Mardin has been occupied and
ruined myriad times, and that the city is composed of different layers of destruction and reconstruction. What looks like the surface of the city, then, is
layered over graveyards and cemeteries, making it attractive to the jinn.

This historical and spiritual imaginary of the urban landscape does not
challenge the hegemonic discourse about the history of destruction and dispossession in the city. Although Mardinites recognize the fact that many of
the occupied houses belonged to Armenians, they refrain from making a clear
connection between the treasure supposed to exist in those houses and the
Armenians who once occupied them. The jinn narratives break up the acute
centrality of the event that caused destruction, and anonymizes the identity
of victims and perpetrators. At best, every displaced person leaves some jinn
behind. Jinn narratives preempt the contemporary meaning of the political
and ethnic identities and rupture their linear temporalities. For, according
to the narratives of Yaşar Bey and Veysi Bey, there aren't any Kurdish, Arabic,
Armenian, or Syriac jinn. Instead, there are Muslim jinn, who are well intentioned and submissive, and Christian and Jewish ones, who are subversive

and aggressive—stubborn jinn that prevent locating and taking possession of treasure. In this sense, cin narratives do not produce critical accounts or articulate different vantage points from which history could be told. Yaşar's narrative does not challenge the official discourse about the Armenian genocide. Instead he refers to his late father's explanation to justify what has happened to the original owners of the house, shifting the responsibility from self to other, from self to the state, and from self to the jinn. At the same time, he renders his knowledge of the jinn as a means to reestablish another sense of justice for the absent other. He rethinks the notion of property rights combining the secular ideology of justice and the religious one. It is the lack of public recognition of the dispossessed that allows Hüseyin, Yaşar, and Veysi—members of the same imagined community—to dare to continue digging. The jinn both remind them of the reasons for their return to digging and help them to endure the frustrations of not obtaining what they seek.

In this chapter I have presented ethnographic narratives about the experience of treasure hunting in the stone houses of Mardin. The encounter with the jinn at the scene of digging, or at the unspecified cracks of old houses, engenders conversations about the limits of agency and about the ethics related to the rules of possession and ownership. At the same time, the encounter reveals parallels between processes that underlie the construction of subjectivity and property regimes. In this space, the jinn operate as the invisible force that guards against the dispossession of property and of treasure left behind by the absent other. The digger-tenants of this ethnography, are the flaneurs of the city, aware of the connections between the house and its landscape, knowledgeable about the architecture of the stone houses themselves, initiated into mysterious ways to decode the assemblage of materials. They read all of these as traces of an unknown that, in their view, is where the real cultural and economic value of heritage lies. They seek to avoid possession by the jinn and want to possess the object that the jinn protect. However, they know that avoiding possession is impossible: they know that someone must be possessed for the jinn to release the treasure they guard. For in those stone walls—where the legacy and heritage of previous owners is embedded—the unknown is concealed from the eyes of the uninitiated.

CHAPTER 4

Living as if Indebted

The day starts at 6:00 A.M. with the sound of the phone ringing. The nun is calling İsa Bey to tell him that the cows from the neighboring village have once again entered their village's vineyards. The grapes are in danger. İsa Bey hears her high-pitched voice and hangs up the phone without listening to the whole story. He already knows what she is going to say. The Kurdish neighbors are letting their cows walk through the fields of their village, a Syriac village named Zaz[1] located near Midyat, a town sixty kilometers from the city of Mardin (see Figure 2). İsa Bey puts on his clothes and wakes up his housemates, Uncle Yakup and İdo. Five minutes later, he jumps into his four-wheel drive vehicle and waits for the others to arrive. It is a chilly, sunny autumn morning. The trip from Midyat to Zaz takes under fifteen minutes. No one talks. İsa Bey slows down when he reaches the fields. He can see nothing beyond the reddish green leaves of the vineyards, which seem to reach as far as the horizon. There are hectares of open fields, open sky, invisible borders, and, somewhere, a single suspicious cow. İsa Bey calls the nun to ask exactly where she spotted the cow. Holding the phone in her hand, the nun goes to the roof of the church and takes another look through her binoculars. We hear the echo of her slippers hitting the stone steps and then curses and complaints. The cow had been spotted north of the road thirty minutes earlier, but it has disappeared. İsa Bey speeds up to see whether they can catch it close to the border between the two villages. Uncle Yakup gets out of the car. An old smuggler, he finds it easy to chase things on foot. Despite his poor eyesight, he knows the village and its borders like the back of his hand. He sleepwalks through the vineyards to find the cow and then calls İsa Bey to report its location and the scale of the damage.

İsa Bey believes that this is the Kurds' most recent harassment strategy. They no longer sneak into the fields to steal fruit and vegetables. Instead, they send their animals—including cows, sheep, goats, and horses—to eat the wheat or grapes and ruin the fields. İsa Bey has asked them not to let their animals enter the vineyard until the end of the harvest season. He has even visited the gendarme station and filed an official complaint, reporting that the villagers of Kayalı and Ortaklı are sending their animals into his community's fields with the purpose of damaging the products. As usual, no one has taken him seriously: not enough evidence to prove that the damage was intentional or that private property has been trespassed. Since his uncertain return to the region, his personal assemblage of networks, connections, and associations has been pulled back toward older conflicts and life tensions with the Kurdish neighbors. And thus he lives haunted by the memories and experiences of violence (Figure 8).

İsa Bey's life is built around routines. He wakes up, chases the cows, handles the requests of the nun and the monk, and finds tools and laborers from the Kurdish villages to work the fields. He also submits documents to the bank and municipality, or petitions lawyers, the state prosecutor, or gendarme forces about the verbal abuse and physical attacks he receives from Kurds; he works on a litigation case related to ongoing disputes over confiscation of land by the state. His phone rings all day long. During the lunch break of European cities, villagers living in Germany, Belgium, and Sweden call him to get the latest news about the village: the weather, the harvest, the cow, the *korucu* (village guard), and the agha are usually the focus of these exchanges. "No one comes here, but they do call and they send money," says İsa Bey. The life of his community has been brutally interrupted. The effects of those interruptions have never really been mitigated.

In İsa Bey's narratives, two of the milestones are the Sayfo—as noted earlier, the massacres of the Syriacs in 1915—and the 1993 displacement of all Syriac villagers at the peak of the conflict between the PKK and the Turkish Armed forces.[2] No one had been living in this ancient village other than the nun and the monk, who had returned in 2000, and four Kurdish families, who never left. The village church was now in the process of being restored and the fields had been planted. However, the rest of the village remains in ruins. The pond in the village square is dry, the burned blackberry tree just never returned to life. İsa Bey, a sixty-year-old Syriac man who has spent thirty years of his life in Scotland and Australia, is back in

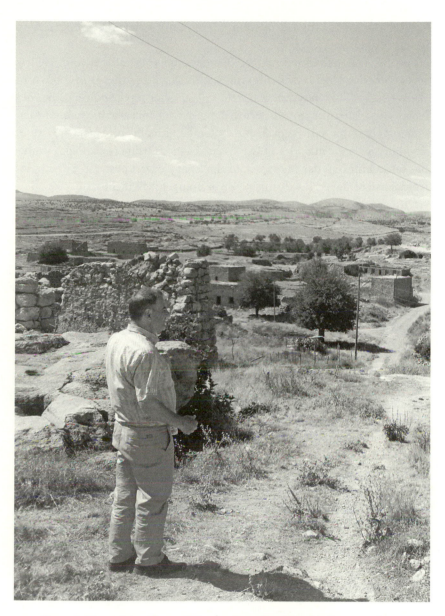

Figure 8. View of the village of Zaz. İsa Bey talks about his future projects.

Midyat with a self-assigned mission: to carve out a new life in the ancient Syriac village.

İsa Bey is not a returnee in the conventional sense of the word. He has never settled in the village because it is unsafe. He stays in the town of Midyat, forty kilometers away from the village, sharing the house with other Syriac visitors. He has not had a house of his own since leaving behind Australia.. At best, for a few months in winter, he visits his parents, who live in Hamburg, where a majority of the Syriac diaspora from Zaz village eventually settled. Despite his resistance to the legacy of the past, İsa Bey cannot avoid feeling trapped inside this mode of living, as if indebted.

This chapter explores the historical and political underpinnings of indebtedness as the mode of existence of Syriacs in the region. We will mostly follow these contortions through the lens of İsa Bey, a Syriac man with Australian and Turkish citizenship who constructs his life story through characters, places, and practices engendered through different modalities of life. Between 2008 and 2015, I shadowed İsa Bey's engagement with the village of Zaz through my visits to Midyat and Hamburg through e-mails and phone calls. These long conversations took place in the tenses of the past, present, and future with characters living in different villages, countries, and continents. İsa Bey documented every aspect of his life in Midyat in the form of petitions submitted to lawyers or officers and phone interviews granted to journalists, NGO activists, and anthropologists. In these narratives, İsa Bey emerges as the witness, representative of villagers who live in diaspora, a potential returnee citizen who engages with all the actors involved in displacement, dispossession, and restitution. His narratives provide evidence for violence-in-continuum not only through the self-evident connections with events in 1915, the 1990s, and after 2000 but also through everyday struggles to stop the process of dispossession and ruination of his village. His daily experiences, which move through mediation, communication, plantation, and restoration, evolve into an archive that collects the personal and collective memories of violence, the day-to-day experiences of confronting the state, the working of the land, and the expectation of fellow villagers whose opportunity to return largely depends on the success of İsa Bey's efforts to re-inhabit their ruined village.

And yet, İsa Bey wants to make a life against the "exception" that has been historically the "norm" in the village. Despite the shadow of the Sayfo, memories that never cease to torment him, he wants to allocate his perception of violence beyond the single responsible of one party, beyond any single purpose, and beyond any single suffering (Scarry 1987). As his understanding of the past constantly changes, he wants to redraw the lines that separate new friends from old foes.

The Context of Violence and Displacement

In his book *Routine Violence*, Gyanendra Pandey (2006:17) writes that the "history of extreme violence is almost always about the context—about everything that happens *around* violence" (my italics). I agree with Pandey's crucial reminder: context matters. Eyal Weizman explores this very dimension through his detailed analysis of the Israeli occupation of Palestinian territory, where he examines the dynamic between the spatial reorganization of borders and the trajectories of political and military conflicts. "The various inhabitants of this frontier," writes Weizman (2007:7), "do not operate within the fixed envelopes of space—space is not the background for their actions, an abstract grid on which events take place—but rather the medium that each of their actions seek to challenge, transform or appropriate." In this space of occupation and dispossession, Weizman argues, "the relation of space to action could not be understood as that of a rigid container of 'soft' performance. Political action is fully absorbed in the organisation, transformation, erasure and subversion of space" (7).

In their comprehensive analysis of the literature of displacement, migration, and return, Stef Jansen and Steffan Löfving (2007) discuss opportunities for producing a critical analysis of "home" in connection with violence and place. They criticize the problematic aspect of both "sedentarist" thinking that posits a normative causality between territory and ethno(nationality) and the free-floating assumptions of the "anti-sedentarist" paradigm that disregards "patterns of territorialization, identification with place and a desire to return to locality of origin" (4). Their main focus has been on engaging with different historical and political processes addressing not only "memories of social and geographical belonging but also *forward-looking practices* of attachment to and detachment from place" (3, my italics). Their work invites an understanding of the ways in which violence and space operate and transform each other; how they resonate through discourses and practices about belonging, subjectivity, and citizenship; and how people who get involved in the processes of displacement and return ascribe different meanings to this relationship (7). This multifarious attachment to places in the here and then is also explored in Sharika Thiranagama's (2007, 2011) ethnographic work on displaced Tamils, in which she illustrates that one's relationship to home is created through the interplay of places and people that connects the political, the intimate, and a sense of belonging.

In pursuit of the analysis of the violence continuum (Scheper-Hughes and Bourgois 2003:5), in the next two chapters, I recast a context made of assemblages of fragmented, repetitive, and selected narratives about "everything that happens around violence." In this domain of "around violence," home does not reemerge as a "timeless entity" (Jansen and Löfving 2007:9). The possibility of home fluctuates between past memories of loss, present conditions of violence, and hope for a better life that is imagined for the future.

I engage here with the performances of Syriacs, who resist the occupation and dispossession of their property. For this purpose we will make our way and witness the unfolding of memories, aspirations, and practices connected to the possession and repossession of collective and individual spaces, such as ancestral land and a prominent monastery that Syriacs associate with their ancient homeland, Tur Abdin. Our paths will map and reveal the context of the past and present history of dispossession that has taken place between Syriacs, Kurds, and the Turkish state. Unfolding these connections in stories of inclusion and exclusion, I write against the "sedentarist" logic ingrained in the episteme and politics of scholarship about the Syriac community (in Turkey and in diaspora), which predominantly represents Syriacs as bearing the historical quality of an authentic ethnic or religious community in Mesopotamia (e.g., Bilge 2001:425; Taşğın et al. 2005). In these accounts the trope of victimhood sets up the form and content of the argument: the violation of space and territory is identified with the violation of identity and community (see Omtzigt et al. 2012; Önder 2012; Özmen 2013), and Sayfo constitutes the Syriac-Assyrian identity (see Çetrez et al. 2012; Atto 2012a; Gaunt 2006; Gaunt et al. 2017; Travis 2017). Here I write against the grain of the reification and essentialization of the Syriacs as the self-contained, self-referenced community of Mesopotamia. While I do not wish to disavow these narratives in any way, nor do I question the veracity of the events that so constitute them, I write against the fetishization of these events because they posit a normative causality between present conflicts and memories of past atrocities. My commitments lie, instead, with exploring the ordinary ethics that emerge from attempts to re-make life despite the enduring and haunting memory of loss.

History of Multiple Returns

Syriacs have been the witness-survivors of "critical events" (Das 1997) that are constitutive and reproductive of the sovereign violence of the Ottoman Empire and the Turkish state. They have experienced displacement, migration, and re-turn as they moved between Kurdish tribes, villages, cities, countries, and con-tinents. The historical origin of Syriac Christianity is situated in both "a Jewish Christian heritage and the gentile Christian milieu of Antioch" (Armbruster 2013:6). The Syriac Christian Church was established between the fifth and sixth centuries. Due to the intense wars between Byzantium and Persia, their homeland Tur Abdin was constantly occupied. Together with Armenians and Nestorians, the Syriac Christian Church moved to the mountains to escape the hegemony of the church of Byzantium. With the Arab occupation in the sev-enth century, they were subjected to further social, political, and linguistic transformations. Despite their significant population, they became a religious minority under the hegemony of Muslim sovereignties (Armbruster 2013:26).

During the Ottoman imperial and republican regimes, the historical life of Syriacs was entangled with the Kurds and Armenians. From the sixteenth century onward, Armenians and Syriacs were engaged with Kurds through patron-client relationships in which Christians provided support to compet-ing sections of the tribal structures in exchange for protection (Armbruster 2013:29; see also Aydın et al. 2000; Yalçın-Heckmann 1991, 2000; Özgen 2007; Aydın 2013). In 1915, the Syriacs in the city of Mardin were exempt from the *ferman* (order) of deportation, while the Syriacs in Tur Abdin and the moun-tains of Tarsus and Hakkari were heavily affected by the attacks and killings carried out by the Kurdish locals. The Sayfo caused thousands of Syriac sur-vivors to escape their homes and move to Syria, Lebanon, and Iraq (see Altuğ 2013). The approximate toll for the Syriac Orthodox is reckoned to be around ninety thousand people, which is estimated to be equivalent to a third of their total population in the Middle East (Armbruster 2013:36). With the estab-lishment of borders arising from the Treaty of Lausanne in 1923, the Tur Abdin region became divided by the borders between Turkey, Iraq, and Syria, as did the Syriac community that remained in the region. Under the Lausanne Treaty, unlike the Armenians, Greeks, and Jews, the Syriac community was not granted the official status of a non-Muslim minority, which would have provided protection for their physical presence as well as their rights to practice, learn, and teach their language and religion.[3] They were not the subject of political negotiations or settlement between nation-states, as was the case of the exchange of population between Turkey and Greece. Rather, in the vicinity of the city of Mardin, the Syriac Orthodox Patriarchate was removed from Deyrulzafaran Monastery and relocated first in Homs and later in Damascus in Syria (Armbruster 2013:38). Their migration from the region to other parts of the Middle East, western parts of Turkey, and Europe continued through the 1925 Kurdish uprisings, the time when the wealth income tax was introduced in the 1940s,[4] the Cyprus events in 1960s, the military coup in 1980, and the military conflict between the PKK and Turkish Armed Forces in the 1990s. Their population in the region dropped from fifty thousand to twenty-five hundred between 1960 and 1995 (Armbruster 2013:7).

Syriacs have not disappeared from the region, but the sense of being invisible, unrecognized, and few in number has historically marked the structure of their feelings as a community. In her remarkable ethnographic study of Syriac identity, Heidi Armbruster emphasizes with acute clarity that "the sense of being historically beleaguered was compounded by indifference in the larger world. . . . They had been forgotten victims of the Christian massacres in Ottoman Eastern Anatolia in 1915–16, a minority without minority rights in Turkey, and foreigners not recognised as 'fellow Christians' in Austria and Germany" (2013:8). In the year 2000, the Turkish government issued a call to Syriacs in diaspora to return to their home villages. As part of the democratization process to fulfill the Copenhagen criteria, the AKP-led government initiated the official registration of individual and state property in eastern and southeastern Turkey in 2004. Syriac diasporic communities seized this opportunity to make official claims about ownership of land that they had left behind and secure official recognition of their historical presence in their homeland. They traveled to the region to witness the registration process in their villages, act as consultative authorities, or explicitly or secretly negotiate disputes with state employees, Kurdish aghas, and lawyers.

Between Life and Death

In 2008, I met with İsa Bey at the residence of the Syriac Association in Midyat, where many Syriacs living in Europe and Syria were provided with free lodging while they visited their home villages. Some were indeed just visiting their villages but others were trying to sell or buy new property in the villages or in the town of Midyat. Some were building new homes in their ruined villages. Others were trying to sort out their documents and deal with the bureaucracy of the cadastral registration. İsa Bey would leave the residence every morning at 9:00 A.M. He always wore a smart suit and carried a plastic bag full of paperwork. He returned each afternoon at 5:00 P.M. after local government offices closed. He was a familiar face to all of the employees in the state's Deed and Cadastral Department following the cadastral registration that had taken place in 2005, he was sorting out the title deeds for each of the mostly Hamburg-residing Zaz villagers.

Syriac families had been forced to leave the village of Zaz in 1993 at the peak of the conflict. The korucus had occupied the village, allowing four Kurdish families to remain. The korucus were from a village located on the other side of the road, close to Perbume Hill, a place remembered for the killing nearly three hundred Syriacs from Zaz in 1915. The perpetrators had brought back the victims' clothes to Zaz, washed them in the pond, and then worn them. Perbume Hill was a forbidden place that Syriacs never visited.

İsa Bey had lost seventy-five people from his extended family on the forbidden hill and on the road near it. He recalled the narratives that he collected for decades from other witnesses.

It was during Ramadan. They broke their fast in the village square that day. They attacked the houses, removed doors, windows, stones, food. A boy who escaped from the hill witnessed it all. He told the rest of the Syriacs hidden in the church building what happened on the hill. He told them not to leave the church. People managed to stay inside the church for a full month. They only left when the Muslim villagers from the other side of the road came and promised not to hurt them if they did. And they didn't. Instead, they forced the survivors to collect the dead bodies lying on the road to Midyat. The majority of them died on that same road looking for the corpses.

The history of the Sayfo was different for each village in Tur Abdin (Gaunt 2006). Some of the Syriacs were protected by their Kurdish covillagers or neighbors. Some were killed after 1915. Some of them managed to join the resistance in the village of Ayn Verd. The majority of the Syriac survivors escaped from their villages after 1915. They moved, finding work in the coal industry that supplied the British Army or resettling in the Al-Jazira Province of Syria, where they were absorbed into village families as children, potential wives, or servants. İsa Bey's grandfather had been one of the survivors who had managed to escape from the church and then lived in a Kurdish village, where he had served the community as a shepherd. A few years after that, when was in the vicinity of Zaz, he had been attacked by one of the Kurdish villagers. İsa Bey's grandfather had stabbed his adversary and then take refuge in the village of Ayn Verd. The family of the dead man found him and demanded that the villagers turn him over to them. When the villagers refused to do so, the family of the victim flew into a rage. As İsa Bey explained, they could not come to terms with the fact that a Christian who had injured a Muslim would go unpunished.

İsa Bey's grandfather escaped to the village of Alike Batti, the infamous tribal leader who continuously fought against the Ottoman State and other Kurdish tribes (Van Bruinessen 1992; Özgen 2007; Aydın 2013).[5] Alike Batti allowed İsa Bey's grandfather to stay and to accompany him during the restless years following 1915. In 1919, Alike Batti was killed and his rival, Çelebi Ağa, was released from the imprisonment. He gathered all his Muslim and Christians subjects under his protection. The legacy of Çelebi Agha—the prostate tribal leader—continued during the republican years and was revitalized by the invention of the village guard system, which, as noted earlier, eventually led to the arming of villagers under tribal protection against the PKK. Alike Batti's supporters were regarded as Haverki while Çelebi Agha's supporters were the Dekşuri.

İsa Bey's grandfather returned to Zaz in the 1920s. He managed to reclaim his family property and gained power as a prominent village leader. He became a fierce supporter of the Haverkis and did not change his position for the rest of his life; he died in the 1970s. İsa Bey's grandmother was also one of the survivors of the Sayfo. She had spent a few years in the servitude of a Muslim family in another village. She was one of the main narrators of accounts of the massacres in the village. İsa Bey was the only son in his extended family and was brought up at his grandparents' house. This had made him an unwitting witness of how his family had remade community life with both friends and foes. According to İsa Bey, narratives about these events were never shared as memories of the distant past. Rather, they were recalled and circulated in order to interpret the events of the historical present, which reiterated itself in different forms and shapes, and revealed its faces of evil and death. The narratives constituted implicit knowledge of daily life that the Syriac survivors used as the means to learn how to live alongside the very perpetrators of violence.

As a leader and prominent landowner in the village, İsa Bey's grandfather had given small parcels of farmland to his landless Kurdish covillagers or neighbors. The Syriacs were the owners of the land, but not the holders of power. "They pretended that they were not the landowners, that they were sharing ownership of the property with the Kurds," İsa Bey recalled. They shared their resources to sustain this shared life: "My grandmother used to give food to the poor Kurdish women from the neighbor villages. They were the grandchildren of the perpetrators, but she never held the crimes of their grandparents against them. She held them separate from the sins of their elders." İsa Bey remembered his grandfather trying to keep the village unified and leaving as little room as possible for intervention by outsiders.

İsa Bey found it difficult to explain the logic of unity and separation between the Haverkis and Dekşuris. Their alliance formed the backbone of social and political relations between the tribes of the region and created a political map between friends and foes. Dekşuris would have voted for the right-wing parties and Haverkis would have voted for the left-wing parties. This was a historical and political alliance that extended from Midyat to Ankara and impacted all political decisions concerning the distribution of the power. It cut across religious differences and was based on tribal loyalties and protector-protégé relationships. The positions of Syriacs and Yazidis were pivotal: they would change sides to maintain the balance between two parties and secure their survival and well-being in an otherwise explosive environment. Unlike many other Christian families, İsa Bey's family had never changed sides. They were always supporters of the Haverkis. However, this does not mean that they enjoyed the full support and loyalty of the Haverkis. After all, the space of coexistence with the Kurds was full of ambivalence and exceptions.

İsa Bey recalled events from his childhood in the 1960s when historical relics from the church—old books and Bibles—were stolen: "Once, they stole a book that had been hidden and wrapped inside a cloth. The piece of string that had been laid over the book was later found on the path to one of the villages." The Syriacs from Zaz found out who had stolen it and filed a complaint in court. The thief was a Dekşuri supporter. Later, the Syriacs withdrew their complaint by request from the ağa of the Haverkis, who intervened in the situation and enacted his own law to punish the thief and force him to pay compensation to the Syriacs. Five years after that decision, the very same agha of the Haverkis created a new alliance with the party of the thief from Dekşuris and forced the Syriacs from Zaz to return the compensation that they had received. For İsa Bey, Kurds always held the right to break and amend a contract.

Boundaries of the Self and the Other

İsa Bey experienced and witnessed injustice for the first time during the years he spent as a student at the Mor Gabriel Monastery, which is in the immediate vicinity of the town of Midyat. "We were surrounded by nature, planting trees, taking long walks in the forest with the monks, and then bumping into Kurdish villagers who were there cutting down trees," he said. "The bishop asked them to stop, and the villagers aggressively rebuked us. I still remember the time when we were forced to be silent. We swallowed our anger. And that is when I felt hatred in my bones for those guys. I could never forget their faces. For me, it did not matter whether it was a household, a village, a tree, or a person. Kidnapping, killing, cutting—all of it meant violating the right to life." İsa Bey felt that people from all sorts of backgrounds committed such violent acts, yet he could not help feeling that he was subjected to all of these atrocities because he was a Syriac. "They forced me to feel this way."

His way of understanding and articulating difference changed after he left the village in the late 1960s. After spending a few years in the monastery, he headed off to Istanbul like many Syriac youngsters of his time. While there was not much of a future in the village, migrating to Istanbul also became a challenge because there was no network to receive him there. Life in Tur Abdin was isolated and remote, fraught with the conditions of survival and obligations of coexistence with the Kurds. Syriacs generally did not know much about the Turks until they left home for military service or migrated elsewhere in the country. By contrast, the elite circle of Syriacs who had migrated from Mardin in the 1950s, and who had become integrated into the minority life of Istanbul, were a world apart from the Syriacs coming from a small town like Midyat and its nearby villages (see Erol 2016). Syriac rural migrants took refuge under the protection of Greek or Armenian families and worked as their servants.

İsa Bey did not have access to special means and therefore lived in dire conditions in various rented rooms. "Our life was no different from that of refugees," he said. "We worked hard and earned little, starved, and lived in dirt and poverty." He was invisible and powerless in Istanbul. But he soon carved out new spaces and gained access to the economic and political circles of the Christian communities in Istanbul. He found a job at the historical market and started learning English from tourists. He broke into the closed circle of the political young Syriacs and was exposed to the ideas of the Assyrian (Asuri) nationalist movement, which by then was articulating a sense of identity and belonging along ethnic lines. Assyrian nationalism had emerged among Syriac communities in Syria and circulated among young people in Istanbul in the shadow of the rise of right- and left-wing nationalist movements in Turkey. İsa Bey followed their journals and also got to know Turkish people from left-wing circles (see Çetrez et al. 2012).

In the 1970s, İsa Bey's grandfather died and the unity of the village started to inexorably crumble. There was no one to replace him. The same decade witnessed the migration of many Syriac villagers to Istanbul and Europe. İsa Bey's most intense encounters with leftist or Assyrian nationalist activists took place after he left Turkey. He once again chose paths that were different from those of the rest of the Syriac community. He moved to Scotland and worked for fishing companies and lived on large boats for a few years. During this time, he moved back and forth between Scotland and continental Europe, where the majority of the Syriac community had settled and became politically active in solidarity with other Assyrian nationalists, leftists who left Turkey after the 1980 military coup. As this time, the Kurdish resistance movement was spreading through myriad political divisions in the region, with groups later merging into the hegemonic body of the PKK.

In 1982, İsa Bey moved to Australia and lived in different parts of the country for two decades. "The world changed after I left Turkey. More importantly, my world has changed. I learned what inequality is and what it does to people very early on in life. I learned new concepts such as the Marxist terms of capitalism, state, land, economy at the seminars I attended in Australia." İsa Bey's exposure to people from Kurdish, Marxist, and Leninist backgrounds had transformative effects on his historical imaginary and memory of the Sayfo narratives that he had heard throughout his childhood in his village.

"I wanted to forget all those brutal stories, but I could not," he recalled. "They had become a part of me. In Australia, I thought about freedom even more strongly." İsa Bey started high school in Sydney, reading English literature, and rethought Sayfo in the light of Shakespeare's writings. "We were reading Shakespeare at school. At first I did not get what was so special about this literature. My own village was full of stories similar to Shakespeare's. Disloyalty was on everyone's mind. Later those stories, particularly King Lear, made me think about the evil aspect of the past as well as other values that make life worthwhile. I started rethinking the meaning of being Syriac through the morals of those writings. There and then, I felt different about who I was."

İsa Bey recorded Sayfo narratives during those years, collecting the stories of survivors scattered across Europe during his visits to see his parents and family in Germany. He also recalled the testimonies of his grandparents. He organized the fragmented narratives of survivors and witnesses. He translated them from Kurdish into Aramaic, Turkish, and English and rethought those narratives in terms of literature, Australia's indigenous history, and debates among Kurdish, Turkish, Armenian, and left-wing activists as well as the political movements of Syriacs in diaspora, which by then had started lobbying for international recognition of the Sayfo as the genocide of Aramaic, Chaldean, and Syriac people (Biner 2011).

Life in Zaz after the 1980s

After he moved to Australia, İsa Bey visited his village only once. He was greeted by Kurdish neighbors who had become PKK supporters. İsa Bey noticed the difference in the tone and content of their speech. They were talking to him in friendly terms, expressing their sense of guilt and regret for their ignorant violent attitudes toward the Christians in the past and calling for solidarity against the shared experience of state oppression. The emergence of the PKK changed the historical and political meaning of the Dekşuri and Haverki parties. Until the 1990s, the Dekşuri were the only party because Haverki supporters disappeared from the scene due to state repression. The Dekşuri supporters lost their power in the 1990s with the increasing superiority of the PKK in the guerrilla war against the Turkish military. Recalling the early days of the PKK movement, İsa Bey recounted: "I was not here during those years, but I know that the Syriacs in our village also had empathy for the PKK. The guerrillas were roaming back and forth between the mountains and the villages. They were talking about shared suffering and inequalities that affected all of us. The state never spelled out those things. The PKK called us brothers and pushed us to question the reality that we could not dare to question until then: Why are our languages forbidden? Why are we not all equal citizens? Why do they [Turks] have schools? And why don't we? These things touched our wounds. However, we still wanted to keep our distance."

The villagers were afraid that they could be targeted by the PKK or the state and wanted to find a middle ground. However, there was no middle ground during the war. On the other hand, how could the Syriacs survive the war without having the arms, knowledge, and networks that the Kurds had managed to bring together? The village of Zaz became a battleground in the 1990s due to its strategic location. It was the site of skirmishes between PKK militants, korucus, and the Turkish military. Syriac villagers were caught in the cross fire and witnessed the brutal effects of these violent clashes. The position of the Kurdish villagers from Zaz was not clear. While one of the families had a son who joined the PKK, the rest stayed in the village, often acting as informants for the korucus or the military. İsa Bey's parents and members of their extended family stayed in the village until 1993, when the korucus forced them to leave. The Kurdish locals stayed, but the Syriac villagers left for different destinations in Europe. For the next two decades, Zaz would remain under the control of the korucus, who would use the houses and land to extend their territorial and economic hegemony. Under emergency law, the korucus as the local militias were employed and funded by the state as part of the support system against the PKK. The villagers who did not accept this role were threatened and eventually displaced. Armed by the state, the korucus turned into legitimized personas of state violence provided with immunity in exchange for their loyalty. The korucus became beneficiaries of the state of exception, which in turn gave them access to legitimate and illegitimate resources. The state turned a blind eye to their excesses in exchange for their guarding of villages against potential PKK invasions.

In Zaz, the occupation led to the destruction of the built environment and the replanting of agricultural land. The stone houses were dismantled and ruined (except for the occupied ones), and the land was reclaimed and used for agriculture. In this new era, while the Syriac owners of the land were migrant-refugees in new destinations in Europe, the Kurdish villagers of Zaz who remained in the village provided cheap labor to the korucus, some of whom made themselves into the new landlords and warlords in the region. They achieved this through political kinships woven with the visible and invisible personas of the state and the ağas as coexisting sovereigns at the margins (see Yalçın-Heckmann 1991, 2000).

Final Call for Return

As part of the post-emergency process, in 2000, the prime minister, Bülent Ecevit, issued an official call to Syriac citizens in diaspora to return to their villages in the region.[6] The call for Syriacs to return to their villages was different than that directed at displaced Kurdish villagers. In the first decade after 2000, the government resisted recognizing the evacuation of the villages as forced displacement. The naming of the event was a contested issue between state agents, NGO activists, scholars, and the locals. There was never an explicit acknowledgment of the force used in these measures. In a similar vein, despite the reopening of the villages and resettlement projects, Kurdish villagers were never fully welcomed to return, as they were perceived as potential supporters of the PKK. Syriacs, then, who had the cultural and economic capital to change the image of the region, were perceived as desirable minorities in the context of restorative justice projects within a setting of violent peace. Although they did not remain indifferent, the Syriac diasporic communities did not feel that they would be protected and were anxious about facing the conditions at their villages. Moreover, return to their homeland was only possible if they could convince their children (who had grown up in Europe) to have a different set of expectations of life and imaginations regarding the homeland.

Still, the idea of return was not unimaginable. The first serious attempts to return home were undertaken by Syriacs who viewed this project as a political commitment. They were the main political agents of the Sayfo-related movement that had started in the 1990s with the aim of gaining official and international recognition for the 1915 massacres of the Syriacs as genocide. In tandem with the Armenians' political struggles, the Syriacs in diaspora turned the denial of 1915 into a battleground over acknowledgment and recognition of their losses in the region (Biner 2011).

While the Sayfo movement became shared ground for all Syriacs living in diaspora, solidarity with the Kurdish resistance divided them and created a new political community that included the generation of young migrants who left the region in the 1980s and 1990s. Referring to themselves as revolutionaries (*devronoyo*), they aimed to define their struggle not only in terms of recognition of the Sayfo but also in terms of the goal of returning to the homeland. This involved developing a vision of peaceful coexistence with other Mesopotamian groups, mainly the Kurds. The collective hope was to establish a new way of life based on equality between Kurds and Syriacs. Despite the cynicism and suspicion of some members who identified themselves exclusively with Assyrian nationalism, as well as of an older generation that had experienced the feudal order with Kurds, devronoyo activists' diaspora managed to instill a new mood with respect to this collective hope (Biner 2011).

In regard to the returnees, the majority of the volunteers who aimed to bring life to this project were Syriacs from Switzerland. Having lived in Switzerland for over two decades, they were able to mobilize strategic economic and political networks to access state institutions and obtain permission to resettle in the villages, transfer economic resources, have their identity cards reissued, and reactivate their citizenship status. The representatives of this unnamed movement spent a few years traveling between Switzerland and Turkey to move their resources and families and build new houses in their burned and evacuated villages. They applied their capital in the restoration of churches and the construction of mansions, most of which were built during 2000–2010. These stone mansions have become symbolic and material reminders of future life erected on the ruins of past atrocities. The neo-Syriac architecture had the look of a modern-authentic castle covered in white stone on the outside and marble inside. The material expression of the return was embedded in the solid and resilient appearance and feeling of stone and marble. This architectural style was consolidated, mimicked, and reproduced by different returnees, mostly in the nonmixed Syriac villages of the Izla region, which became hubs for state and transnational visitors and a showcase for the reparative relationship between the Turkish state and Syriac citizens. As the state was opening up opportunities to start a new life in destroyed places, the recently reconstructed Syriac villages offered a different idea of place than the evacuated villages with mixed or only Kurdish populations. New stone mansions showcase new economic and social inequalities between Kurds and Syriacs. In what amounted to a blatant policy of "positive discrimination" in favor of Syriacs, the government did not block these relocations.

However, İsa Bey's village was neither a showcase for neo-Syriac architecture nor a destination for a political project developed by Syriac activists
or the state. As I mentioned in earlier sections, Syriac villagers had left Zaz
and only four Kurdish families stayed in the village. Occupation by korucus
made it impossible for Syriac villagers to return.

The Eligible Witnesses

In 2005, Syriac villagers from Zaz who were living in Hamburg received a
phone call from Midyat that sent them into a panic. The caller was a Kurdish man from another village who informed them that the cadastral survey
was about to end, and that the korucus had convinced the cadastral officer
to register the land under their own names. The villagers took immediate action and paid an urgent visit to the Turkish Consulate in Hamburg to halt
the procedure. Petitions were faxed to the cadastral officer. In the meantime,
they needed to find a few people who could go to Midyat and act as witnesses
for a second cadastral survey in the village.

It was not easy to find eligible people because they need to be Turkish citizens with valid ID cards. The younger generation had rejected Turkish citizenship or was not familiar with the location and ownership of the land. The
majority of the elder Syriac villagers who had left Zaz in 1993 were living in
Germany as refugees with the right to permanent residence and housing and
unemployment benefits. They had neither citizenship nor passports. In 2000,
İsa Bey moved to Germany from Australia to live with his parents. He was
eligible to join the survey committee because he held both Australian and
Turkish citizenship. Yet he chose not to do so for some time and decided to
watch the process from close up. In the end, the villagers managed to find
the people they needed to enter Turkey and act as witnesses during the cadastral survey. Upon their arrival, they got in touch with a local lawyer and
submitted petitions to the head of the cadastral survey. The survey was repeated with a new group of six witnesses, two of whom were Kurds and the
rest Syriacs.

One month later, the villagers in Hamburg received official notification
of the results of the cadastral survey. The land was officially registered as the
property of Syriac villagers. However, the new cadastral map was totally different from the map that they remembered. The cadastral officers had not registered the parcels under the names of the people in accordance with the

testimony provided by the Syriac witnesses. Six hundred parcels were registered under false names and the majority of the parcels were registered under
a false category that would eventually affect the economic transactions between the state and property owners related to tax payments and state benefits. In addition, the Kurdish covillagers had managed to expand their land
on paper by claiming ownership of parcels in the vicinity of the mosque.
Neighboring villagers had also violated the historical borders and expanded
the territory of their villages at their expense. In addition, the cadastral officer had changed the historical names of the parcels and registered them
under new names. He had replaced Aramaic names with Kurdish ones. Iron-
ically, the official cadastral map was Kurdified by the Kurdish cadastral officer of the Turkish state, erasing the historical memory transmitted through
parcels that bore the name of a significant person, location, or event. The witnesses had not noticed these changes and therefore had signed the official
documents. The Syriac elders had been satisfied with the outcome of the
process and had not scrutinized the results because no major dispute had
arisen during the survey. They had appreciated the fact that the Kurds had
not created any obstacles. "They perceived it as a favor and prayed for their
goodness from morning to night," said İsa Bey, who was annoyed by their
submissive attitude.

İsa Bey felt Syriac elders acted like slaves. Kurds used to call them "our
Christians" (bizim hristiyanlar) and the elders responded to that name. He
despised the phrase because he felt that it suggested the Kurds' possession of
the Christians. "Kurds used to perceive Syriacs as their property and our elders have internalized [özümsediler] it," summarized İsa Bey. The Haverki-
Dekşuri distinction held for this generation, and they were acting in
accordance with the loyalties, anxieties, and prejudices that were attached
to those historically embodied positions. In addition, they did not have any
experience dealing with the state bureaucracy. They knew the land. They had
the visual memory of different types and sizes of fields, the kinds of grapes
that demarcated the vineyards, the material texture of the borders that divided the parcels within and across the village. They knew the names of the
locations operating as the reference points. Yet they could not decode or
transfer their visual memory into written codes. The cadastral map did not
have any meaning for them. In addition, they were in a rush because their
return flights were scheduled to leave only a few days later. İsa Bey summarized the situation as follows: "They had only from Tuesday to Friday to
sign the sixty-eight hundred documents required for the completion of the

registration of seventeen hundred parcels. They had to write, 'I have read the documents and sign four papers for each parcel as the final approval.'" The witnesses signed and approved all sixty-eight hundred documents and took their flight to Hamburg on Saturday confident that—even if they never again returned—they had completed an historical mission that would allow them to obtain official title deeds to their land.

The Return of Cash

İsa Bey called the head of the cadastral office in Midyat to discuss the mistakes on the cadastral map. The officer rebuffed İsa Bey, telling him that they should consider themselves lucky to get any deeds to land that they didn't put to any use. He was in effect pointing out the limits of recognition of Syriacs' rights over the land. What difference would it make if İsa's land was registered as the property of Ibrahim when İsa and Ibrahim were just two names listed on paper documents with no presence on the ground? At this stage, the discussion was not only about the violation of ownership rights of the Christian minority citizens but the recognition of the right to the land of absentees. The Syriac villagers of Zaz were paper citizens, virtual landowners who did not have the confidence that was necessary to return to their village to start a new life.

It is at this point that İsa Bey decided to take a stand. Almost forty years after he had left Zaz, he was in Midyat as the official representative of the Zaz villagers. After he gained the notarized approvals of seventy villagers, his first mission was to amend the cadastral map and convince the cadastral officers to revise it. There were two possible paths: he could either go to court, which meant making a cash payment of 5,000 Turkish liras to the lawyer for each case, or pay the unofficial fee to the officers responsible for the cadastral survey and title deed. The fee for the latter was not set, but depended on each officer's demands. Cash functioned as a hidden agent that mediated communication between the actors: unregistered cash was passed from the villagers in Europe to lawyers, cadastral officers, korucus, and aghas in Midyat.

This was by no means a new form of interaction between the Syriacs, Kurds, and the state. Bribery was an old form of communication in the region, one that often took the form of a debt or gift. As İsa Bey put it, "Kurds

made Syriacs feel indebted for everything that originally belonged to them."
After 1915, Syriacs had been forced to sell their property in exchange for food
or their abducted children. After they returned to their villages, they had been
forced to buy back the very same land from their Kurdish neighbors. A similar logic was in place when dealing with stolen property, particularly animals: the Kurds would reportedly steal animals belonging to Syriacs and then
claim a cash reward in exchange for finding them. The conscious act of keeping the agha informed about these daily disputes was an important aspect of
the debt economy that required careful behavior on the part of both parties.
The agha was charged with returning belongings to the Syriac villagers, which
cultivated indebtedness even further.

As the migration of Syriacs to Europe accelerated in the 1970s, the meaning and means of these transactions changed, shifting from property such
as land, houses, and animals to cash. The cash flow was dynamic and slippery,
crossing into different social and material networks. The Syriac villagers who
had lived under tribal rule tried to survive as refugees and migrants under
the immigration policies of European countries. Regardless of the source of
income, Syriacs of that early generation maintained their relationships with
the aghas, korucus, and other acquaintances, sending cash as gifts. In the
absence of ordinary shared time and space and daily economic exchanges,
the cash-gifts kept the accounts of debts alive among tribal actors who had
clear positions in a protector-protégé relationship. At the peak of the conflict
with the PKK, Syriac villagers had sent cash to all of those actors as protection fees for their property.

After 2000, with the official registration of private property, cash had been
used as the nondiscursive means to negotiate and prompt consent, particularly with state officials. These transactions did not only take place in Midyat.
Cadastral officers began taking short trips to European cities in 2004 in order to visit Syriac friends-fellows-customers, whom they had come to know
through the cadastral survey process. This prompted a practice of forced hospitality from Syriacs in diaspora to the cadastral officers. Syriac villagers
acquiesced, hoping that this would protect them from the state bureaucracy
and free them from discrimination when it came to claims of citizenship
rights. They assumed that the hosted officer would play the role of the mediator with the state. However, this forced hospitality failed to resolve the
problem. Money maintained the relationships between those who left and
those who remained, but it did not create a permanent space for potential

returnees. Instead, it simply reproduced an economy of indebtedness between the different subjects.

Being Syriac, Becoming a Citizen

İsa Bey was fully aware of the spectral and speculative effects of cash. He sought out a different relationship with the state. He wanted to work through nonmediated rules of citizenship that facilitated access to rights and benefits. In 2004, the AKP government had introduced new legal and economic policies designed to recognize material loss and cultural rights jeopardized by the repressive regimes of previous governments. These policies were not designed to recognize the collective rights of the victims or the injured, nor were they a way of acknowledgment off the state's responsibility for the violation of human rights. Rather, they were implemented, publicized, and documented as economic and legal exchanges between individuals as citizens and the state. In an effort to establish itself as a charitable, paternal, yet neoliberal state, the AKP government channeled economic resources to the landowners in order to encourage the use of agricultural land. It also created government-sponsored NGOs to support individual leading projects and disbursed funds to support low-income families and provide compensation to displaced villagers. The sources of cash multiplied and were justified under the rubric of state benefits (see Yörük and Özsoy 2013).

Unlike the majority of the Syriacs, who avoided dealing with this process, İsa Bey was determined to find out about public benefits and integrate his villagers into this citizenship economy, which required a physical presence, command of local and official languages, and the energy to tackle the state bureaucracy. More important, it involved the daily challenge of documenting their history of absence and presence in the region. As the official representative of seventy villagers in Zaz, İsa Bey collected all of the documents as proof of landownership and applied for state funding for agricultural support. He then encouraged villagers to apply for benefits under the Compensation Law 5233, which promised to compensate citizens who had suffered material and immaterial losses during the military conflict between the Turkish state and the PKK. Sixty villagers submitted applications to the Turkish consulate in Hamburg. In order to apply for compensation, one had to gather official documents that would prove the incidents of violence in that period. During his visits to Midyat, İsa Bey visited all of the state offices, gave them the exact dates and locations of the events, and managed to collect the documents that registered the "terror-related" incidents in the village. Included among these was the bombing of a minibus full of korucus, the killing of PKK guerrillas, and the physical destruction of the village through rocket attacks. He did not dare offer testimony of the events, but reminded the officers about them by describing his research. Those interactions with the state officers were charged with different emotions and judgements, which also had an effect on the way they performed their duties and treated the applicants. I discuss these interactions and their implications in further detail in Chapter 6.

İsa Bey gave all of the documents to the lawyers, who in turn submitted his and his family members' petitions to the commissions. The application was rejected by the commission members because they said that they had not provided enough evidence of the alleged atrocities in the village. İsa Bey wanted to push the case further and asked his lawyer to apply first to the administrative court (idari mahkeme) and then, as necessary, to the Council of State (Danıştay). He left the file in the lawyer's hand and focused on other village-related work. As a result, the lawyer missed the deadlines. He gave İsa Bey the bad news with dry apologies. İsa Bey did not get upset. He was used to this kind of negligence. He was trying every possible avenue to seek recognition and rights within the legal terrain. Two years after the completion of the cadastral procedure, the treasury filed a complaint against a few villagers who had allegedly registered state land under their names. Around the same period, the children of a Syriac woman from Zaz who was later abducted by and married to a Kurdish man from Ortakli also filed complaints against the Syriac villagers for having occupied and registered land that originally belonged to their mother. As the representative of these landowners, İsa Bey followed their cases in court, submitting the necessary documents to lawyers and reporting back to the villagers, who were constantly calling from Hamburg. He also responded to the insults of the Kurdish villagers who were irritated by his work. His struggle for recognition was not only with the state but also with the Kurdish korucus who had occupied the village since 1993.

The Village Guards

The violent acts committed by korucus (village guards) were disregarded and considered part of their efforts to defend against a potential PKK invasion of the villages. They had become warlords and strongly resisted the idea of leaving their position of power by giving up their arms.[7] The korucus occupied the village of Zaz between 1993 and 2005. They worked the land, rented parcels to people from other villages, and received state benefits to support their agricultural work. One korucu settled in Zaz with his family. The rest moved back and forth between two or even three villages. They chose the muhtar (head of the village) from within their ranks and controlled information about the daily procedures between the villagers and the state.

The official registration of the land to Syriac villagers was not binding for the korucus. They wanted compensation for their investments and potential losses over the land they occupied in the village. The prices of the estate began to increase in 2005 and reached their peak in 2008. There was high demand and lack of supply. Loan sharks and real estate agents, most of whom were Kurdish villagers who had managed to stay in their villages during the peak time of the conflict, were the main beneficiaries of this speculative economy. The korucus required Syriacs to pay 100,000 euros for the return of their occupied land. This calculation also included the cost of returning the benefits that they were receiving through agriculture and other land-related support payments granted by the state. The local head of the gendarme officers, the agha, and the elder Syriacs agreed that the korucus should be paid. İsa Bey resisted paying the korucus. His main goal was to create a sustainable economic cycle in which they could use the cash to invest in agriculture and make a living by selling their products in the market.

Resisting İsa Bey's nonsubmissive attitude, the korucus refused to leave the land. In addition, they continued to hire people from nearby villages to work on it. Compensation was open to negotiation and accounts were not yet settled. Withdrawal would have to be slow. Between 2008 and 2011, the korucus made decisions about the land including what they would plant and who would be hired to work. In the meantime, they expected the Syriacs to share the state support provided to them for the agricultural land. İsa Bey and other Syriac villagers were applying for agricultural support as the official owners of the land and paying the fees and costs related to farming while the korucus were harvesting and making use of the crops. After 2011, the forced consensus turned into a battle over the right to use the land. The korucus agreed to withdraw, but then reoccupied the released areas and ploughed it all before İsa Bey arrived with other Syriac villagers. It was an old rule that whoever ploughed the land first had the right to sow it and then take the harvest. The korucus had ploughed land that they promised to leave or collected the harvest that Syriacs had planted (when they were not sending their animals to farmed land resulting in the destruction of crops). They would not give up their claims to land easily.

Addressing the "State"

Any trace became useful to justify a connection to the land. This is illustrated by the fierce dispute over pistachio trees. Having planted pistachio trees during the occupation, the korucus claimed ownership of the trees and their right to collect the harvest. The land did not belong to them, but the trees planted on the land were their property and they had the right to return to Zaz to collect their products. While İsa Bey found the situation unacceptable, the Syriac elders wanted to find a middle ground. A few years before, Uncle Yakup, an eighty-year-old Syriac man, had allowed the korucus to collect the pistachios without informing İsa Bey. Others were comfortable with the idea of sharing the land and other state benefits that they were receiving as official owners. İsa Bey was tired of these sticky attachments that betrayed feelings of fear, dependence, and submission. The elders' interventions reproduced these unequal relationships with the Kurds, especially with the members of the extended families of the agha. He strongly felt that they were in denial about the historical and political necessity to create a new way of life, governed by a different logic of coexistence that was not based on exploitative power and submission to the will of aghas and the korucus, and instead reasserted their full right as full citizens.

İsa Bey started writing and submitting petitions regarding the pistachio dispute. For every insult, attack, robbery, or land occupation, İsa Bey appealed to the vali (local governor), gendarme forces, and local prosecutors and filed and archived copies of his petitions. He also disseminated an account of the dispute through newspapers and other media channels. The crux of the matter for him was to document and transform the perception of these violations from incidents to events, from public secrecy to public truth, and hence to seek recognition for the Syriacs' precarious conditions and protection for their well-being. İsa Bey sought this recognition in order to make the present possible and liveable in the midst of the (un)homely space of loss rather than somewhere far from the scene of the crime. The recipient of this daily call was not the long-lived tribal persona of the agha or the explosive, hegemonic hands and eyes of the pro-Kurdish party or the PKK, but the state. He did not trust the pro-Kurdish party to mediate. Although they had a more inclusive understanding of coexistence based on recognition of difference, party members were still far from objective when it came to resolving the land disputes. He felt that they would either pass judgment in favor of their supporters or delay a final verdict on the matter. Regardless of the significant transformations of the political landscape, İsa Bey was searching for a different path that would free him from the familiar feeling of entrapment and confinement. He sought to de-Kurdify his relationships with the state.

Delivering complaints to state officers was not a new practice. Syriac villagers had done so in his grandparents' time, though the process was often blocked by a tribal figure. In contrast to previous generations, İsa Bey did not give up his aspiration for justice. The act of drafting the petition in the official language and delivering it to a military or state officer by hand, knocking on their door to follow up on his inquiry, and facing the challenge of calling them to task was part of his process. İsa Bey was seeking state recognition and protection for all of the violations that he was subjected to as a Syriac Christian citizen. He was putting forth the idea that the state was a coherent and consistent entity that belonged to everyone. He gave voice to this imaginary whenever he returned from one of his petition-submission trips.

The gendarme forces never took his complaints seriously and implicitly asked him not to waste their time on banal incidents such as the pistachio case. The valis often dismissed his claims and sometimes received them with uneasiness because of the pressure that they were receiving from the central government in Ankara due to the noise that Syriac Christian political lobbies were making in diaspora. If he did not receive a response, İsa Bey would contact journalists and publish pieces in the newspapers. The visibility of these incidents made the military officers and local governors even more defensive. They made public statements assuring the public that were providers of the necessary support and protection for the recently returned or settled Syriac Christians, thus calling to question incidents reported in the media.

At the level of personal encounters, both the military officers and valis were getting impatient and angry with İsa Bey's insistent calls for help. They accused him of distorting reality and circulating fake stories of violence to attract public attention and even to discourage other Syriacs from returning to their villages. The korucus found his unwillingness to submit to the tribal order outrageous. They ordered him to give up his complaints and withdraw his petitions and let them manage the land. In the legal realm, İsa Bey's petitions to the prosecutor were never accepted. All of his cases were rejected due to lack of evidence, as if nothing had ever happened, as if he did not work the fields, as if the occupiers from the same village had not stolen from him, as if no one knew about it. The door to litigation was closed to him. He regularly submitted his lists of demands to the gendarme station with statements that included the names of the people who stole the crops, ploughed the land, cut the wood, and released their animals in the fields. He continued to insist on holding state institutions responsible for mediating all of these disputes.

In his view, the goal was not to report the neighbors to the authorities but rather to submit complaints about daily acts of injustice. For İsa Bey, the difference between those two acts lay in the transparent quality of his methods and the implicit knowledge that Syriacs had to find different ways to coexist with their Kurdish neighbors. It was vital to include the Kurdish neighbors in the farming and production process and incorporate their labor. He hired people and vehicles from the neighboring villages to restore the vineyards and plant pistachios, sumac, and wheat. The goal was to balance income and expenses and create a sustainable economy that would rely less on cash flow from Germany and Sweden. İsa Bey worked alongside two former korucus who were publicly known as Thief (Hırsız) Ahmet and Hadji (Hacı) Mehmet. They were not from the families of the previous occupiers. They needed jobs and land to plant in order to meet their own needs. İsa Bey needed labor and connections so that he could participate in the local economy.

Indebted, Again

In 2013, İsa Bey managed to complete the full planting and harvest cycle. Thief Ahmet and Hadji Mehmet worked the fields with him along with half-blind Uncle Yakup, who despised the Muslims. The korucus had not vacated the houses, but they were not living in the village or on the land. The sumac was stolen, and the cows were let into the vineyards. İsa Bey submitted more petitions about these recurring matters. Yet he was content. After all these years of waiting for their withdrawal, İsa Bey had to harvest what he could sell in the market or replace it with another crop. Thief Ahmet was in charge of taking the grapes to market in Batman and Hadji Mehmet was assigned to finding customers who would be willing to exchange red grapes for white ones. İsa Bey and I were on our way to collect payments from the people in the market who bought wheat from the village.

We drove to the market square in Midyat. İsa Bey entered the shop. I waited outside. He returned ten minutes later, angry. He counted five hundred Turkish liras into my hand. This was half of what he had expected to receive. The other half had dissipated into the void of the debt economy. One of the korucus owed five hundred Turkish liras to the man in the shop and asked him to settle his debt using the payment that was to be made to İsa Bey. The man followed the guard's orders, cutting the amount he was to pay İsa Bey in half. In the end, İsa Bey paid the debt of the korucu against his will. His subversive acts intended to beat the debt economy were countered by petty acts of revenge that belittled the exchange value of what was produced in the field. Who was indebted to whom? We drove back to the village. İsa Bey felt humiliated by the way he had been treated in the market. The daily abuse was ruining any hope of a new form of coexistence. It was the same, always the same. We noticed the silhouette of Hadji Mehmet in the vineyards. He was walking with a group of men, negotiating with another Hacı who was trying to bring down the price for the grapes. The Hadji customer was arguing that they should give him a lower price because he would need to give alms (zekat) for the poor before the eid (bayram). The discount should be considered a contribution to his payment of zekat. Hadji Mehmet told the man that the property belonged to Christians and that they did not pay zekat as part of their religious obligations. İsa Bey cut off the conversation, telling him that the grapes were no longer for sale. Hadji Mehmet tried to smooth things over, taking the man to his car and giving İsa Bey room to breathe.

This has been the evil banality of İsa Bey's life. Despite his efforts to work through the past and make a present, there was no space for İsa Bey to breathe and live in the village. The past traveled through moments of confrontation with the present in the militarized and occupied space of the village. İsa Bey's daily struggle to repossess the land and win recognition of acts of injustice subjected memory and experience of coexistence to ongoing negotiation and contestation. The attempt to return to an occupied land brought İsa Bey into a new form of dependency on his Kurdish neighbors. He attempted to awaken the latent agency of the Syriac villagers in diaspora who dwelled in the presence of past attachments to the memories of the Sayfo and the tribal rules of the agha that survived cycles of violence. In so doing, İsa Bey refused to act like the protégé of the agha or the Christian of the Kurds or the minority citizen of the Turkish state.

He simply strove to create an ordinary life in his ruined village, to transform life by interrupting dependency-based relationships, that is, replace the attachment to the ağa with an attachment to the land. Thus, İsa Bey's attachment to the land is not only a manifestation of transgenerational memory of loss and violence but also an active and ongoing, future-looking relationship that has mobilized historical energies and forces to transform the space from a site of ruination and dispossession to a home to be repossessed. By opposing the mediation of the Kurdish korucus, aghas, officers, or politicians, İsa Bey enacted his citizenship rights and insisted on acting like a full-fledged citizen who could directly address and communicate with the state and military officers.

İsa Bey stood against the gift-debt economy. The elder Syriacs who were sending gifts to their Kurdish neighbors would agree with Marcel Mauss (1990) that every gift was offering the social ground for obligation. They involve reciprocity. Every gift demands a gift in return. The Syriac elders were hoping to receive protection and assurance in exchange for their gifts. The gift economy between the Kurds and Syriacs was constitutive of relationships within and across the communities (Douglas 2001). İsa Bey would not disagree with this analysis. However, he would claim that such exchanges do not involve gifts but rather the perennial act of paying debts. Syriacs were both the debtors and donors. The debts based on protection fees were not calculable—they were immeasurable, and actually unpayable. The debt economy, in İsa Bey's view, had only produced enslaved subjectivities that engendered further dependencies, exploitation, and failure to acknowledge and recognize past atrocities and opportunities for a different life.

İsa Bey wanted to consolidate the property-tied subjectivity in order to change the meaning of every component in the current equation. Syriacs should be recognized through their entitlement to the land. He believed in the causal connection between "being" and "having." He wanted to provide stability for himself and his community by stabilizing the relationship to property. His plan was no different than that of the property regimes of the nation-states that established the notion of individual property and tied people to specific places through censuses, naming practices, written registers, and cadastral surveys.

For the first time, there was an expectation of returning to and remaking the home because of the cadastral survey and land registration. İsa Bey's

expectation of normal life was tied to his hope of a functioning "state" (Jansen 2013) that would recognize him as an ordinary citizen with the right to
live, possess, and feel at "home." In the absence of a legal infrastructure that
would serve as a mechanism of restorative and retributive justice, İsa Bey attempted to replace the historical and material means of indebtedness with
the language of law and citizenship. He searched for a new ground on which
to materialize his labor of return, his search for justice. In that struggle, the
ghosts of the past were not only the Kurdish neighbors and their heirs, all
linked to the perpetrators of acts on the other side of the hill. The memory
of his grandparents, who managed to survive the Sayfo and who returned
and repossessed the land and the community, was also constitutive of his attachment to the land. This cruel attachment kept him trapped in a daily
struggle with Kurdish neighbors, some of whom were occupiers–korucus and
some of whom were landless peasants in search of means that would allow
them to make a life out of their endless sense of precarity. He was aware of
the social and political inequality between Syriacs and the Kurdish neighbors. He recalled the memories of life in Australia that reshaped his reflections on poverty, brutality, and betrayal. Yet his daily struggle with the Kurds
did not allow the ghosts from the past to be released. His attempts to recover
boomeranged. The petitions served as a sort of diary that was erased the moment it was turned into official documents. His complaints, which were subject to the disavowal of state officers, added up to the accumulated memory
of loss that included the testimonies of survivors, daily interactions with the
Kurds, and ongoing conversations with villagers in diaspora. The possibility
of thinking about property in a different light vanished. His attachments to
the land became even more cruel and obsessive and turned into a vicious cycle that he was forced to endure. However, this political and psychic struggle
did not turn the village into home for İsa Bey. Even if İsa Bey attempts to reinhabit the world by keeping the land alive and working through "poisonous knowledge," he remains homeless.

CHAPTER 5

Beneath the Wall Surrounding the
Mor Gabriel Monastery

In the summer of 2008, the land registration process moved to the Kurdish villages near the Mor Gabriel (Deyrulumur) Monastery, one of the most important shrines of the Syriac Orthodox Christians. The cadastral survey led to a furious dispute over the boundaries between the monastery and the neighboring Kurdish villages, in the vicinity of Midyat. The dispute ended up in the cadastral court (kadastro mahkemesi) which later on engendered further legal battles between the monastery foundation, Kurdish villagers, and the state. The monastery was accused of encroaching on state property because of the wall built in the 1990s to protect its territory. The area occupied by the wall and some of the land inside of the wall were officially regarded as belonging to the Forestry Department. Three hundred court cases were opened during the legal battle between the monastery foundation, Treasury and Forestry Departments, and the neighboring villagers. The monastery representatives won the legal battle that they waged against their Kurdish neighbors over the consolidation of the borders between the monastery and the villages but lost against the state. They faced the real possibility of being forced to give up 60 percent of their territory. Having exhausted all of the domestic legal channels available from the cadastral court to the Court of Cassation (Yargıtay), the monastery representatives ultimately took their case to the European Court of Human Rights.

In September 2013, Prime Minister Recep Tayyip Erdoğan issued the final verdict on the dispute. He revealed the decision as part of his declaration of the democratization package (demokrasi paketi) promoted as the first of the legal and political measures to resolve the Kurdish conflict. The political focus was moved from the peace talks to the legal dispute with the Syriac

Christian monastery. The frame of the peace process (barış süreci) was shifted from the Kurdish issue to the minority issue. Erdoğan's final verdict challenged the Supreme Court ruling by promising to return the disputed land to the Mor Gabriel Monastery Foundation. The government's decision was an attempt to control the unintended consequences of the legal process. The wall surrounding the monastery became the battlefield on which state officers, Syriacs, and international actors confronted each other. Soon after the first court hearings, Syriacs in diaspora started the "Action Mor Gabriel" movement, which sought to keep the case in the spotlight by organizing demonstrations in different European cities (see Arıkan 2011; Atto 2012a, b). By mobilizing its network of contacts, the movement was able to ensure that a steady flow of diplomats, lawyers, and legislators from different EU countries attended the hearings. As a result of this legal battle, an event that had started as a local land dispute grew into a case of minority rights that was discussed well beyond Turkey's borders.[1]

The media and academics have treated the case as yet another violation of the property rights of minorities in Turkey. Syriacs, particularly those in diaspora, identify with the monastery and portray it as the symbolic and material embodiment of their history. In these narratives, the monastery has been the mirror of a self-sufficient ethnic or religious identity.[2] The attack on the monastery was perceived as an attack on their presence in the region. They have explained violence as obvious and expected through preexisting formations of antagonism. There was no reference to other spaces, rules, and networks that historically mediated and transformed different forms of relationships constitutive of the life of the monastery. The monastery was situated as an omnipresent historical and spiritual entity beyond and outside the context, recalling Gyanendra Pandey's insightful remark that the context was "about everything that happened around violence" (Pandey 2006:17).

Three hundred court files that were opened during this process created a thick cloud of complexity over the matter that made it difficult to uncover the intermingled relationships between subjects that relate to each other through historical processes of dependency, submission, repression, and mediation. This chapter engages with the partial and limited representation of this complexity, which goes beyond the hegemonic discourses of both the state and the Mor Gabriel Monastery that are reformulated as the tension between illegal occupation of state property and the dispossession of the ancient land of the indigenous Christian community. Revealing the practices and memories that arise from the legal battle over the natural and built environment surrounding the monastery, the chapter explores the (il)logic of the historically and politically embedded relationships of violence that "takes place" (Herscher 2010) through sacred and daily spaces shared and contested by Kurds and Syriacs. The monastery reemerges from this ethnography not as a backdrop or a spiritual space of a self-referential ethnic or religious identity situated in a nonqualified temporal zone of ancientness. Here, the monastery emerges as a mediator constitutive of material, political, and historical networks that translate and transform the legal and political demands that reproduce the boundaries between self and other, and between self and the state.

The Social and Political Life of Mor Gabriel Monastery

Founded in 397 AD, the Mor Gabriel Monastery is one of the most important shrines in the Syriac Orthodox World and embodies both historical continuities and ruptures in the history of the region.[3] Despite massive out-migration of Syriacs due to the Sayfo in 1915 and later events leading to the political and economic marginalization of the Syriacs who remained, the monastery has continued to be an active religious shrine. It houses nuns and monks and provides religious and language education to Syriac children in the region and in the diaspora. For Syriacs who live in Turkey, the significance of places like Mor Gabriel is best captured in the following statement by a monk: "We do not have a state. Instead, we have monasteries which act like states, working for the survival and well-being of our people." Though the status of the monasteries as representations of Syriac identity may be contested among diasporic Syriacs who refer to themselves as Assyrians with a particular emphasis on that ethnicity and nationalism as the pivot of their identity (see Çetrez, et al. 2012; Önder 2012), monasteries and churches are regarded as a collective site of struggle and resistance for the right to exist in the historical homeland, Tur Abdin (e.g., Atto 2012a, b; Omtzigt et al. 2012).

Mor Gabriel Monastery is located in the village of Kafarbe, twenty kilometers away from the town of Midyat. The village was historically populated by Kurds and Syriacs until Syriacs left the village in the 1970s. The majority of the Kurds remained in the village. The relationship between the village and the monastery was absent in the public discourses about the legal dispute over the land. When I asked the Syriacs in diaspora about the history of the village, they recalled Sayfo as the main historical reference in narrating the memories of coexistence that were imbued with feelings of both hatred and gratitude toward Kurds. Some Kurdish villagers helped their Syriac neighbors to escape; others worked with Kurdish aghas from outside villages and broke their promises of protection. During Sayfo, all of the monastery inhabitants, most of them monks and nuns, were killed. A Kurdish family from an outside village whose members had been directly involved in the massacres of the monastery inhabitants settled in the monastery. In 1922, Syriac and Kurdish villagers from Kafarbe fought together to expel the perpetrators from the monastery. A new bishop was appointed in 1925, and in 1936, the monastery was reregistered as a religious foundation under the new Turkish state.

The memory of the social and religious life that existed in the monastery during the first three decades of the republic was laden with images of poverty, including monks engaging in agricultural work and collecting donations from Syriac villages in order to meet their basic needs. The monastery faced a new series of attacks in the late 1960s. These were perpetrated by the Kurdish aghas. The process leading up to these attacks was not explained in the narratives, but informants did recall that the leading Syriac figures first sought legal protection by filing court injunctions and later withdrew the cases when they realized that the attacks had behind-the-scenes support from the vali.

In the 1970s, disputes with surrounding villages over land intensified. This intersected with the start of the conflicts between Syriacs and Kurds in Kafarbe, which led to the first flow of Syriacs to Europe. In 1978, the government attempted to close the monastery on the basis of accusations that it provided shelter for Armenians from the Armenian Secret Army for the Liberation of Armenia. Syriacs in diaspora responded with protests. The closure was deferred. In the 1990s, the monastery residents were accused of providing shelter to PKK guerrillas. In 1997, the vali invoked his full authority guaranteed under the emergency law and closed the monastery with the claim that religious education given to Syriac children was illegal because—unlike Armenians, Jews, and Greeks—Syriacs do not have official recognition as minorities and are thus not entitled to the special treatment of minorities set out in the Lausanne Treaty. The decision prompted massive protests by the communities in diaspora, which escalated to demonstrations and hunger strikes in several European cities. In the post-2000 era, when Syriacs were reconsidered as desirable minority citizens capable of restoring the image of this underdeveloped and terrorized geography, the position of Mor Gabriel Monastery has changed in tandem. Mor Gabriel, this time, emerged as a site of political and cultural pilgrimage by government officials, military officers, diplomats, human rights activists, and party leaders. The monastery became a stop on their itinerary as one of the magnified sites of tolerance, democracy, and multiculturalism in Turkey.

Land Ownership Disputes Surrounding Mor Gabriel Monastery

In 2005, the cadastral land registration process began at Mor Gabriel Monastery. Soon after, the work was halted because it was claimed that Kurdish neighbors were attempting to occupy land that allegedly belonged to the monastery. This led to a series of negotiations between the monastery and the surrounding villages. The monastery alerted the government and European institutions to the possible seizure of the property. The call mobilized powerful political networks and put the land registration process on hold.

This was not the first cadastral survey and land registration of the monastery. The first attempt was undertaken following the foundation of the Land Registry and Cadastre Directorates in 1936. That year, the new Turkish government ordered foundations to declare their assets and properties. According to a statement signed by the bishop at the time, the monastery owned "22 fields without water access, two vineyards, 10 wells, the monastery building, and the surrounding lands for which there were no title deeds" (Bilge 2012:214). Large-scale measurement and registration began in the 1950s, when aerial photographs were employed. In the 1990s, the technocrats assessed the results of the 1950s registration and measurement as not reliable and concluded that incompatible measurement systems were used, hence a significant part of Turkey's territory had not been properly measured and registered (Tozman 2012:142). After 2000, as Turkey began its accession into the EU, cadastral survey and land registration efforts resumed. Eyewitness accounts, official state documents (including records from the Ottoman era), title deeds, and ownership certificates were accepted as proof of landownership. Private companies were hired to conduct measurement and survey work, and the entire effort was financed by the World Bank. Property owners have the right to object to the decision within the first ten years of registration (Tozman 2012:143–144).

In July 2008, the streets of Midyat were full of Syriac visitors who had traveled to the region to witness the registration process in their villages. Some were trying to repossess their property while others wanted to buy new or occupied property. The appearance of Syriacs in the market prompted speculation, the swift circulation of money from pocket to pocket, and a steady rise in prices. The negotiation process was delicate and involved state officers as well as estate agents who served as the town loan sharks. As a Syriac returnee from Germany put it, "This is an expensive process. One should come to Midyat with a full pocket and knowing beforehand how much to pay, whom to pay, and what one is expected to pay for." The reference to "whom" points to the presence of mediators, mainly the agha or the korucu.

In Midyat, the heads of the korucus collaborated with the local tribal leader, Çelebi Agha, who derived his power both from tribal rule and the state. As mentioned in the previous chapter, his family has historically espoused the pro-state position in the polarized political structure of the region. That position has historically redefined and reproduced itself solely on the basis of the emergence of the oppositional parties of Haverki and Dekşuri. Çelebi Agha, as noted earlier, was historically one of the leaders of the Dekşuri supporters. The power of the family was not based on landownership. Instead, it was based on its capacity to inflict both symbolic and physical violence, define the boundaries between "just" and "unjust," and establish order.

The Çelebi family maintained its power over some of the Kurds as well as Syriacs through a protector-protégé relationship and continued to be the main arbiter in local conflicts. Its members extended their networks, occupying formal political settings and holding positions in formal institutions such as the national parliament, the intelligence service, local governments, hospitals, and the courts (see Yalçın-Heckmann 2000; Özgen 2007). Syriac elders view the Çelebi family as a prominent and respectable authority. Çelebi Agha provided protection to Syriacs in the aftermath of the Sayfo. Until the mass migration began in the 1970s, Syriacs held protégé positions and established attachments of submission and solidarity with the Çelebi family. As mentioned in Chapter 4, in diaspora, Syriac elders maintained contact with the eldest member of the Çelebi family through symbolic and material gestures such as giving calls at religious feasts, sending money as wedding presents, and offering tributes in return for acts of mediation and approval of village activities. During the land registration process, Syriac elders continued to ask Çelebi Agha to mediate disputes over property.

In the midst of all the activity associated with property buying and selling in the region, rumors circulated that the process of land registration would move to villages near and around Mor Gabriel. According to these rumors, the monastery had reached an agreement with one of the neighboring villages but remained engaged in a dispute with a village on the northwest border. It was suggested that the Kurdish villagers were trying to squeeze money out of the monastery in exchange for the parcels of land that they controlled. The monastery representatives and the Kurds from the neighboring villages held negotiations over the right to the disputed land, trying to reach a consensus before the official start of registration. Some felt that Kurds were trying to prolong the negotiations and that Çelebi Agha intervened in the process.

The cadastral officers paid their first visit to the village in the company of gendarmes in late July 2008. Kurdish men and children from the neighboring villages gathered together brandishing axes and knives, ready to cut down the trees growing on the disputed land. Witnesses from both sides arrived. The witnesses from the second Kurdish village claimed that the monastery wall was the border between their village and the village of Kafarbe. The Kurdish muhtar of Kafarbe argued that the border between the two villages was five kilometers away from the wall surrounding the monastery. Accepting the first claim would violate not only the property rights of the monastery but also of his village. The representatives of Mor Gabriel presented a document, dated in 1937, that showed the agreement between the headmen of all the villages. The letter involved the names of the locations in Kurdish "Germik Kulki Mico and Keveri Ceyzo" in the east, "Berihi Bessaani" in the west, "Miştaka Pire Kefiri Hizni" in the north, and "Kekula Hamziki" in the south, marked as the border points between the village of Kafarbe and other neighboring villages. The document was signed with the fingerprints of the village muhtars of the time.

To the dismay of monastery representatives, cadastral officers established that the border was to cut through the middle of the disputed land in a line located two kilometers from the wall. The monastery representatives attempted to contest the decision in the cadastral courts, but the appeal was swiftly denied. The final decision of the cadastral court led monastery representatives to change their strategy. The first step was breaking the rule of silence and revealing information in order to gain public support. The immanent logic of the relationship between Syriacs and Kurds, and particularly with Çelebi Agha, was made public. In the meanwhile, Çelebi Agha visited the bishop in the monastery to express his uneasiness about the growing publicity and the tone of the letter that the Syriac-Assyrian member of Parliament in Sweden sent to the Turkish Ministry of Interior Affairs. The matter should be resolved between the monastery and the villagers. Other actors should not intervene in the internal matter. Çelebi Agha's visit did not convince the representatives of the monastery foundation.

Soon after, the bishop and the muhtar of Kafarbe village decided to continue with the litigation. They decided to apply to the administrative court to review the decision of the cadastral court on the consolidation of the borders between Kafarbe and the neighboring villages. To recap the dispute: The muhtar of Kafarbe and the monastery representations claimed the border was five kilometers away from the wall surrounding the monastery. The cadastral officer found a solution by drawing the border through the middle of the disputed territory, two kilometers away from the wall. What was behind these numbers? What was hidden through the strong desire to keep the possession of the "original" claim?

The Witness

"The violation of monastery borders is the violation of village borders and that means it is the violation of our honor [namus]," Muhtar Ahmet said during our first meeting at the monastery in 2008. As the muhtar of Kafarbe, he was the strongest supporter of the Syriacs in the border dispute with their Kurdish neighbors. Muhtar Ahmet's position was unique. He was attached to the Çelebi tribe. "We belong to him [Çelebi Agha (ona aidiz)]," he said, indicating his absolute loyalty. Muhtar Ahmet was employed as a korucu for a few decades under the Çelebi family. He also served on the Executive Committee of the local branch of the AKP. According to Muhtar Ahmet, Çelebi Agha's family always protected the Christians and respected their decision on the border consolidation. The AKP government was not responsible for this conflict over the monastery land. He believed that the AKP had managed to bring safety and tranquility to the area and sustain a new order of justice under which landowners who repressed the poor and vulnerable were no longer in power.

Muhtar Ahmet was the only Kurdish villager who was actively engaged in the cadastral survey and the litigation process that followed defending the monastery's ownership of the disputed territories. The monastery sat within the boundaries of his village, so any chunk of land outside the shrine would remain under his protection. Muhtar Ahmet believed that the neighboring Kurdish villagers wanted to appropriate and loot the Christians' property.

Friends and relatives from these villages with whom he had made a pilgrimage were now telling lies and making unjust claims over property that did not originally belong to them. Muhtar Ahmet recalled a conversation that he had with one of his close friends from the disputed villages as follows: "I said to Hadji [Hacı], 'Hadji, I recognize your authority in the witness of God and Mohammed. I will accept whatever you claim in regard to the boundaries of the villages. Is this disputed area yours?' Hadji responded, 'No, it did not belong to my father. It is not part of my village. But why wouldn't we snatch it from the Christians?'"

According to Muhtar Ahmet, the cadastral officer witnessed this conversation but ruled in favour of the villagers. The cadastral officer was feeling under threat. Supporting the claims of the monastery, Muhtar Ahmet turned himself into a target for the rage, revenge, and anger of his Kurdish neighbors. He could not serve as an arbitrator between the Syriacs and the Kurds. Rather, he acted as a human shield to protect the monastery and his village from occupation and abuse by the Kurdish villagers who were accusing him of betraying his Muslim relatives and friends in exchange for a payoff from the monastery. "They tried to kill me few times on my way to the village," he said. "They told me they would shoot me if they saw me in the courtroom."

Muhtar Ahmet based his position on three separate claims. The first involved certified documents that established the boundaries of the monastery. These dated back to Ottoman and early republican times and included aerial photographs and agreements signed by the villagers in 1937. In addition, in regard to the conflict with the Forestry Department, Muhtar Ahmet confirmed that the aerial photographs from the 1950s showed the area as green and identified it as forest land. The monastery foundation never held deeds over the land, but they owned the trees that appeared in those photographs. "The area looked green when they took those photos from the planes in 1950s but we [the villagers of Kafarbe] cut down those trees and turned that land into fields so that we could plant chick peas and oat," explained Muhtar Ahmet. "We did not have any money, so we used the land to feed ourselves and grow products to sell. We paid the state for the use of the land. The monastery paid taxes on the areas that they farmed. In those days, the state did not care what we did on this land."

His second argument was based on his historical and political imaginary of "we." The history of his village was constitutive of the history of the Christians and Muslims who moved from place to place together. His grandparents brought in four Syriac families and settled them in their village in order to increase the population and strengthen its defense against other Kurdish tribes. The village was evacuated three times because of food scarcity and fear of armed Kurdish tribes.

"We [Kurds and Syriacs from Kafarbe] all lived in poverty," he said. "We spoke the same language. The Christians of Kafarbe village spoke Kurdish. Only the brides who came from other villages spoke Turoyo. We had a smaller population than the surrounding villages, so the neighbors saw us as easy to swallow up. We always helped the people in the monastery when they had trouble with their neighbors. They would have occupied and destroyed the monastery if we had not supported them. We protected the monastery and the village. We all died defending this land."

In 1915, the Faliya family invaded Mor Gabriel Monastery. They killed monks, nuns, and villagers and occupied the property. They held it until 1922 when the Kafarbe villagers organized and returned to save the monastery from occupation. "The family was part of a Kurdish tribe [aşiret]. They were outsiders. They lived in the monastery until they escaped to Syria," said Muhtar Ahmet. He was talking about the Sayfo without naming it such. "This was not a single event of killings," said Muhtar Ahmet. "In those days, this region was covered with all sorts of conflicts. It was like today's Syria. . . . We were all scared of the new government [the recently established Turkish state] and we all escaped to the other side of the border for a while."

According to Muhtar Ahmet, solidarity between the Syriacs and Kurds in Kafarbe held until the Syriacs started emigrating in the 1970s. The historical protector-protégé relationship took a new turn in the 1980s with the start of the conflict between the PKK and the Turkish Armed Forces. The Syriac villagers escaped the war and left for Europe and yet sent financial support to the monastery. The monastery foundation used those funds to expand, repair, and restore the property. This prosperity was shared with the Kurdish villagers. "They helped us too," said Muhtar Ahmet. "They provided whatever we needed for the village. They even funded the construction of a new mosque in the village. We do the same for them. I take care of the church in the village. I keep it clean and do not allow it to be used by anyone for other purposes."

In the 1990s, Muhtar Ahmet became a korucu. The korucus from Kafarbe provided the village and the monastery an extra layer of protection from state violence, but their presence also turned them into targets of the PKK.

Muhtar Ahmet's son was shot dead by PKK guerrillas in one of the neighboring villages. "I could have destroyed that village," he said. "The military officer would have allowed me to do whatever I wanted, but I did not. If I had known who the real perpetrator was, I would have gone and shot him, but it would not be right to take revenge on the entire village. I made myself forgive all of the villagers. But, they could not stop themselves from claiming ownership of two more trees." There was a delicate balance hidden in those relationships that Muhtar Ahmet did not want to disturb. The neighboring villagers knew who had shot his son, but they did not reveal his name. Muhtar Ahmet worked with his neighbors as a korucu under the rule of Çelebi Agha for many years. Open hostility could have deadly effects. Muhtar Ahmet was wise enough to know the rules. The justice that he sought for the monastery allowed him to keep the ground open for an unnamed struggle without ruining the loyalties to other forms of sovereigns enacted in the body of the agha and the state. This was one of the threads underlying the multiple meanings of the occupation of the monastery land, which he identified with the occupation of his territory and attack on his honor.

Muhtar Ahmet had an implicit double standard in regard to the historical presence of the monastery. He was in full support of its claims over the land. The monastery provided material and political protection if not for him for his village through the continuous flow of visitors, goods, and cash from Europe. At the same time, Muhtar Ahmet believed that the Kurds would remain on this land and that the Syriacs would vanish one day. His notion of "us" changed, taking on different meanings. Muhtar Ahmet expressed his insights for the future as such: "I told the bishop in the presence of the judge that I would not accept it even if the bishop agreed to give away these parcels of land. I will not intervene in their monastery but I can intervene in the right to use and possess this land. It has been appropriated and protected with our blood. This land is our blood. At the end of the day, Christians are guests here. Over the next few years, they might all go away, but the land should and will continue to be part of our village."

The Return of the Perpetrators

"I was walking down the street. I felt someone's shadow come over me. Who was he? I approached him and asked who he was and why he was after me," said Muhtar Ahmet. The man who was following him was from the Faliya family, which as just discussed, had occupied the Mor Gabriel Monastery and massacred the monks and priests in 1915, then remained in the monastery until 1922. Few people from the family were now back in Midyat. They were informed of the disputes over the monastery land, though. They were looking for ways to make claims over parcels that remained within the territory of the monastery. The members of the Faliya family organized meetings with the muhtars of the Kurdish villages surrounding the monastery, who agreed to support their claim. They also informed Muhtar Ahmet that they would file a claim against the monastery. Muhtar Ahmet was furious. Decades later, he found himself negotiating with the descendants of perpetrators who had massacred the residents of the monastery and the village. He told the Faliyas that under no circumstances would he collaborate with them and that they could defend their case in the court if they had documents that would prove their ownership of the property. "Give up your claim or get ready to face the fire," warned Muhtar Ahmet. The struggle would be a legal or an armed one. Muhtar Ahmet's sense of justice was interwoven with Islamic rules, tribal rule, and an obsession with documents that emerged from the long litigation process that created endless attempts to search out and present evidence of ownership of the land at stake.

According to Muhtar Ahmet, after long negotiation tours in Ankara and Midyat, the Faliya family gave up and left town without officially engaging in the legal process. They could not find any documents to serve as proof of their claims. The return of the Faliya family had opened up different possibilities for the future of the litigation. For the Syriacs who had close kinship connections to Kafarbe and intimate knowledge of the massacres that took place at the monastery, the reappearance of the Faliya family could be used as further proof of the Sayfo. Had the Faliya family managed to file the claim of ownership of the disputed land, some of the leading Syriac figures from diaspora who were closely following the case would have brought up the need to first address past atrocities. The material and bodily ruins of the Sayfo that were scattered all around the towns and villages of the Tur Abdin region haunted the political and historical imagination of both the Kurds and Syriacs concerning their past losses as well as future expectations. Mor Gabriel Monastery was mediating the reemergence of political imaginations, historical memories, and future desires for material, political, and spiritual existence moving through the real and imaginary possession of the land.

Seeing the Land Through the Wall

In regard to the litigation process, Muhtar Ahmet and the monastery representatives applied to the administrative court (idari mahkeme) for review of the decision of the cadastral court (kadastro mahkemesi). Despite their deep distrust of the court system, they assumed that the litigation would at least avoid the closure of the case and give the monastery representatives additional time to find other solutions. The monastery foundation's petition before the administrative court intensified the dispute. The refusal to drop the legal battle confined the monastery representatives into a legal imprisonment.

One week later, the muhtars of three neighboring Kurdish villages signed new petitions and delivered them to the local prosecutor. Written in a provocative language, the petitions accused the monastery of organizing missionary activities, illegally providing language and religious education to children under the age of twelve, sheltering unidentified individuals, receiving money from unknown resources, and last but not least building a wall on the forest land that belonged to the state. In the petitions, Muhtar Ahmet was accused of abusing his authority. The prosecutor only took up the issue of the wall and filed a complaint against the monastery for occupying state property.

The history of the wall was unclear. The monastery representatives shied away from clarifying the reasons for its construction. The wall was often referred to as a permanent part of the monastery's architecture, as if it dated back to ancient times and a new wall was added to the old structure as a security measure in response to the threats and attacks of the 1990s. In other conversations, the wall did not exist until 1990. The acceleration of the conflict and the continuous flow of financial support from the diaspora made the construction of the wall seem like a plausible idea. The wall was built gradually between 1992 and 1997. The monastery residents discussed its presence as a daily necessity that facilitated the life of the people in and outside the monastery and provided protection for the trees, plants, cows, and goats that belong to the monastery. In their view, the wall served both Syriacs and Kurds as it reduced the daily disputes. The wall functioned as the domestic-private barrier between the interior life of the monastery and the outside world. Its presence was never questioned by government authorities until the recent submission of complaints by Kurdish villagers. The monastery representatives were frustrated. While they were seeking legal protection against the abuse of their Kurdish neighbors, they found themselves involved in legal battles that accused them of having illegally occupied state property. The role of the occupier was shifted from the Kurdish villagers to the monastery foundation.

The new charges against the monastery initially created panic and revitalized feelings of distrust particularly among the Syriacs in diaspora. However, a short time later, the visibility of the case in the national media engendered confidence and pride. The dispute was framed as another violation of the minority rights in Turkey. Discussions focused on the brutality of the tribal order and in particular the village guard system. Süleyman Çelebi, who was the son of Çelebi Agha and a member of parliament from the AKP, denied the claims of Syriacs over the disputed land, condemning them for contaminating historical truths. Public support for the monastery swelled when Kurdish politicians and activists entered the fray: forty Kurdish lawyers offered to give defense services free of charge. The leader of the pro-Kurdish Peace and Democracy Party (Barış ve Demokrasi Partisi), Ahmet Türk, visited the monastery and gave a speech apologizing for the atrocities committed by Kurds against Syriacs during 1915. The bishop of the monastery kindly rejected the offer of the Kurdish lawyers to avoid the conflation of their case with the Kurdish cause (Biner 2015).

The Syriacs had not expected the trial to proceed. The prosecutor based his argument on two articles: Cadastral Law No. 3402 and Forest Law No. 6831. According to the Cadastral Law No. 3402, land that was not used for agricultural purposes for over twenty years would be reregistered as state property. According to the Forest Law No. 6831, land that looks green in aerial photography would be registered as forest land and become state property. A total of 260,000 square meters of land within the monastery walls and 60,000 square meters of land outside the monastery walls were registered as forest and thus treasury land (Oran 2012:203–204). In addition, the wall itself occupied 276,000 square meters of the forest land, which justified the claims of the lawsuit against the Mor Gabriel Foundation. The cadastral court in Midyat issued a final verdict on behalf of the Forest Department regarding the aerial images from 1952 that showed the land in dispute to be green and thus categorized as forest and state property. The monastery foundation representatives were found responsible for illegally occupying state property. The wall was the material evidence of dispossession.

There were further claims regarding the "illegality" of the wall. The Treasury Department made a new claim regarding the twelve plots (244,000 square meters) that were registered as monastery land during the cadastral survey. The cadastral court in Midyat rejected the case, but the Court of Cassation (Yargıtay) overruled that decision, referencing Section 14 of the Cadastral Law that states, "when a plot of non-registered land is claimed by someone who can prove that he has been its de facto processor for at least 20 years, this land cannot exceed 100,000 square metres in dry areas, whereas the land registered here is 244,000 square metres" (Oran 2012:205). The decision of the Court of Cassation was exceptional as it negated the very same law that allowed to register more than 100,000 square meters also in case of the submission of tax records prior to 1982 (205). The monastery foundation had official documents to support the claim over these disputed parcels. It registered this land as its property under the 1936 declaration ordered by the government. In addition, the monastery foundation had paid taxes on this land since 1937 and kept the tax payment slips as the proof of the transactions. The cadastral court of Midyat rejected the claim of Treasury on the basis of these documents, but the Court of Cassation supported the Treasury on the basis of the lack of those documents. In its letter to the monastery foundation, the court reported that the official documents that were claimed to be attached as proof of ownership were not found in the file. They were simply absent. The monastery foundation responded to the request by resending copies of the very same documents.[4] However, the resubmission of these materials did not change the final verdict of the Court of Cassation. Eighty acres (244,000 square meters) were transferred to the Treasury (205). The tension between the local court and the Court of Cassation continued throughout the process with the disappearance and disregard of the documents provided as proof of the continuous engagement with the disputed land. Without these documents, it was impossible to provide proof or ensure the accuracy of local knowledge. Neither the transmission of oral accounts that relied on visual knowledge of the landscape nor written documents such as tax slips, the 1936 declaration, or the written consensus between the villagers mattered in the decision-making processes of the Court of Cassation.

The trials over the territory occupied by the wall continued for three years. In losing to against the Forestry Department, the monastery faced the possibility of being forced to give up 60 percent of its core property, the space currently enclosed within the wall. The final verdict of the court carried the struggle back to the starting point. Despite all the attempts to redefine the struggle in the context of the global discussions of rights and justice, the legal dispute was lost as a result of the litigation over the monastery wall. The representatives of the monastery foundation have taken the case before the European Court of Human Rights (Oran 2012:205).

In September 2013, Prime Minister Recep Tayyip Erdoğan issued the final verdict in the case, promising to return the disputed land to the monastery. The government used the case to consolidate its power by exerting its authority to draw the line between the legal and illegal, internal and external. Accordingly, the wall has been recast as the mediator of the "exception." The government endorsed this decision as a tangible product of what it called the democratization package (demokrasi paketi), as evidence of the ongoing peace process (barış süreci) in Turkey. The resolution of the Mor Gabriel issue should be interpreted as part of the government's 's attempts to restore justice and reconciliation in the region. From the perspective of the monastery agents, however, the case was not yet closed because the government returned only twelve parcels of disputed land and excluded the area occupied by the wall and the outside, which was officially registered as forest land. Another eighteen parcels remained disputed. The legal battle with the Forestry Department eventually reached the European Court of Human Rights (see Oran 2012; Gusten 2015).

The Mor Gabriel case was imbued with "travels of the law" through different courts, legal orders, communities, and states (see Benda-Beckmann et al. 2005; Eckert, Donahoe, et al. 2012). The dispute that began in the vicinity of the wall took on multiple meanings. From the cadastral court, it traveled to the Court of Cassation, and finally the European Court of Human Rights, engendering iterations that led to new interpretive processes that revealed the relationship between personal and community values, feelings, and the interpretation of notions of right and law (Eckert, Biner, et al. 2012:15). Politics had migrated to the courts, "where ordinary political processes are held hostage to the dialectic of law and disorder" (Comaroff and Comaroff 2006:26). The confrontation between the monastery representatives, the Kurds, and the state turned into "lawfare" (Comaroff and Comaroff 2006:30). This lawfare did not lead to justice, which is what the Syriacs had imagined and hoped for. It instead led to the violence of the law that facilitated acts of political coercion and subordination. The disjunction between law and justice resonated in the gap between the hope and aspiration that people invest in their use of law and law's "mundane translations of hope into procedures" (Eckert, Biner, et al. 2012:9).[5]

This gap was filled differently in the cases of İsa Bey and Mor Gabriel. It is worthwhile to make this comparison in order to understand how "exception" operates through the law and how it constitutes the limits of recognition of positions and agencies. İsa Bey's struggle and Mor Gabriel's endless trials took place during the same period. İsa Bey wanted to use the law to express his desire for justice and demand protection against the dispossession of private and collective property. In the absence of official mechanisms of transitional justice, he used the law to situate himself and his community against the rule of the tribal order. His faith in state law moved in tandem with other negotiations of the daily conflicts that continued to develop with the Syriac elders, state officers, and Kurdish neighbors: negotiations that he could not halt. His case was not about resistance to legal orders that were often articulated within the discussions of legal pluralism (see Benda-Beckmann, Benda-Beckmann, and Eckert 2009). Rather, it was about revealing injustice and gaining recognition for the past and present histories of exclusion that he represented as a member of a Christian minority with an endless experience of exploitation and as a landowner with enough ambition and optimism to reclaim the ownership of thousands of hectares of land against the backdrop of the economic and political inequalities of the violent peace. İsa Bey did not see these positions as mutually exclusive. He was reclaiming what has always historically belonged to his community. His promise to the community that he would set wrongs right prompted his hope for and insistence on resort to state law.

However, in a Kafkaesque twist in the story, İsa Bey was not allowed to enter the court. Every attempt that he made to seek justice in court failed due to a lack of evidence. He could not protect the physical boundaries of his village from invasion and occupation by the korucus. His insistence on serving as the visible witness of dispossession was resisted. Meanwhile, the Mor Gabriel Monastery case followed a different path. The legal battle between the state and the Syriacs was not uncommon. The land registration process that started in the middle of the first decade of the century generated a proliferation of legal cases due to the claims made by the Treasury Department regarding the land of the Syriac villages. The Syriacs claimed that they stood to lose a considerable amount of land in this process (see Tozman 2012). This seemingly similar situation followed an explosive path in the case of Mor

Gabriel Monastery. The monastery representatives' willingness to engage in litigation to defend their boundaries locked them in endless confrontations with the Kurds and the state in the courts. Every file opened up another chapter, led to another trial, forced the production of more evidence through witness testimony and documents. The legal struggle over the Mor Gabriel Monastery also provided political and moral justification for a collective struggle based on Syriac identity. For Syriacs, the trial was not only about protecting the physical boundaries of the monastery. It was a battle with the Kurds and the Turkish state, a quest to gain recognition for what has been taken away from them, to consolidate the boundaries of their property and establish the political and existential boundaries between self and other, and self and state. The wall was the material and political expression of that goal. The wall was the embodiment of the linear border that would be fixed, not movable or subject to constant change through the passage of plants, animals, and people. It would be a permanent border, not one that would expand at the will of others. The state used the law to intervene in that space of hope, to challenge that sense of possibility, to change the meaning of the physical and political boundaries. The state and Kurdish neighbors wanted the wall to remain "not rigid and fixed at all; elastic in constant transformation" (Weizman 2007:6), a permeable barrier that would allow for daily negotiations, transactions, violations of the rule, and exertion and invention of new exceptions, one that would constitute and regulate the historically and politically embedded relationships of dependency and subversion. The government, prime minister, legal experts, cadastral surveyors, Syriacs, Kurds, aghas, international actors, and the media all play their part in the collective organization and transformation of the monastery as the medium of confrontation and (non)reconciliation. Though the legal battle empowered Syriacs by generating international recognition of their historical presence and material heritage and helped them to seek protection against the repression of the tribal order and the state, it did not bring an end to their liminal position with regard to their full entitlement to property rights. While the wall sheltered them against the physical intervention of their Kurdish neighbors, it failed to grant them autonomy against the political intervention of the state.

CHAPTER 6

Loss, Compensation, and Debt

We did not know what to expect of the law. We
informed all of our members to come and give their
testimonies. Villagers found it difficult to believe that
the state would accept its responsibility and compensate
for the damages incurred by the Armed Forces. They were
suspicious of the purpose and the consequences of the
law and . . . they were uncertain about how to complain
about the state to the state. . . . We were not sure whether
these petitions would ever be evaluated.

—Extract from an interview with a lawyer from
a human rights organization

In 2004, the Turkish Parliament passed the Law on Compensation for Losses
Resulting from Terrorism and the Fight Against Terrorism. The law was designed to compensate citizens who had incurred material damages as a result of the military conflict between the PKK militants and the Turkish
Armed Forces between 1987 and 2004. In the preamble, the aim of the law
was explained as providing compensation for the damages in the context of
"bolstering trust and rapprochement between the state and its citizens." Compensation was to be granted for losses resulting from physical damage to
movable and immovable assets as well as losses that resulted because a person was denied access to his/her property during that period. Loss of life and
injuries were also included in the compensation categories, but nonpecuniary damages were not. Compensation would be awarded by mutual agreement between the applicants and the provincial committees known as damage

assessment commissions (zarar tespit komisyonları), which were staffed by local public officials and the vali in the provinces of the conflict zone. In the case of signing the "friendly settlement" (sulhhame), applicants would be awarded compensation in exchange for renouncing their right to litigation. Applicants also had the right to reject the award and reapply to the administration or appeal the decisions of the damage assessment commissions to the Supreme Court. Litigation in the European Court of Human Rights (ECHR) was only an option once the individual had exhausted all internal legal procedures (Kurban 2007; Kurban et al. 2007).

The deadline for applying for compensation under the law passed in 2008. Complaints about the form and content of the law have been covered in the media. People often complained about the low level of compensation and the rejection of files and threatened to take their cases to the European Court of Human Rights. Very few applicants resorted to litigation to appeal the decisions of the commissions. In 2006, the government sent a report to the European Court of Human Rights on the applications made under the Compensation Law from people who had previously filed petitions with that court. Evaluating the mechanisms and results of these assessments, the European Court of Human Rights ruled that the Compensation Law provided an effective domestic remedy and that applicants must exhaust this procedure before filing action in Strasbourg. On the basis of this evaluation, the court returned all pending applications (see Kurban 2007). Following this decision, the issue of state accountability and individuals' right to reparative justice have become an internal affair between the lawyers, the displaced villagers as the petitioners, and the local bureaucrats of the damage assessment commissions (Biner 2012, 2013).

In the previous chapters, I explored how Kurds and Syriacs have historically coexisted through (re)production of as-if-indebted relationships. In this chapter, I turn to debt-producing mechanisms that exist between the Turkish state and Kurds. Focusing on the legal procedures related to acts of compensation, I argue that the Turkish state uses the law to transform reparative justice mechanisms into debt-producing mechanisms. Here, *debt* refers to the material and intangible relationship that the Turkish state has established with Kurds through which militaristic state violence transforms itself into forms of dispossession. How does compensation as an act of reparation transform the relationship between the state and citizens? How is it converted into debt? Who is indebted to whom?

The Turkish state has never officially acknowledged the human rights violations that took place under the emergency law between 1987 and 2002. No state perpetrators were held legally responsible for these acts of violence, which were often justified as the inevitable consequences of the fight against terrorism. Starting in the mid-1990s, human rights lawyers brought individual cases of Kurdish citizens involving the burning and evacuation of villages, torture, disappearances, and killings before the European Court of Human Rights. The court accepted the petitions and in some cases found Turkey responsible for failing to provide a domestic legal remedy to compensate the villagers or hold security forces accountable for the violations (Kurban 2007:128). In such cases, the state was ordered to compensate the victims through pecuniary and nonpecuniary damages and to pay for their legal fees and expenses (131). The other component of this picture was the increasing number of military or police officers who were engaged as permanent state employees and the conscripted soldiers who had died or were injured during the conflict with the PKK. Under Anti-terror Law No. 3713 of 1991, the state granted veterans disabled in the struggle against terror "material and symbolic entitlement such as job replacement, interest-free housing credit, medals of honor and firearms licenses" (Açıksöz 2012:10). In addition, some brought lawsuits before the courts and asked for compensation for their injuries and losses from the Ministry of Interior Affairs or the Ministry of Defense.

After 2000, the state never gave an official apology for the economic and moral injuries that had devastating effects particularly on the lives of Kurdish citizens, or attempted to establish a political and social infrastructure for the possibility of revealing the "truth" and identifying the perpetrators and victims of the 1990s. Rather, the state eluded accountability for violations of citizenship rights by crafting legal devices designed to tackle claims of damages and losses under the scrutiny of supranational organizations such as the United Nations High Commissioner for Refugees and the ECHR during the EU-accession process (Biner 2012, 2013).

In this context, the AKP government designed the Compensation Law to provide benefits to citizens who had incurred material damages as a result of the conflict between 1987 and 2004. It covered all civilians except for those who had been convicted under the Anti-terror Law. As I mentioned earlier, the preamble of the Compensation Law did not derive from recognition of the accountability of the state, but rather, according to the Official

Gazette from the "doctrine of social risk based on the objective responsibility of the state" (cited in Ünalan et al. 2007:92). People who had suffered damages were compensated as a "requirement of justice and of the principles of a social state based on the rule of the law," regardless of whether the state was accountable for the damages (90–91).

The Compensation Law was turned into an effective tool to refashion the credibility of the Turkish state in the international arena. The accountable, care-taking, and justice-delivering images of the state are constituted in particular against the scrutiny of the European Court of Human Rights and other supranational organizations (cf. Wilson 2003; Slyomovics 2009).

The state reconciled with the global norms of accountability and created inner mechanisms to cut off access to international institutions of justice. More importantly, the state used the Compensation Law to reproduce its power as the main provider of all the material and immaterial benefits, holding the "doubled edge sword of protection and violence" (Kelly and Shah 2006:251). Here, I argue that at the margins of Turkey, where daily life was structured around conflict and competition between the state and the PKK in the struggle for control and hegemony over the people and the territory (Das and Poole 2004), the state used violence not only to struggle against the PKK but also to sell protection of access to its resources and from its possibility of violence (see Shah 2010).

In the sections that follow, I describe the ways in which the legal procedures related to compensation were enacted after 1999, moving from the ways the Compensation Law was implemented and perceived by the damage commission members, lawyers, and applicants in Mardin to the parallel yet less visible mechanisms of compensation cases known as "compensation recovery cases" (rücu tazminatı davaları). Drawing on comparative analyses of both types of processes, I show how the Turkish state uses reparative justice mechanisms not to meet "burning needs for acknowledgement, closure, vindication and connection" (Minow 1998:106) but rather to engender debt-producing mechanisms that mortgage not only the past but also the present and future of Kurdish citizens.

Compensation Law

The procedure started with the submission of a petition to the damage assessment commissions in the provinces of the conflict region. There were several ways to file a petition. Petitioners could file individually at the vali's office. They could apply via a joint commission established by human rights organizations, and migrant associations or lawyers with power of attorney could file the petitions with the vali's office on behalf of their clients. Lawyers were significant agents in this process, filing most of the petitions. They collected and submitted documents as proof of damage, and followed the progress of the case on their clients' behalf. They standardized the petitions, which involved a formulation of the cause of damages and the construction of categories of material losses, and they followed the process of documenting and registering the damages and losses by the expert teams and documenting the evaluations by the damage commission members.

The damage assessment commissions were established as the main implementers of the Compensation Law. They were responsible for processing applications, assessing damages, establishing payments, and preparing settlement statements or protocols of nonagreement in cases in which applicants refused to sign statements and decided to take the commission's decision to the administrative court. Commissions were chaired by the vali and composed of seven other members, five of whom were public officials from the provincial public departments of health, finance, agriculture and rural affairs, health, industry and commerce, and public works and housing and a lawyer who was appointed by the bar association. The commissions also included a police officer as the secretary who was responsible for receiving the applications and documents. The vali's role was to represent the state. The police officer and the vali were the only nonlocal public officials on the commission. The rest of the members were the local bureaucrats, both Kurdish and Arab, some of whom had family members who were going through the same process and awaiting a decision.

In principle, the commission's decision would be based on the documents submitted by the applicants to support their claims, including probate decisions, autopsy reports, incident reports and deeds,[1] the reports provided by the gendarme forces on the conditions of the village (whether it was evacuated during the conflict), and reports of the members of subcommissions of local experts who visited the villages to assess the damages and losses claimed in the applications. After approving the eligibility of the applicant and verifying the presence of the required documents, the commission would award compensation based on the reports provided by local experts from the subcommissions. Until 2006, the damages were calculated according to the estimated amount indicated in the subcommission reports. This often resulted in inconsistent and incoherent decisions in terms of the compensation amount, which in turn not only engendered tensions among villagers but also jeopardized the credibility of the damage assessment commissions. In 2006, the government set up a calculation model based on a standard values table that indicated an upper and lower limit of the value for certain types of property, including houses, farmland, gardens, trees, and wheat stock. A computer program was developed to calculate compensation by multiplying each item of damaged property by a value that fell between the upper and lower limits of the standard values table. The commission members would rely on the report of the subcommission on the assessment of the damaged property. Yet they were to choose the upper or lower limit of the value of the chosen property and use the data processor to calculate the compensation.

A short conversation I heard between a commission secretary (a policeman) and one of the other commission members provides insight into how personal judgments were used to set these limits in both a literal sense and a figurative one. As we will see below, while the experience of violence was reduced to the calculation of property, the computer program would mingle the subjective decisions of commission members with the mundane stresses of daily life in a government institution in the conflict zone.

> *Police officer:* How many kilos of grapes does a vine produce?
> *Commission member:* No more than ten kilos.
> *Police officer:* I calculated the cost of the damage based on fifteen kilos.
> *Commission member:* That is too much, but don't waste time
>   changing it. We have to be at the meeting in fifteen minutes.
>   Make a cut from the total production of other trees. Are there
>   apricot trees on the list of the claimed items?
> *Police officer:* Yes.
> *Commission member:* Drop it from there. Calculate ten kilos for
>   each apricot tree.
> *Police officer:* OK, I will do that.

Applications involving death, disappearance, and bodily harm were also subject to the personal judgments of the commission members. In principle, as was the case for compensation for the movable and immovable property, the law set the compensation amount for the death and bodily harm based on civil servant coefficients: 14,000 Turkish liras for death; 2,000 Turkish liras for injuries; 1,000–21,000 Turkish liras for disabilities.[2] Here the amounts were fixed, with no upper or lower limits regardless of differences of class, age, or gender. The law stated that all of the applicants who were affected by "terrorism" and "the fight against terrorism" were eligible to apply. Members of the military and police forces, public officials, korucus and displaced villagers would be granted the same amount for death, injury, or disability. The homogenizing principle of the law created symbolic equality among the dead and erased the distinction between victim and perpetrator. Yet there was still a rule to draw the boundaries of exclusion. According to the law, people who were convicted under the Anti-terror Law or who had received compensation from another source (this refers to the European Court of Human Rights) were not eligible for compensation. In the case of the former, this was because they were held responsible for the event that led to damages and injuries. This was the most sensitive issue for the commission members I interviewed in 2009. In their view, other criteria (here they refer to the availability of the required documents) were always open to negotiation but the exclusion of those convicted under the Anti-terror Law should by no means be transgressed. The commission members further interpreted the noneligibility criteria and extended them to the relatives of convicted individuals and PKK guerrillas, creating new "exceptions." The criminal records of male relatives of female applicants would be checked before a decision was issued in order to avoid "abuse of the law." It was not uncommon for the applications of the families of guerrillas to be rejected without cause.

There was a similar attitude toward cases of anonymous killings and disappearances. Some lawyers reported that compensation was granted only for cases in which the act was reported as murder by the PKK and Hezbollah and had been taken to the National Security Court (Devlet Güvenlik Mahkemeleri) Most of the applicants who could not provide incident reports or autopsy reports were denied. As one of the lawyers explained, "During the early years, we could not receive any compensation for anonymous killings. The commission members were prejudiced. They considered the victim and their relatives to be potential terrorists. In the later years, they changed their attitudes and agreed to award compensation in a few cases of disappearance and killings. We still do not know the reasons behind these decisions. Maybe they received a secret message from the state, maybe there was a warning from the European Court of Human Rights observers. But it is still difficult to get compensation for these cases."

Even administrative court verdicts that contradicted the commissions' decisions did not change the defensive interpretations of the cases of the disappeared and anonymous killings. As revealed by an experienced lawyer, recently, one application involved the case of a man who was shot dead in 1992.[3] The commission refused to provide compensation to the family, arguing that by attending the protest where he died, he bore some responsibility for the events that caused his death. The family carried the case to the administrative court, where the decision of the commission members was disapproved and the file sent back to damage assessment commission. "We expected that the commission members would object to this verdict and take the file to the Council of State (Danıştay). Yet they did not move. Either they forgot or they decided to act as if nothing happened," the lawyer said, describing the uncertainty of the situation.

The uncertainty of the law and the arbitrariness of the authority were not exceptional at the margins of the state (see Das and Poole 2004). There were numerous examples of arbitrary, inconsistent, and exceptional decisions by commission members as civil servants. According to the lawyers, these inconsistencies were not only between commissions in different provinces but also within the same province, and even within the same commission. There were many cases in which a commission would apply totally different criteria in its evaluations of the files from a single village. In some cases, commissions would accept the remnants of houses and burned trees as evidence of the evacuation of the village, while in others commissions would only consider the incident reports drafted by the gendarme forces to be reliable sources of evidence. In still other cases, while commissions would agree to pay for material losses, they would reject payment of compensation for the people who died in the same village, claiming that the incident happened before the date indicated in the law.

The lawyers often interpreted these differences as being due to the political views of the vali, who chaired the commission and allegedly influenced the decisions of other members. As mentioned above, with the exception of the vali and the police officer, the commission members were local public officials who were in the midst of everyday political struggles. Their class, ethnic background, and experience of violence as witness, victim, or perpetrator would mingle with their attitude of showing conformity and proving their loyalty to the vali as the top representative of the state in the province. One of the commission members explained the logic of their decision making as follows: "The decisions relied on our knowledge of the region, sense of justice, and, most importantly, our conscience. The law was enacted without any infrastructure or well-defined rules. We did not evaluate these applications on the basis of one of set of rules. Our main principle was to act in order to arrange settlements. We tried to protect people as much as we could and give them compensation even if they left their villages earlier than the start of the conflict. The war affected everyone. Everyone lost something here. But people started to ask for more than what they had lost. We are not prejudiced against anyone but we also have responsibility to protect the state."

Conscience and *justice* were words the commission members used repeatedly to explain the logic of their decisions. In that context, morality did not lie in making coherent and consistent decisions regarding the judgment of the applications. Their responsibility against the state and their awareness of the political reality of the region were pushing them to develop a private sense of justice while transgressing the law and at the same time reinforcing the boundaries of the state by reiterating the notions of loyalty and care. As one of the commission members related:

> I have done everything to be just. Someone who left his village a hundred years ago applies for compensation under this law, or the korucu claims that his sister was shot dead by an anonymous person. I know that this murder was a crime of honor, but the korucu wants us to treat the case as an act of terrorism. I reject such petitions. Or a man has been convicted under the Anti-terror Law and, hence, his wife files a petition. I immediately ask the secretary of the commission to check the criminal record of this woman's husband. If he was convicted, I refuse to assess the petition submitted by his wife. The Compensation Law clearly states the criteria of eligibility, of who is or isn't eligible to apply for compensation. In the future, inspectors will come to review our decisions and they will ask whether we have ever received petitions from terrorists or their families. These rejections are the proof of our law-abiding decisions.

In the view of the commission members, the inconsistencies were related to the lack of infrastructure and the initiative they needed to take due to the absence of a well-codified legal structure and the political and economic polarization in the region. Exceptions were by no means indicators of unjust, noncredible, or abusive practices. These interventions were necessary in order to define and redefine the boundaries between legal and illegal and just and unjust and to provide protection both for the state and for the injured yet "abusive" citizens.

Seeking Resources Without Justice

> I agree to receive compensation [as determined by
> damage assessment commissions] for the damages
> and losses incurred as a result [of] terrorism and [the]
> fight against terrorism. I hereby declare and confirm
> that my losses as assessed by the commission have
> been compensated either in kind or cash.

> —Extract from the declaration on the friendly statement

Despite the strong sense of dissatisfaction regarding the decisions of the commissions, the majority of the applicants were inclined to accept the compensation, and renounce their right to litigation. People only resorted to litigation when their cases had been rejected or the compensation offered by the commission was exceptionally low. According to the lawyers, this was related to the applicants' financial situations and the high costs and long waiting periods associated with litigation. It was not unusual for six to eight years to pass before applicants exhausted domestic legal options and reached the point where they could appeal to the European Court of Human Rights. Though these observations are important, they do not explain the rationale behind the acts of submission and more significantly the renunciation of the right to litigation. In a protracted war zone where there is full and open support for the Kurdish resistance movement and where the PKK is the leading party for the Kurdish struggle, why would people submit to law and sign agreements renouncing their right to litigation? What does this submission reveal about the relationship between the state and the Kurdish citizens?

The people I interviewed for this project in 2009 who had applied for compensation under the new law and later agreed to accept it were often the displaced Kurdish villagers who moved to the city of Mardin in the middle of the 1990s, in the aftermath of the evacuation of their villages by the military forces. They were open to articulating their experience of violence, support for the Kurdish struggle, and disapproval and fear of the militarized solutions of the government. In effect, they had a wider imagination of the state that not only involved the police forces, military, government, and civil servants. In their view, the state has the potential to permeate into any polity including tribal families and the branches of the pro-Kurdish political party and turn opponents into traitors. Although they "fetishized" the state through the imaginary and experience of violence, threat, and care, they were fully aware of the power relations, networks, and dynamics that existed behind the fetish as the mask (cf. Taussig 1997; Navaro-Yashin 2002). There were many people who were politically involved with the struggle or who had family members who joined the PKK and at the same time had jobs as civil servants. They did not view their double act of subversion and submission as a conflict. Their eagerness for the benefits was based on hope of economic and political survival and feeling of resentment and anger for the violation of their rights and the nonrecognition of their identities as Kurdish citizens. In their political imaginary, the Turkish state was obliged to provide them with resources in exchange for the violence they had been subjected to for decades. As sharply epitomized by an elderly Kurdish man, "Should the state not subsidize this region, these mountains explode [bu dağlar patlar]. And the state knows that."

In order to avoid dealing with the bureaucracy, most villagers filed their applications through their lawyers with a power of attorney. They would then wait for a call from the lawyers on the processing of the file or receipt of compensation. The collection of the documents was a stumbling block because the majority of the applicants did not feel secure about revealing information about the material aspects of their lives. There was a significant gap between their willingness to provide their testimony and their reluctance to search for the documents that would serve as proof of the damages suffered. There was also a gap between their political attachment to the movement and their pragmatic outlook on life. According to the lawyers who worked on these cases, some people were worried that receiving compensation would mean accepting a blood payment in exchange for their losses and betraying the main cause of the movement. Others were hesitant to reject the compensation out of fear of insulting the state. The more pragmatic applicants were worried that they would not receive the compensation they claimed because they had already generated expenses or made investments based on the expectation of receiving money from the state.

The lawyers were the crucial actors in this political and legal process. They drafted standardized petitions that often consisted of a short explanation of the loss claimed accompanied by a list of the damaged or lost properties. Where applicable, they included the names of the dead or injured and the requested amount of compensation for material and intangible losses. In most of the applications, the perpetrators were not identified. While some of the lawyers attributed responsibility to the Turkish Armed Forces, others decided not to do so for pragmatic reasons. This concealment was based on rumors that applications which stated that the evacuation of the villages was handled by the Turkish Armed Forces were denied or delayed indefinitely. The effects of these rumors were magnified by the parallel implementation of another procedure that took place over the course of residents' return to the villages.[4] In order to obtain the official permit of entry to the villages, displaced villagers were obliged to indicate that that the village had been evacuated by PKK militants. In the view of the applicants and their lawyers, people who had signed these statements before applying for compensation received larger awards.[5] This was one of the main rules of the "market for protection" (cf. Shah 2010:166) whereby the state promised protection in the form of "nonthreat" in exchange for signatures that would provide legal protection for the Turkish state against the accusations that it had violated international agreements.

The villagers were all aware of the implicit rules of negotiation that the state imposed on returnees, which involved signing statements that identify the PKK as the perpetrator, volunteering to collaborate with the military, and voting for the government party. However, they were not sure about the legal implications of the Compensation Law and how it differed from the previous projects of the government concerning the return to the villages. The intervention of lawyers as mediators in the procedure, the absence of a legal setting where they could provide their testimony, and the lack of an official apology or acknowledgment of the incidents of evacuation and displacement obscured the terms and conditions of submitting to the law as well as the meaning and the long-term implications of receiving compensation. In this political context, the applicants perceived compensation as another form of charity supported by the EU. The imaginary of connection between the state as the charity giver and the EU as the funder blurred their understanding of the implications of the law. They were not sure who was paying for their losses and damages or who they would have to take to the court if they decided to reject the payment. Despite their suspicion of the purpose of the law, the main concern of the villagers remained focusing on the resources and ascertaining how to get the greatest amount of compensation in the shortest time. They were again in the same dilemma: how should one get one's share from state resources without fully submitting to the state, without fully being visible or legible?

Makbule, a fifty-year-old Kurdish woman, was living with her children in a town on the Syrian border. She was brought to the village by her mother-in-law and married to her husband when she was thirteen. Her husband's family became involved in the struggle early on. She said, "I came to the village without knowing anything about it [the struggle]. I grew up witnessing death and disappearance, first that of my husband and then those of my brothers-in-law and nephews." She left her village with her extended family in 1993 after her husband was found dead. Soon after, the entire village was evacuated and her family's home and fields were burned. She was the sole breadwinner, caring for her children with the help of her in-laws. Makbule was politically active and took part in all of the demonstrations and meetings organized by the pro-Kurdish party. She felt that after everything that happened to her family, she had nothing to lose: "I walk in the front row at every demonstration. The police know me, and I know them."

When asked about the possibility of returning to the village, she recalled the rumors that she had heard about recent returnees: "We cannot return. The soldiers would not allow anyone from my family to settle in the village again. They not only burned our house, they bombed it—they destroyed it. From time to time, we go there to pick fruit from the remaining trees and visit relatives who recently returned." Makbule was aware of the Compensation Law. She had heard about it from her brother-in-law. She gave him the documents required for the application that he said he would submit on behalf of his father for the whole family. She expected to receive her share: "Before my brother-in-law was killed, he told me that he would apply to Europe to ask for money for our damaged property. He asked me to give him the deed to the property that I had inherited from my husband. I did as he asked. However, after he applied on behalf of the whole family, he was killed. When I spoke with the lawyers, I learned that his application had been accepted by the commission and that his wife would receive all of the money for the property, including that which belonged to me and my children."

Makbule was not clear on the legal and bureaucratic details of the application process or the source of the compensation. Information about the Compensation Law was conflated with other "rights" discourses that involve filing an application with the European Court of Human Rights and seeking recognition of the violation in Europe. Like many displaced Kurdish villagers, Makbule thought that "Europe" is the agent to recognize the violation of rights and grant compensation while the state is the agent of negotiation in "exchange" and in "return" for rights. She was not aware of the terms of the law that required that she renounce the right to engage in future litigation. Based on her experience of surviving the war, she knew that one should be aware of the terms for receiving anything from the state. "We know how our neighbors have returned to the village," she said. "They do not want to admit it, but they signed the papers that say that the PKK did it. They signed them and resettled. They signed them and they got the money." What was immoral for Makbule was not to receive the money from the state. As the sole breadwinner of the house, she was desperate to get her share from her sister in-law. What was not acceptable for her was to get the money in exchange for signing the documents that declared the PKK as responsible for the evacuations. She was in peace knowing that given his political commitment, his brother-in law would not do that. She did not want to think otherwise.

Rıza Bey was in a similar limbo. He also lost his house during the evacuation of his village and was committed to the resistance movement. He grew up in western Turkey and moved back to his village after the conflict began. His was the first house to be burned in the village with all his belongings inside. The family moved to the closest city. During that period, his daughter joined the PKK. In 2000, he helped the migrant association make a documentary about his village. This was the first documentation of the burning of his house and the evacuation. When some of the villagers wanted to return to their homes after the year 2000, they were asked to sign statements indicating that the PKK was responsible for their losses. "I did everything I could to convince the villagers not to sign those statements," he said. "I went back and forth every day. But I could not convince them. They signed the agreements, and when they applied for damages under the Compensation Law, the ones who had signed those documents got more money." According to Rıza Bey, after the villagers returned, everyone and everything was different. Even, the most nationalist villagers (Kurdish nationalists) were now trying to get along with the korucus. Despite his resentment toward the returnees, he also filed an application to claim damages for what he lost during and after the evacuation of his village.

> Most of the field that belonged to us was already confiscated by the state and registered as state property. I did not have proof of all of the belongings I had in the house. I thought about rejecting the money and taking the file to the European Court of Human Rights, but if the state paid compensation, that means that the state accepted its respon-

sibility for burning all of the villages. If the state accepted its responsibility, then I thought I could not take my case to the European Court
of Human Rights any longer, so I accepted 1,000 Turkish liras. But
this is not about money. No matter how much they pay, it will not
bring back what we lost in this war. At this point, I trust neither the
state nor the people here.

Ahmet Bey had similar anxieties about his new life in the village. He believes that people returned for different reasons. Some wanted to take back
their land while others had political motivations. Regardless of their reasons,
they were asked to identify which side they had supported during the conflict and prove their loyalty to the state. Soon after he returned, he began to
struggle with the implicit rules of negotiation imposed by the state. He was
forced to collaborate with the military and asked to act as the local informant.
He refused to take on that role. After few months, the soldiers entered his
house by force, claiming that he was hiding weapons and bombs. "They found
bombs in my house, but I wasn't the one who hid them there," he said. "That
was the cost of refusing to collaborate. However, they could not prove anything." He was imprisoned and released five months later without a convic-
tion. He was not willing to give up his struggle to survive in the village. He
made basic repairs to the house and received free building materials as part
of the government aid distributed to those who wanted to return. Before he
was imprisoned, he submitted his application and supporting documents to
the lawyers in the Human Rights Association (İnsan Hakları Derneği) He
never received a response. However, he discovered that a family that had lived
in the same neighborhood after the evacuation received a huge amount of
money for land that did not belong to them. How did they do it? Ahmet Bey
was trying to leave the experience of imprisonment behind. His new challenge was to find out how to make use of the state resources. The life of a returnee was inscribed on a thin line between the struggle to get settled and
the challenge of existing as a political and legal being without being subjected
to violence. Returnees struggle against being displaced again physically and
emotionally, and the foe was not only the state. In this context of political
uncertainty, neighbors, fellow villagers, and family members could all become enemies, establishing alliances with different faces of the state in order
to receive immunity and protection in exchange for their loyalty.

From the perspective of human rights lawyers, the state has been the only
winner in this situation. The passage of the law allowed it to escape the

political scrutiny of transnational organizations as well as the major expenses related to the payment of sizable awards ordered by the ECHR. If the applicants had declined the friendly settlements, the files would have been taken to the administrative courts and the damage assessment commissions would have been stripped of their function. More significantly, the court system would have been incapable of dealing with the excessive number of cases, which would have justified recourse to the European Court of Human Rights. The political aspirations of the human rights activists were not fulfilled. The applicants accepted their compensation with a pragmatic attitude and the expectation of gaining access to state resources that they perceived as a form of charity given their awareness of the market of violence. Lawyers often signed the friendly settlements on behalf of their clients. The political commitment to documenting the truth was blended with the dream of obtaining cash and getting their share. This in turn made them major stakeholders in the economy of reparation. The law was valid for a finite period and the conflict was suspended for a time. The uncertainty of the future gave way to the opportunism of the present. It is within this political context that the Compensation Law reproduced symbolic and material relationships between Kurds and the Turkish state based on a history of bribery, disavowal, abuse, and subversion.

Recovery of Compensation Cases

The process for applying for compensation for the injuries suffered between 1987 and 2004 ended in 2008. However, the Compensation Law remained the sole legal instrument for providing reparations for all future material damages resulting from "terrorism" and the "fight against terrorism." After 2004, military and police officers, korucus, and civilians who suffered material and intangible damages would be subject to the terms and conditions of the Compensation Law and would have to submit petitions to the damage assessment commissions instead of taking the matters to court.

There was also a second form of compensation that underpinned the relationship between the Turkish state and Kurdish citizens. It was known as compensation recovery cases. These cases involved compensation paid by the state to members of the Armed Forces for injuries and losses incurred during the fight against the PKK beginning in the 1990s. These transactions have never fully settled the matters in question, but instead have led to a new cycle of litigation in which the Ministry of Defense or Ministry of Interior Affairs as the payer of the compensation sues the other party in the conflict, in this context, the pro-Kurdish party activists or the PKK guerrillas, in order to recover the compensation that the state had paid to the police or the military officer or to their families.

These cases were not grounded in special articles of the Anti-terror Law or the Compensation Law. The right to litigation for compensation recovery was instead based on Article 41 of the Law of Obligations (Borçlar Hukuku), which states: "A person who wrongfully harms another intentionally, negligently or imprudently is under the obligation to compensate the other party for this harm." This provision is mostly used by insurance companies to recover any compensation they make to their policyholders from a third party when the responsibility of the third party has been proven. A classic example is a traffic accident in which the policyholder has little or no fault and the liability of a third party is established. The state adopts a similar logic. Acting like an insurance company, it uses this procedure to regulate its relationship with its citizens in cases concerning material and intangible damages incurred as a result of acts that were committed during political protests, marches, and demonstrations. In the case of injured Armed Forces personnel, the state pays compensation to its staff members and then recovers it from third parties whose actions have been proven to have caused the damage to public property and officers.

The compensation recovery case process is as follows: first, the ministry sends the file to the lawyers at the Treasury Department with accompanying information on the identities of the perpetrators allegedly involved in the incident against the Turkish Armed Forces. The lawyers investigate the financial situation of the accused person or people and document all of their assets. They then file a lawsuit with the civil court (hukuk mahkemesi), wherein the accused is asked to cover the compensation that has been paid to military staff. The lawyers start the legal procedure prior to the final decision of the criminal court (ceza mahkemesi) that determines the responsibility of the accused person for the claimed deeds. However, the final verdict of the civil court relies on the decision of the criminal court. Should the criminal court find the defendant responsible for the injury and penalize the defendant, the civil court immediately finalizes the case and forces the accused to make a payment to the relevant ministry. The payment is meant to include reimbursement for the compensation with interest and the court expenses. The consecutive decisions of the criminal and civil courts turn the accused into both a criminal and a debtor. His or her debt becomes an inclusive and inevitable part of his or her sentence. Yet the life of this debt is not contingent on the life of the militant. The debt stands even if the militant died at the scene of the incriminating event, or afterward.

His or her name remains on the list of responsible parties included in the file sent to lawyers by the ministry. The fact that the person's responsibility for the alleged injury has not and cannot be investigated and judged at the criminal court does not block the ministry's request to file a compensation recovery claim. While the decision on the criminal responsibility of the dead militant for the act is put on hold, the state uses the civil law to perpetuate the crime-punishment-debt relationship: it forces the militant's family, usually the parents, to take responsibility for their child's deeds. Following the orders of the ministry, state lawyers track down the heirs of the militant and bring a lawsuit against them in the civil court, seeking repayment of the lingering debt, which would amount to the recovery of the compensation paid by the state to the Armed Forces.

According to human rights lawyers, despite the complicated implications of these practices, the state has not broken the law. Rather, in the absence of the accused militant, the state has circumvented the general principle of the criminal law (ceza hukuku) that stipulates the connection between the individual, the crime, and the punishment and instead justifies its claim on the basis of the inheritance law (miras hukuku), which rules that heirs inherit both assets and liabilities, including the debt of the deceased. The liability for the debt was what made them subject to the verdict of the civil court for the reimbursement of the compensation. Through compensation recovery cases, the state has been using the force of the law to redefine the connection between the families and the dead militant, between the heirs and the corpse, and to craft forced ties through the legally invented relationship of indebtedness. In this context, the families of Kurdish guerrillas are imprisoned by debt until they find the means to pay the state.

This confinement has neither spatial nor temporal limits. Once these files are opened by state lawyers, they remain open until the debt is paid. The state generates urgency around the recovery of the compensation paid to military or police officers or their families by requiring state lawyers to bring these cases to the court within one year of receiving the files from the ministry. Should the lawyers miss the deadline, they fall into the status of debtors and are held liable for the damages. Despite the pressure applied by the state, compensation recovery cases take a long time to close. Reaching the families can be difficult because they tend to be scattered or to have settled outside Turkey. Some do not register their current address. The trials often take place without the presence of the family members. State lawyers appear in court as claimants representing the ministry, and most families are not notified. They often learn about the debt only upon receipt of a letter containing the terms of the final verdict, which can come years after the death of their children. The closure of the cases can also be delayed due to the continuous deferral of the final verdict by judges who avoid making decisions that go against the will of the state, leaving the case in limbo for an unlimited period of time. In the interim, the parents of the dead militant might pass away and in turn leave younger members of the family liable. Their inheritance includes both the memory of past violence and the future debt of siblings who died in the war against the state.

Upon receiving the final verdict, the families can choose to follow one of two paths. First, they are advised to apply for the renunciation of inheritance (reddi miras), which involves disclaiming their legal connection to their children and hence the obligation to inherit their debt. This route has a temporal constraint, as the renunciation can only be done within a certain period of time after the death of the person. More significantly, the families often feel divided between the urgency to escape the heavy burden of the debt and the desire to remain loyal to the memory of their children. They are also informed that they have a right to appeal the decision of the Civil Court to the Council of State (Danıştay). Such appeals can be based on a lack of evidence for the injuries and the alleged crime or fault of the dead militant.[6] If their appeal is refused, they are forced to pay the debt including court fees, the compensation paid to the military or police officers or their families, and the interest that accumulated starting on the day that the transaction between the state and the injured families was initiated. If the family does not have assets or other financial means that can be appropriated, they are given the status of "aciz" (not able). Even this status as someone who does not own property does not exempt them from the debt. The file is never closed. The debt does not vanish. It lingers behind the scenes, continues living and breathing in the files, and inhabits the past, present, and future of the family as the material ghost of protracted violence.

The Treasure Department requires its lawyers to return to the file every five years and reinvestigate the financial conditions of the "aciz" family to see whether the family members have accumulated any means that could be confiscated in order to settle the debt. The lawyers follow orders. Before they move to their next post, they leave notes in the folders reminding their successors of the time line to be followed in order to reactivate the process of hunting down the debtors. As the gatekeepers of the law, state lawyers continue to wait for the reemergence of the debtor.

I suggest that the analysis of state violence in Turkey requires looking into legal practices related to the political economy of conflict, which in turn involves revisiting the relationship between loss, compensation, and debt. Through the implementation of the Compensation Law and compensation recovery cases, the state has effectively operated as if it were an insurance company, generating new forms and domains of debt-producing management and creating its own internal mechanisms of investment in death. This mode of compensation-debt economy has served the redistributive logic of the neoliberal state, which accumulates capital through dispossession, effectively continuing its war against the opposition by economic means (Harvey 2004:64–65). The state used the Compensation Law to dispossess those who had suffered losses during the conflict of the right to appeal to a transnational institution for justice. It also managed to standardize its own compensation system—at rates much lower than those used by the ECHR—and calculate the economic and political costs of death and life in the context of "the fight against terrorism." This maneuver functions as an effective way of reducing the official expenses spent by way of compensation and, as envisioned and stated in the preamble of the Compensation Law, to "prevent the sudden enrichment of the applicants" who filed claims to the ECHR. In this political context, the rule of recovery (rücu) operates as a complementary practice, supporting the accumulation logic of the neoliberal state that redistributes capital by converting the compensation paid to the Armed Forces into the debt that would be paid by the Kurdish families of dead militants.

David Graeber (2011:121) defines debt "as an exchange that has not been brought to completion." Debt brings inequality into relationships and creates a forced bond between two parties such that they cannot walk away from each other. Yet, Graeber notes, "There is no such thing as a genuinely unpayable debt. . . . We call it a 'debt' because it can be paid, equality can be restored, even if the cost may be death by lethal injection" (120–121). Maurizio Lazzarato makes a counterargument that in contemporary capitalist societies, "debt is a promise of repayment and therefore concerns open and indeterminate time, the radical uncertainty of the future which the logic of probabilities cannot anticipate or control" (2015:86–87). With the formation of states, empires, and monotheistic religions, Lazzarato (77–78) argues, debt becomes unpayable, is unreimbursable, and turns into life debt. The relationship between creditor and debtor is continuously sustained with the extension of capital and is never settled as it enables political domination and economic exploitation. Hence debt can never be paid through "monetary reimbursement," but only, as he emphasizes, with reference to Walter Benjamin, through "political redemption" (84).

Following Lazzarato's critical analysis, I argue that the debt the families in these cases are made to pay is also unpayable. It is not reimbursable. Using the rule of recovery, the state produces legal violence that mortgages the past, present, and future of the families. The state uses the relationship of indebtedness to disclaim its responsibility for the loss of lives and to pass the cost of that violence on to its opponents. Legal violence seeks to transform all losses into material transactions between debtors and creditors. It establishes the families as subjects who are accountable for the pain and losses that they suffer and forces them to take responsibility for actions that are not their doing. While the Compensation Law justifies the monopoly of the state to execute and then repair the effects of violence, punishment through compensation recovery instills guilt and fear through a relationship of indebtedness. While the Compensation Law erases the accountability of the state and sets the rule of the friendly settlement in exchange for the renunciation of the right to litigation, the compensation recovery cases create an unmovable and permanent relation between the state and families of the dead militant as the inheritors of punishment in the form of debt.

The state uses law and debt to channel the force of the past on the present and future and redefine the limits and form of continuity and responsibility between citizens and generations. In this context, neither the state nor the military and police officers were imprisoned for violent acts that caused the destruction of the environment and lives of Kurdish citizens. Nor were their families held responsible for the compensation paid to the Kurdish citizens who applied for and received compensation in exchange for the loss that they incurred during the conflict. Only Kurdish citizens were held responsible for the acts of their older and younger relatives and held liable for the recovery of any compensation that was paid.

The bodies of dead militants were often not returned to the families; they either disappeared or were buried by PKK militants or the Armed Forces in unknown locations. Families received the news of the deaths of their children through PKK networks and channels or an official letter from the government that registered and certified the death. These families were forced to

continue their lives suspended between mourning for their loss and melan-
cholia for the absence of the grave. Even though the person responsible for
the action was absent, and even in cases in which no body was made available for burial, the state used the rule of inheritance and recovery to define
what would live on from that incident and what would haunt the people who
were left behind. As the rule of inheritance became the key component of this
forced contract, its renunciation became the only clear path to escaping the
obligation of this bond. In other words, the erasure of the legal debt was con-
ditioned on the parents' renunciation of their bond with their child. The
debtor-creditor relationship would be voided through the legal dissolution
of the parent-child relationship. The state was offering another opportunity
for closure by forcing the families to disown their children, which would in
turn mean disowning their connections to themselves.

In June 2015, the city of Mardin was immersed in the victorious atmosphere of the general elections, which had ended with the unexpected victory of the pro-Kurdish People's Democracy Party (HDP) and resulted in significant losses for the AKP. This was a moment of consolidation of the city's political choices, as the HDP had also won in the local elections a few years back. Those Arabs, Syriacs, and Kurds who had voted for the HDP this time around were in the process of rearranging their position, shifting their historical and political antagonism into a form of proximity and solidarity. The political will for an alternative form of coexistence was real, as real as they could bring themselves to believe in. There was both hesitancy and suspicion. At the time, no one could predict what would happen to the city under the full hegemony of the Kurds, or, more significantly, what would happen to the peace process once Erdoğan had lost his majority.

In parallel, the war in Rojava was going on at full strength, attracting many youngsters across the city and the region to its cause. The war would come to occupy and overwhelm both the spaces of hope in the future and the place of death in the present. In June 2015, the members of MAYA-DER, an association grouping together those who had lost relatives in Mesopotamia, were on alert. Huddled inside their office, they watched the news from Syria, expecting each next phone call to report another local resident who had recently lost his or her life Rojava, along with instructions about when and where the deceased's family should pick up the body. Local representatives of the state were turning a blind eye to the process, in practice allowing the delivery of bodies as if they had come from some far-off war in an unrelated location. In these final days of the fragile peace process, they were also turning a blind eye to attempts by HDP activists to set up cemeteries for PKK guerrillas in the skirts of Bagok Mountain.

In the meantime, the city was hosting the Mardin Bienal exhibition. The theme was *Myths*. The rooms of the old Armenian houses were filled with memorial art installations: photos of the houses' original owners and other residents of the houses. One of the installations featured a coffin against recorded laments sung by a deceased Armenian woman who had spent her life in a nearby village as a Muslim convert. The display explained that she had wanted these laments to be sung at her funeral, something that had not taken place. In 2015, years after her death, the woman's last wish was being fulfilled in an old Armenian house as an art installation of the Mardin Bienal on the very centenary of the 1915 Armenian genocide. June would be the final month of mourning for these ungrieved lives, even if mourning as a public act had condensed into performance rather than felt grief.

The signs that the peace process was stagnating in the region were there, but nobody really predicted how stagnation would unfold. A month and a half after the election, in July 2015, a suicide bomb attack by ISIS in Suruç, a border town on the Turkish side, resulted in the death of thirty-three members of the Federation of Socialist Youth Associations. These university students were on their way to Rojava—to help reconstruction efforts in Kobane and had stopped in Suruç to make a press statement. Their assassination was followed by the killing of two policemen in another border town, Ceylanpınar, two days later. This second assassination was claimed by a self-organized group, the Apocu Fedailer (known in English as the Apoist Team of Self-Sacrifice) who argued that the assassinated two policemen had been acting in connivance with the ISIS forces. The PKK, which initially appeared to endorse the attack, subsequently declared that the official PKK had had no involvement whatsoever in the second event.[1]

These happenings triggered a spiral of unchecked violence. This was not a return to the conflict of the 1990s but a new type of war fostered by transformed conditions, ideologies, and practices that had developed in the previous fifteen years (Ertür and Martel 2016). The war theatre had shifted from the mountains where guerrillas hid to the towns and cities s in the Kurdish region that had declared "democratic autonomy," a status coined by the leader of the PKK, Abdullah Öcalan. Democratic autonomy amounted to a paradigm shift within the tactics of the Kurdish movement: rather than a continuation of the struggle for a Kurdish state, it called on local political actors of the Kurdish movement to establish stateless spaces, involving their own legal, educational, economic, and defense systems, through the setting up of elementary schools, courts, and alternative economies (Akkaya and Jongerden 2013; Jongerden and Akkaya 2016; Darıcı 2015, 2016; Leezenberg 2016).

Democratic autonomy was not a recent idea. Over the course of the previous decade, it had been much discussed as a new form of political practice in the Kurdish region. The circulation of discourse about democratic autonomy and the mobilization of political activists in urban areas had by then already led to mass imprisonments in both the eastern and western parts of Turkey (Mandıracı 2016). Within an increasingly hostile political scenario and lacking the organized political cadres required to develop the legal, educational, and economic systems that would make such an alternative system of governance possible, the discourse had become idle and contentless. However, in southeastern Turkey, in the aftermath of the Suruç bombing, HDP mayors and other activists declared the status of democratic autonomy in specific towns and neighborhoods. Consequently, democratic autonomy became a radical call to battle for the politicized youth of many towns and neighborhoods, who confronted the police using stones and Molotov cocktails in order to materialize a self-governance movement (Darıcı 2016). These youths generated the Patriotic Revolutionary Youth Movement (Yurtsever Devrimci Gençlik Hareket)—took on the responsibility of defending these autonomous spaces and became the frontline actors in the war against the Turkish state in the region (Darıcı 2015, 2016).

The war then took on the form of a round-the-clock, uninterrupted curfew whereby civilians were forced to live, bear witness, and survive in the midst of continual cross fire between the Kurdish youth and Turkish security forces. Neighborhoods turned into open battlegrounds the security forces could not enter due to deep trenches excavated by the armed youth. This prompted the Turkish state to bulk up the operation by sending in military and police reinforcements, leading both to fierce violence, the destruction of infrastructure and buildings, and the loss of many lives (Amnesty International 2016b; Office of the United Nations 2017).

Locals, unable to bury their loved ones who had perished in the cross fire during the curfew, were forced to live together with their dead (Zengin 2015). It became a physically and emotionally complicated mission to reach the dead bodies of the youth. Families would go from hospital to hospital, leave their DNA samples, and wait for the prosecutor's call informing them where their relatives had been interred. People who had died in Nusaybin were buried some 650 kilometers away, in Erzurum, while those who had perished in Cizre were buried 400 kilometers away in Elâzığ, in existing cemeteries that are customarily used to inter people who do not have relatives (Söylemez 2016). There were still other cases where DNA samples had been mixed up and matched with the wrong bodies, where the families had been called to identify their children, thus coming face-to-face with a grotesque error committed by a state nurse, a doctor, a technician, or someone in a forensic lab. These mismatches demanded amendment,[2] which in turn required filling in forms, making requests, and waiting long hours in corridors of morgues. The state had created a new bureaucracy around these bodies, one that framed them as not to be found, not to be recognized, not to be grieved. Families then strove to undo this procedure, subjecting themselves to all sorts of ethical encounters with state bureaucrats. "How many of these children have died? I want to know. I want to count them. How many?" asked a friend who had spent the 131 days of the curfew without leaving her home in Nusaybin.

Gleaning the Aftermath Through Messaging

The final curfew ended in July 2016, marking the loss of the battle. The PKK guerrillas withdrew from the cities and moved the conflict back into the mountains. Buildings in the conflict areas were demolished, whether they had been damaged or not. The neighborhoods of war were cleared of anything personal—bodies, houses, cemeteries. All were ruined equally, the new and old dead all jumbled together under the rubble of the buildings. The state transformed these areas into construction sites for houses built by TOKI, the Mass Housing Administration, and changed the norms for compensation payments. As a result, people could only make claims on the basis of Compensation Law 5233 for damage to personal belongings within the houses, not for the immovable property itself. The state agreed to reimburse the damages of the immovable property by allocating a TOKI house to the claimant. If the value of the TOKI house was higher than that of the damaged building, the property owner would be offered credit to pay the difference. In this way, claimants became indebted to the state (Amnesty International 2016; Housing and Land Rights Network 2016).

I did not visit the region in this period. I was in London, keeping myself sane with the hopeful patience of an expectant mother, writing this book on the politics of life before the war resumed. Between July 2015 and February 2017, I kept in touch with my friends through WhatsApp calls and conversations. Most of my friends were from the city of Mardin. Although the city was not under curfew, it was only fifty to a hundred kilometers from other towns that were kept under curfew for months. Mardin was also the head-quarters of the new war, accommodating large numbers of police and military stations, residences, hospitals for the dead and wounded from both sides, and a temporary population of displaced peoples from the surrounding towns.

Our first WhatsApp conversations began immediately after July 2015. Ayşe wrote to me in August: "Mardin is like a ghost town. All the hotels have been shut down. There is a huge silence. There were a few, small-scale pro-tests on the new road, but now even they are quiet. The phones are not work-ing properly. The internet connection is very slow. They say that they will install receivers at specified locations. We are being watched. We are being followed." She continued, "People are leaving the town for İzmir, Istanbul. Mostly Arab families are leaving. They are full of rage against the Kurds. They say, 'We gave our city to Kurds. We served it to them on a golden tray. Now they are everywhere. This is not a place to live any longer.' I am tired of ar-guing with them. It gives me a headache. I've lost all faith in people."

"We can't communicate," another friend wrote. "We either live in silence or in the loud voice of *heval* ['friends' in Kurdish, referring to the activists of the pro-Kurdish party]. They tell us how to feel, how to see, and what to do. They tell us how to understand this war. They tell us how they have gone through equally bad days before and how they managed to survive back then. They make me feel alienated. I feel like a stranger in this town. I've lost my voice. I don't know what to think any longer." The same day, she sent me a photo of a family—friends we had in common—standing in front of a su-permarket. "There is a pause in the curfew for few hours. They will shop and return to Nusaybin," she wrote. "Why do they return? Why do they go back to the curfew area?" I asked. She responded a few hours later. "Would I re-turn? I don't know. I can understand why they do it." Silence. A few weeks later, I wrote to her on the day the prominent human rights lawyer Tahir Elçi was killed in Diyarbakır. "Are you in Diyarbakır?" I asked. "I am in the morgue," she answered.

A month later, she sent another long message. "Yesterday evening, the left-ist trade union held a demonstration. We were forty people in total. It was a great protest. It started at 12:03 and ended at 12:09. Six full minutes. No po-lice, no journalists. Not a single one. That pissed me off." I asked why the police had been absent, speculating "Maybe, they want to leave spaces for a few minutes of breathing. Maybe they know that such acts will not cause any mobilisation." She interrupted me. "Maybe they"—referring to the security forces—"just slapped us with the big lie on the face, the one we live in and make ourselves believe in. And we are so blind that we can't even recognize it. I can't even breathe during these demonstrations. Half of those people in the crowd"—referring to the pro-Kurdish party activists—"don't feel anything. At the end of the day, do they really care who is dying over there?" I could not respond. I could not even ask a question. I was out of context. She went back to her silence again, leaving me with her frustration and my own curiosity regarding the murkiness of the situation.

We could not communicate. The language between us had collapsed. I was convinced that it was no longer possible to understand what was happening. Who were these youth? What was happening behind the trenches in those towns that had remained under curfew for months? What was the purpose of this war? I stopped looking at the images and news on social media. All conversations over WhatsApp turned into small talk of everyday routines, sounding and feeling as though they were outside the zone of explosions.

The curfew in the Sur neighborhood of Diyarbakır ended in March 2016. That same week, my second daughter was born. We named her Irene, *peace* in Greek, Mara, *one of us* in Zaza, a Kurdish dialect. A few weeks later, I began again with WhatsApp communication, sending photos of Irene Mara to my friends in the region, sharing with them the kind of hope that had filled me with her arrival. I yearned to break out of the asphyxiating sensation of being voiceless, out of this life lived, even in my separate and distant space in London, within the unspoken normalcy of violence.

I came up with the idea of us informing one another of our everyday lives through the use of images and sound files. The idea was to create an archive and a shared common memory so as to resist the normalization of violence. A close friend started sending images and sound recordings from ordinary spaces and times carved out of the city's emergency. Not regularly. Whenever he encountered them, whenever he remembered, whenever he wanted to get out of that space. Images of high cement walls surrounding police stations, police residences, military zones. The sounds of ambulances. As emblems of daily life in the new war, a montage of short films depicting the movements of riot control vehicles (toplumsal olaylara müdahale aracı, TOMA), funeral cars, and earth diggers, all in the same frame. Images of blocked routes and roads in the wake of each explosion that residents physically felt or heard about.

Then came the photos of new cafés and breakfast places that had opened across the city. Café Pause was decorated all over with colorful umbrellas. "Café Pause. Notice the name," wrote my friend in his WhatsApp message. Then another photo followed of a stone house transformed into a branch of a well-known breakfast café chain restaurant from Diyarbakır. "The one in Diyarbakır is closed after curfew hours. So now people are coming to Mardin to have breakfast," he said in his note. We finish our exchanges with few references to emotion. In the archives, messages summarizing the sadness, anger, irritation, laughter over our confused feelings are rare.

Several days later, more photos arrived of the alleys of Mardin. Mimarbaşı Sarkis Lole Street as noted earlier, the street named after a famous local Armenian architect, had also been covered with colorful umbrellas. What did color mean in the midst of this violence? Who was insisting on covering the empty stone streets of Mardin with these umbrellas? Was this some surreal disavowal of what had been taking place? A few months later, my friend sent images of posters about an event entitled "A Meeting of Storytellers in Mardin" with a note saying, "I listened to the story of Mem û Zin [a well-known classic Kurdish love story] in a coffeehouse covered with Atatürk posters. The owner is a guy with a tattoo of three crescent moons [the symbol of the Turkish ultranationalist party]. The event ended with the slogan 'Peace will come through the old stories.' The shop owners were the happiest in the audience; they had had a chance to sell some of their wares."

News and images arrived about some explosions on the road to Kızıltepe, a town just fifteen kilometers outside of Mardin, and then another inside the town just before the Ramadan celebrations. "I passed by the point of the explosion half an hour ago," a friend wrote. "I was lucky. People in the area returned to their shopping few hours later." There were images of luxurious cars at night celebrating the Beşiktaş football team's victory. Further news and videos came in about the opening of a night club, Sefa, in the old city, frequented mostly by the children of Kurdish landowners.

The last to come were snapshots of the biggest mosque, situated in the city's public square, by the park. Named after one of the wealthiest families from a nearby town, who had funded its construction, the permission to build the mosque in the middle of the central public park had been issued by Ahmet Turk, the prominent Kurdish politician and former mayor of the province of Mardin. The park had recently been renamed 15th of July Democracy, after the 2016 coup attempt. Life was tranquil under the new state of emergency.

The city of Mardin was only so far from the towns and villages that lived under curfew.

Returning to Mardin

In early 2017, I returned to the city of Mardin during yet another interlude, this time between the lifting of curfews in the towns and cities and the staging of a referendum on the new constitution. The military conflict was again playing out between PKK guerrillas and the Turkish military in mountainous areas and villages, some just ten to fifteen kilometers outside Mardin. Those municipalities governed by the HDP had been seized by the state. Mardin's municipal workers, the provincial mayor and co-mayors of the city were arrested, as were the mayors of other Kurdish towns and cities in the region. The provincial vice governor had been installed as mayor and more than half of the city's previous employees, all of whom had been pro-Kurdish party activists, had been fired. The municipality building was moved to another site at the edge of the city, across from the military barracks.

This was my first visit to Mardin while the city was under a "state of emergency," declared after the coup attempt of 15 July 2016. It was my first time experiencing the city in close proximity to the tangible effects of violence. How could I draw a distinction between the near and the far, the intimate and the public, the past and present when violence was taking place every day via legal and nonlegal means? My friends were expressing their sense of confinement in fragments as follows:

"I can't breathe."

"They have weakened our will and desire to live."

"We pretend as though we were dead."

"We are physically alive. But in fact we live like the dead in this occupied city."

"I am unhappy, we are unhappy. Each time, I believed that it couldn't get any worse than this. It did."

"We are all thinking about the same thing. We are all talking about the same thing. All the tables in this café are covered with whispers, covered with mumbles. We have accumulated and endured so much bad energy that we are ready to explode. We would in fact feel much better if we could explode. But we don't, we can't. I don't know how we continue to live, how we continue to bear it."

In February 2017, people's talk was frantic, punctuated by long silences and loud voices from the TV. The fare of daily small talk ranged from diets, hairdressers, concerts, and recently opened cafés or music halls to the latest news on the imprisonment and release of friends, relatives, and colleagues. The violence of the past two years was not spoken about. "Everything happened before our very eyes. We turned away, but we could not escape it. Our eyes saw it all," said a lawyer whom I spoke to. Being a witness to the brutality without having agency to stop it: they felt that this was the violence the war had subjected them to. There were no secrets, no hidden facts, no official discourse or practice to ensure that the violence would remain clandestine, covert, illegible. The state was explicit in enacting and justifying its violence. What was more open to speculation and both hurtful and frustrating were the positions of the HDP and the PKK about the war. What was the rationale for this war? Why had it been initiated and fought by the youth? What did they hope to gain from it? Why had they put citizens in this cross fire?

Meaning in what was lived and lost was lacking.. There was no space to move in under the state of emergency. There were not many activists left outside the prisons. Social life continued in the cafés, nightclubs, concerts, and shopping malls, without local or foreign tourists, yet with the odd visitor. The bus stop billboards were covered with the posters of an astrologist who conducted business in the shopping mall on Sundays, providing alternative narratives of the future for a people waiting without prospect or expectation.

The Arab locals were in a rush to return to their usual political positions, ones that served to differentiate them from what they considered to be the subversive, ignorant, wasteful Kurds. This was not their war. To them, this was a war among Kurds, a war between Kurds. Both the murderers and the victims were Kurds. What they were doing in the Kurdish towns was a crime. From their point of view, the state had and deserved to have a legitimate right to perpetrate violence in defence of sovereignty. Life without a strong state would be no different than life in today's war-torn Syria. Not to the mention the fact that the Kurds had wasted their one opportunity, provided to them via the support of other local communities. They had acted as though they were living in Kobane, Syria. They had lost the sense of what was expected of them. For the

Arab locals, the experience of the past two years had only served to reinforce the truth of their understanding of the Kurds, demonstrating that their assessments were not made from feelings of prejudice or superiority, but from an intimate knowledge of coexistence with the Kurds. "The Kurds have a saying: It is not me who knows all, but my gun," noted an elderly Arab Mardinite.

Hüseyin, a long-time resident of Mardin and one of the people involved in old house excavations, was waiting in front of his new restaurant nightclub. He was dressed in a suit and sported an AKP party badge and a Turkish flag pinned to his lapel. In this period of exception, he had found an opportunity to turn his coffeehouse into a restaurant. He was now an active member of the local branch of the AKP. Although he remained unconvinced about the party's discourse and wary of the new methods of occupation in the city, he was fully aware of the necessity of staying within the vicinity of its supporters. Already the owner of two shops in the city in addition to the new restaurant in the Old City, Hüseyin spent his entire day participating in AKP meetings, and waiting in a queue to apply for aid for his children's education. He had also managed to get the support of the Mardin Museum for the restoration of his house.

He was taking all the right steps for the survival of his life spaces; the rest was unrelated to him. He thought that people arriving from cities under curfew—Cizre, Nusaybin—should return to their homes. If they didn't, the authentic urban life of Mardin would be quickly ruined by their alien rural presence. No reference to the events, curfews, dead youth, new security forces. Hüseyin preferred to stay within the safe discursive zone of the 1990s, not in the way he interpreted the return of violence, but in his views on the return of the other, the return of the Kurds as if they were the displaced villagers of 1990s. His concerns were grounded in the way the *gundi* (villager) began to take shape in the eye of a *bajari* (urbanite). Meanwhile, the Old City had become a ghost town of empty shops, the vacant, ruined stone buildings now mostly occupied by Syrian refugees, who had taken up what seemed to be permanent "temporary" residence there.

The excavation business continued, however. Or so said Veysi Bey, the prominent digger discussed earlier, during our last meeting. Excavators were careful about entering military zones. The Mesopotamian Plain was not as expansive as it used to be for the diggers, but it was possible to continue the practice within the Old City. Surrounded by a crowd of onlookers, tenants who had recently rented a stone house dug up the interior so as to reach the tunnels, until the wife of the owner noticed the strange commotion around the house.

During times when excavation could not take place, treasure hunters continued their business by selling items from their previous digs, such that the usual circulation of cash and invisible income did not disappear. As part of the war economy that continued relentlessly on both sides of the border, certain towns became known as marketplaces for the illicit trade in archaeological objects. While the market value of stone houses had plummeted and the construction economy was on the verge of collapse, excavation remained immune to the state of exception. Now new buyers were on the lookout for cheap property with the expectation of reselling it at a higher price in a few years' time when the violence reverted to nonviolence.

İsa Bey tried hard. Cultivating his strategy of resilience against the ever-changing conditions of the war, he invested his time and energy in planting and harvesting the land, diligently protecting the fragile order of his life. He wanted to believe that he could carry on without getting involved in events. He was sorry about people's suffering, and yet again, it was not his war. It had never been a war of Syriacs. He received fewer visitors from the diaspora abroad. The military and the local governor responded less and less to his calls for help against the usual harassment of the Kurdish villagers. They were "occupied with terrorism," the military officers kept telling him. Because İsa Bey's village was gradually slipping into the high-risk area of the map, they were not allowed to intervene. Still he documented every grape, sumac, and almond that the Kurdish villagers, his usual suspect list, stole from him.

İsa Bey left for Germany a year later upon the loss of his father and has been unable to return without leaving his mother alone. He has continued his struggle from afar, documenting the daily violations as told to him by his neighbors, korucus, and sending them to the same officials as before. This was a lost cause. As his korucu neighbors reentered the war, their alliance with the military was restored. The local forms of sovereignty that had existed before were reestablished, and as before, they had limited authority to execute exceptions. İsa Bey was forced to wait in Hamburg for the day he could return to Midyat.

"Nobody Wanted to Die. . . . Nobody Wanted to Take Responsibility"

My Kurdish friends were frustrated. They were speechless, in search of interpretations with which to make sense of the means and ends of violence to which they were now subject. They expressed their sense of loss either through a critique of HDP policies, at the time in control of the municipalities, or through an attachment to the Kurdish movement. In trying to save reason from the madness of collapse, they speculated. Was there space in this politics for critique? If so, why was the HDP-controlled municipal employee in charge of burial sites arrested on high corruption charges? Why had he been involved in corruption in the first place? Why was the degree of his corruption not moderate as was the case with members of other political parties? Why had the corruption involved funeral materials and not the purchase of flowers or trees? They bought coffins made of the cheapest drywall. Imagine what might have happened if a heavy corpse had fallen through the bottom of the coffin box. A friend circulated a YouTube video unrelated to the region of the scenario he had just described, for him a visual confirmation of his point. We were talking about death without referencing death. Could this be separated from terror's talk? Had everyone lost sight of the distinction between fact and fiction?

After watching the video together, we returned to politics from yet another angle. My friends, HDP voters and former municipal employees, were angry about the HDP-governed municipality's irresponsible actions, its negligence, its ignorance of the residents' needs. Most of the municipal employees hired under the party's governance were not even from Mardin, they complained, and knew nothing of the city's complicated social dynamics. Many municipal employees had been hired because of their close connection to or support for the mayor in blood feuds his tribal family had been involved in over the past thirty years. Or they were employed because they came from the families of PKK martyrs or from social circles connected to the higher echelons of the HDP. Municipal employment was given to relatives as recompense for their loss to PKK martyrdom and tribal blood feuds, thereby ensuring temporary access and a legal right to a regular salary. Moreover, municipal jobs secured social and political mobility and profit for the recipients, prompting further inequality, expectations, exploitations, and corruption. The jobs were like gifts between protectors and protégés.

None of the dynamics was new. They had evolved out of political mobilization taking place within the peace process. The already unequal power differentials were increasing due to the distribution of benefits and handouts by the AKP government, the HDP, and the PKK. The problem was that the distribution of cash in the form of salary and credit shifted the power relationships between party members. This is turn had transformative effects on the partisanship of political actors, contaminating and poisoning relationships. İlyas, a thirty-year-old Kurdish man, was also a vehement critic, holding the HDP and the PKK responsible for the loss of hard-won political and cultural rights secured over the course of the three preceding decades. As part of the generation of 1990, he had grown up not only witnessing the resistance, but living for it. He pointed to the dissolution of the common bonds militants and activists had for one another during his time: "We were disciplined and sensitive to the presence of danger, and we acted accordingly. The influential figures of the last phase haven't had our sense of responsibility to the people and the movement. They wanted to be heroes. They wanted the prestige without having to take responsibility for their actions."

İlyas formulated this critique in questions: What would happen if the worker in the gardening department was appointed as head of the municipal urban planning department? What would happen if a loan shark was accepted into the local branch of the party? Who had misinformed the PKK about the people's determination for democratic autonomy? Who convinced the youth to join in the fight? In İlyas's view, Mardin was nothing like Kobane: "Nobody was willing to die. Nobody was willing to lose. If a hundred thousand people had gathered together and surrounded Cizre, Nusaybin, and Sur, this would not have happened. People here didn't do what they did in Kobane. They didn't resist. They didn't give back. They didn't want the war."

Melek had similarly bitter feelings about what they had been forced to live through. She was a staunch activist who had given three decades to the cause. She had lost many friends and relatives over the years. She struggled to continue a normal life between the different phases of the conflict. She got married, had children, looked after her parents, took emotional care of her younger sisters and brothers, and worked temporary contracts to make ends meet. Despite her exasperation with the inner dynamics of the party, she never questioned her relationship to the movement. That was the one unbreakable component of her otherwise precarious life. In recent years, as she lost hope of gaining recognition for her dedicated party work, she had taken time out for her children instead. Yet she planned to return whenever she was called for duty, at this stage not for heroism, but out of loyalty to the people she had lost, respect for those who still fought, and enthusiasm for the possibility of autonomy.

She had difficulties, however, in understanding the ideas of Abdullah Öcalan. Living in such a patriarchal city, she never grasped the mechanics of how gender, class, and ethnic equality could be achieved at the local level.

She had read his writings, kept herself informed of the debates, attended the meetings. She never got the picture clear in her mind, subject as she was to all manner of life ruptures—the mass arrests of activists, the loss of jobs, the imprisonment of her brothers, events she was not willing to reveal. She had suffered from the hierarchy in the party. It was her deep attachment to the movement that served to put up with the sovereign presence of whichever pro-Kurdish party was then in vogue.

I met Melek at her house. Her town had not been under curfew and its residents did not support the PKK's decision to proclaim the town's autonomy. They had stated plainly that there was no strategic position from which to establish resistance within the town. Because the town was full of informants, there was no space to move, organize, or resist. Those least suspect turned out to be informants. This poisoned the sense of solidarity they had built together. During the bleakest period of the 1990s, people used to put themselves in harm's way just to protect the bodies of others. Now they would cower behind their closest friend if caught in cross fire.

Although Melek did not shirk responsibility—she responded whenever called to attend a meeting—she had lost all faith in the party. She was emotionally drained by the raw opportunism that ruled the town, she said. Many had made a huge profit from those who had needed to break the curfew. Others had raised the price of rental properties for the people who left their town and who needed a temporary place to stay. Extended families who could not afford a bigger place would stay in a single room together.

We began our exchange in her house. As the conversation got more intense, she spoke more softly, mumbling and whispering her account of the war scenes from the previous year. A friend being shot at the corner of her house. People throwing bags of donated food as a protest against HDP members of parliament. Conversations with her husband about what they would do with their children if the town were placed under curfew. She did not pause for breath, but continued as if in one long sentence.

I suggested we go out for some fresh air. Because going for a walk required a purpose, we decided to visit her brother, who was preparing for the opening of his book café. He was also a staunch activist, unemployed since his release from prison. This was his first attempt at setting up a business for himself, done with the support of his sister and friends. We spent a few hours discussing various options for the café's name and a potentially attractive menu. No talk of politics.

Cafés were the business of the day, carving out public spaces in the visible where people could go to sit, talk, and consume. We saw a few more cafés known as cake houses on the way to visit another brother her home, just beyond the military zone and the police residences hidden behind huge cement walls. You had to zigzag when following the green path that forces pedestrians to pass by these barbed wired, wall-like structures without getting too close. The path forced you to look at the military site as if it didn't exist, eyes avoiding the building altogether. The green security corridor ended with a cake house, one corner of which was covered with meter-long white ribbons hanging at the entrance and neon lights inside. Clean, fresh, and appetizing; surreal, frightening, and devoid of meaning.

Melek's second brother was there, sitting with his friends. He came out to greet us, joined us in our café talk. We compared the location of their brother's café with this one, discussed opportunities for setting up and improving the business. They were talking in a different tense, not the future tense. Everything was in the present, using the Turkish modals—the optative mood for expressing wishes (*dilek kipi*), the imperative mood for giving directions (*emir kipi*). How do you talk about an investment outside the future tense?

We arrived home at Melek's. One of her relatives was there, a young woman in her twenties sitting in the kitchen, looking through scraps of paper. Melek introduced us hastily. Handan was the daughter of Melek's cousin. She had lived with her family in Nusaybin. They had spent two months in Melek's house during the curfew, then returned to their home, Handan explained. "My father did not want to leave his house. He forced us to stay until the soldiers came and told us to evacuate that same day. We left the town under their escort but then returned home secretly. My father could not bear to stay anywhere else."

Handan was calm, talking and folding pieces of paper and putting them in an empty yogurt pot. She was learning German. She needed to pass the language exam in order to get a visa and join her husband there. They had married last November. Her dowry had already left for Germany but she was still there, studying German. She had written German words on the scraps of paper and was looking at them, trying to remember their Turkish translation: *brot* = *ekmek* (bread), *haus* = *ev* (house). She was supposed to memorize fifty words a day. Fifty words is a lot to learn in one day, I said. I was mesmerized watching her way of checking her homemade flash cards and talking about the curfew. I tried to guess the meaning of a couple of words, recalling my basic German, tried to think of what to say to her, or what not to say to her. The German language was an unexpected shield for the two of us. The common ground found in alienhood allowed us to bear the intimacy of our discussion without the need to speak in Turkish. We continued taking words in and out of the yogurt pot. I couldn't wait, though. Knowing what she had witnessed, I couldn't help myself. If what happened in Nusaybin was not a secret, what exactly did I want to know?

"Did you know that the curfew would start?" I asked. "Yes, we did, we were expecting it. We locked ourselves inside the houses and there came a point where we felt so restless that we just wanted it to happen, even if we had to die. And it did." The intonation of more German words punctuated her talk. "We had just the right amount of food. The day our meat stock came to an end, we were asked to evacuate the house."

"Now let me ask you, what do you think is the best way to learn a language?" she says.

"Try to learn fewer words and use them every day in written sentences or in small dialogues. Otherwise, you will too easily forget them."

"I could speak in German with my husband on the phone. That would help."

"Yes. It might. How did you find your house when you got back? Was it damaged?"

"Ours was in . . . good shape. It was set in between two buildings and there was no damage. We were lucky that they didn't use it. Some people found their entire house ruined or looted or covered in shit. There was a daughter and a mother. A bomb exploded when they opened the fridge."

Silence.

"It was like living in World War II. We witnessed a real war."

A real war. Her parents had returned to their house. She had no plans to do the same. She had to pass the exam. That was her only concern. Her life was waiting for her in Germany. The night passed in silence. We ate what Handan had cooked in the afternoon. She would have baked a cake had she not had homework to do. Melek and I sighed, looking at each other. The TV was loud, the Turkish channels announcing news about the recent military operations in our vicinity. We were surrounded with the invisible fire that nobody would talk about. Waiting in despair.

Melek's feelings went further than simply disappointment. She was angry with all the public figures, people who were part of the movement, local activists, parliamentarians from the pro-Kurdish party, PKK leaders. This was a waste of people, rights, places, hopes built up over the past thirty years. She felt emotionally displaced by what she had been left to witness. She was mourning not only the loss of those who died in the war only a short while before, but also the loss of the deep attachment she had had with the Kurdish movement that was still such a part of her.

She was lost in a void. "After what happened last year in Cizre and Nusaybin, I feel as though I've lost my God, lost my religion," she said. "I can't even bear to see their faces. Nobody took responsibility for what we went through. People were furious when the members of parliament visited towns under curfew. They felt that they had been abandoned. They felt that they were being abandoned."

She was also constantly asking herself questions about responsibility and reasons. "Whose decision was this? Why did they follow this path?" There were countless rumors. Some claimed that the locals from Kurdish towns sent loud messages to the PKK indicating that they could declare self-autonomy and defend their territory. Some claimed that the PKK had forced the people, especially the youth, to take action, telling them not to expect the resistance to be fought by the guerrillas alone. Some claimed that the PKK had initiated the battle on the Turkish side of the border in order to protect Rojava from Turkish Army attacks. Like many long-term activists, she was not convinced. That she could not convince herself was the existential crux of the war this time around.

The new war had altered the cost of the war for the Kurds. Over the long term, the cost was unjustifiable. They had been subjected not only to state violence, which they had grown up with, but also to the violence of the PKK. This last battle had ruined the prospects for a better life, the prospects of establishing an autonomous state. It had wrecked the future of a generation. Perhaps this was the "generation in debt" described by Leyla Neyzi and Haydar Darıcı (2015) with reference to those Kurdish youth brought up on a sense of indebtedness to the PKK for its struggle for independence. The "generation in debt" was now dead.

For some who had experienced the curfew, their critique of the violence lay in the materiality of its destruction. The cost of the war was measured not only in the intangible loss of Kurdish youth and the sacrifice of one's child for the endless struggle, but also in the material losses incurred. The costly loss of immovable property in the towns and cities. While they had become used to the evacuation and burning of the villages and the loss of houses and farmland in the remote areas, the loss of immovable property in the towns and cities where they had invested significant capital was new. For the first time in the history of the conflict, they were fighting the insurance companies, who refused to pay out claims for agreements signed between local agents and property owners a mere day before the start of the curfews.[3] For the first time, they were promised houses in exchange for their demolished property. For the first time, they were offered loans for those promised houses whose declared value was higher than the value of their demolished houses. But it was not the first time they had been in debt. The transmission of cash in the form of loan, credit, project funding, agricultural support, and compensation was an established form of relationship between the state and its citizens in the region. The state created debt-producing mechanisms designed to entangle its historically dissident and disloyal citizens in an interminable cycle of moral and economic indebtedness. While the terror of the last two years ruined the residents' attachments to their former social and political collectives and blasted away the visible spaces of the political, the material relationships remain. For certain residents who had witnessed, survived, and stayed put to live among the ruins, talk about the material dimension was their way of critiquing violence.

By Way of Conclusion

This ethnography is the result of a long-term study of the politics of life and death in a border province of Southeast Turkey. By tackling the experiences, discourses, and imaginaries produced in the suspended temporality of the of intensive military conflict between the PKK and the Turkish state, it has engaged with its complicated postemergency effects on various social, political, and emotional realms of life. This postemergency period involved an amalgamation of governmentalities including militarism, neoliberalism, multiculturalism, the tribal order, and the political experiment of democratic autonomy. It also galvanized the promises and projects created by multiple sovereigns—the PKK, the pro-Kurdish parties, the state, tribal families, and the Syriac Christian Church—in pursuit of reconstituting political hegemony through drawing of new boundaries with the other—whether enemy, perpetrator, or collaborator. The postemergency period became a time of violent peace, made up of partial attempts to construct a sustainable coexistence between different sovereigns and their dispossessed and dissident citizens.

This postemergency state embodied the desires of citizens to build a better life and their will to mobilize the means and resources necessary to secure recognition of what they had witnessed, survived, lost, and been dispossessed of. Nothing felt impossible in this uncertain time and space even despite the lack of a political basis for peace-making. While there was no legal infrastructure to settle the accounts of past atrocities, the region witnessed a surge in lawyers pursuing property cases and compensation files. While there was no imaginary, no language, no practice of peace, there was a boom in democratization packages and peace talks, many of which were never publicized. Both citizens and the state appealed to the same projects as the means to survive and the way to implement restorative justice. The state repetitively channeled cash for heritage making, restoration projects, compensation, and other forms of credit to encourage agriculture, cadastral surveys, the creation of NGOs, and their projects. Almost obsessively, those citizens who applied for credit, compensations, funds, and loans.

The political and social order, on the other hand, became a veritable minefield. The state arrested pro-Kurdish activists and randomly destroyed the lives of those Kurds deemed to be suspicious. Reconfigurations of the militaristic repressive state ran alongside the neoliberal economy, together driving inequalities of power across the region. The state reproduced itself through these repetitive acts of governing its people as a territory. Materiality in the form of cash, labor, and property became the means of propagating and reproducing indebted relationships. People strove to build a better life, with a sense of cruel optimism,. A sense of repetition hung over the entire period. As Isaias Rojas-Pérez (2008:255) argues with reference to political violence in Latin America, "violence repeats but also differentiates itself in postconflict settings."

The collapse of the peace process became a sign of the fragility of the sociopolitical transformation that had occurred over these years, of which the postemergency period was itself the result. The official project of remaking Mardin as a World Heritage Site expired. The politics of recognition lost political and economic value on the local, national, and global scene.

Neoliberal multiculturalism was ravaged by neoliberal militarism. As the Kurds were being demonized, the Syriacs were left without protection. The city was reoccupied under a new hegemony of those Muslim Arab families who were AKP supporters. These reconfigurations did not take place in the absence of law. Rather, the acts of dispossession founded on the degradation of rights to life and property were all rationalized under the legitimizing force of the law. In the aftermath of the 2016 coup attempt, the law became the means to implement a state of exception. The declaration of a "state of emergency" deteriorated all social imagination and expectation for justice or retribution.

In pursuit of making tangible the relationship between violence and subjectivity, I have taken the analysis beyond the discussions of the public sphere, identity, ethnicity, and religion that predominate in Kurdish and Syriac studies. I have looked for other spaces of the political and ethical and have found them in human and nonhuman mediators of ordinary experiences in the region. These mediators operate as agents that transform and structure violence and ordinary ethics. Engaging with them allowed me to understand the complicated interactions that reproduce the historical relationships between subjects and sovereigns. In this way I learned that the search for treasure, encounters with the jinn, heritage restoration project, the efforts to document the ownership of property, and compensation claims, among others, structured different forms of life at the margins of the Turkish state.

In each of the preceding chapters, I have attempted to gather those fragments that reveal the link between the daily occurrences of violence, the complex undertakings that seek the transformation of loss and the reinhabiting of life, and the violation of the space of the other. These ordinary occurrences and spaces encompass not only those hopeful acts of managing loss but also the paradoxical contradictions that allow for the coexistence of construction and destruction, as well as possession and dispossession. Ruination, both as an act of ruining and of being ruined, has been present in all the narratives that make up this ethnography.

The book is my attempt to write against the grain of identity politics by offering alternative frames of reference through which to explore the politics of recognition, both of and within communities. A long-term engagement with many subjects instilled in me a historically grounded understanding of interethnic and interreligious relationships. I studied subject positioning not by essentializing ethnicity or religious identities or by examining the normative conditions that produce subjects as recognized victims or perpetrators. Instead I focused on how multiple historical and political contingencies allowed such subjectivities to emerge, fade, return, and transform. The personal and collective histories of Kurds, Arabs, and Syriacs living together in Southeast Turkey, therefore, have been presented and represented in this ethnography not through their protagonists' static and coherent relationships to the state and to the other, but through their intimate, fugitive, and compulsive connections with the dead and the living. Their fragmented accounts speak not only of how they inhabit life, but also of how they inhabit death, double accounts that reveal the limits of what can be possessed, desired, and grieved for in a life lived inside the endless cycles of violence.

NOTES

Preface

1. The state of emergency (OHAL) that was declared in eastern and southeastern Turkey as a response to the armed resistance movement of the PKK initially started with legislation on July 1987 and was extended every four months, forty-six times. It covered thirteen provinces in eastern and southeastern Turkey: Adıyaman, Bingöl, Bitlis, Batman, Diyarbakır, Elazığ, Hakkari, Mardin, Muş, Siirt, Tunceli, Van, Şırnak. Starting from the end of 1994, the OHAL region started to be narrowed down. It was lifted completely in November 2002.

2. The Mardin province with a population of 800,000 is divided into ten districts: Mardin (central district), Derik, Kızıltepe, Mazıdağı, Midyat, Nusaybin, Ömerli, Savurlu, Yeşilli. The main bulk of this ethnographic study was conducted in the central district of the Mardin province, referred to as Mardin city. In 2012, the central district of Mardin was renamed Artuklu, and Mardin was reserved to name the metropolitan province. These name changes on the official map are not reflected in this ethnography as my interlocutors always used Mardin to refer to the central district that is composed of two parts: Upper Mardin (Yukarı Mardin) or Old Mardin (Eski Mardin) and the New City (Yenişehir). For that reason, Artuklu as the recent official name of the central district of Mardin will not appear in the narratives of the book. In a similar vein, my interlocutors always used the Kurdish and/or Syriac names to refer to towns and villages, particularly in the Tur Abdin region. Due to the history of the occupation and dispossession and displacement of the communities in the region, certain names vanished from the daily use, while others became the hegemonic reference for the locals who remained. The official Turkish names were only used for the bureaucratic encounters and procedure. The battles over the names have continued to this day and had a very tangible effect on the process of cadastral survey and land registration (see Chapter 4). In the text, for consistency, the place-names will appear in their Turkish transcripts. On the maps, the place-names will be indicated with their Kurdish, Syriac, and Turkish (official) names. In Figure 1, the places-names in the Kurdish region of Turkey are given both in Kurdish and Turkish. In Figure 2, all the place-names appear in Syriac (transliterated) with the legend that also provides the Kurdish and the official Turkish names for the places on the map. For transliteration of the Syriac names of the villages, I have used the following references as the main resources, http://syriaca.org/place/70 .html and Brock (2011; 466–467), http: //syriaca.org/bibl/1.

3. The community's self-designation in Aramaic is "Suryoyo" or "Suroyo," which is translated as "Syrian" in English and "Süryani" in Turkish. However, the subjects of this

ethnography, mainly diasporic communities, use two separate terms, Assyrian and Aramean/Syriac, to refer to themselves. The use of these terms signifies a split within the community brought about by the ongoing struggle over the historical roots of their identity. The term Assyrian has been used most effectively among the nationalist activists in the diaspora. This discourse is based on the historical imagination and construction of a sense of continuity with the Assyrian empire. Syriacs, on the other hand, identify themselves with the Arameans and reject the historical connections with the Assyrian empire while defining the Aramaic language and Christianity as the most crucial components of their identity. Throughout the book, I often use the term Syriac as my main interlocutors choose to define themselves Syriac (Süryani).

4. The different names used to refer to the 1915 Armenian genocide throughout the book convey how my different interlocutors refer to the events themselves.

5. Except for İsa Acar who requested to appear in the book with his real name, the names of all interlocutors have been anonymized for reasons of confidentiality. Except Zaz (home village of İsa Acar) and Kafarbe (the village where the Mor Gabriel Monastery was located), all the village names have also been changed.

Introduction

1. The Shemsis referred as sun-worshippers by the neighbors is one of the ancient communities that lived Mardin for centuries. Their name is derived from the Semitic word for sun (shemes). Accordingly, the Shemsis are also referred as part of the Armenian community before they converted Christianity at the beginning of fourth century (Aydın et al. 2000: 79). The nonconvert Shemsis were strongly pressurized by both Syriacs and Armenians as well as the Ottoman state to convert into monothestic religion, They converted to Christianity in the nineteenth century. In Mardin, the local inhabitants, especially people living in the Savurkapı neighborhood at the south end of the old city refer to the Shemsis as the previous residents of the neighborhood.

2. There is a vast literature on the causes and effects of the Kurdish conflict. However, the sociological and anthropological studies conducted in 2000s were particularly significant to explore the relationship between violence and subjectivity. Among the most crucial examples, see Özgen (2003) for one of the first sociological analysis of the memory of the state violence in the construction of the state, identity and tribal boundaries. See Aras (2013) for a full ethnography on political violence and trauma in the region. See Darıcı (2013, 2016) and Neyzi and Darıcı (2015) for significant ethnographic accounts of the subjectivities of youngsters who have grown up in, lived in, felt indebted to, and died during the protracted conflict-explore the emergence of a new generation that searches for grounds to act upon the emotional, material cost (*bedel*) of violence. See also the unpublished PhD dissertations of Yıldırım (2010) and Özsoy (2010) for significant analysis of the bedel. Yildirim's ethnographic account also provides an acutely significant and unique analysis on the construction of the gendered militant activism in the region. Nazan Üstündağ's (2013) work is an invaluable critical analysis of the state violence on the construction of gendered identities within different settings of the violent envoirement. Hakyemez (2017a) and Düzel (2018) provide well-thought

and delicate accounts of political and gendered subjectivities through the memoirs and diaries of the Kurdish political prisoners and women guerillas. For inspiring analysis of gendered subjectivities through different forms of cultural expressions, within the everyday spaces of the Kurdish conflict, see Şengül (2013) Schafers (2017). These studies open up space for discussion of the ethical and political issues that emerge from the Kurdish resistance movement and shape the emotions, practices, and discourses of daily life in the conflict region.

3. According to the recently published reports, since July 2015, around four thousand people were killed as a result of the clashes between the PKK and Turkish armed forces. (http://www.crisisgroup.be/interactives/turkey) and five hundred thousand people were displaced from their homes in the Kurdish towns and cities that remained under curfew. See https://www.amnesty.org/en/countries/europe-and-central-asia/turkey/report-turkey/

4. See Yeğen (2010, 2015) for an analysis of the discursive transformation of discussions of conflict in the region. See Scalbert-Yücel and Le Ray (2006) for an expanded and critical analysis of Kurdish studies. See Güneş (2012) for detailed historical and political analysis of the Kurdish resistance movement and the PKK in Turkey. See Jongerden and Akkaya (2012, 2013, 2016), particularly their work on the transformation of the discourses and practices of the PKK. Jongerden and Akkaya's articles provide detailed, comprehensive, and significant analysis of the Kurdish resistance movement.

5. The most important anthropological analysis of the memory of the 1925 uprisings is in Özsoy (2013).

6. During these years, these policies also affected other minorities of the republic.

7. For a critical analysis of the politics of minorities and majorities, see Tambar (2013, 2016). Parla and Özgül (2016) provide a significant discussion of the political contingencies that underpin the formation of the categories of minority and majority. For a comparative analysis, see my own discussion of the Syriac communities in diaspora (Biner 2011).

8. For an ethnographic study of fear and political violence in the Kurdish region, see Aras (2013). Neyzi and Darıcı (2015) present an analysis of the effect of political violence on the construction of youth subjectivities. The significant differences between Aras's approach to political agency within the Kurdish movement and that of Neyzi and Darıcı are worth considering. Aras's account draws a picture of a paralyzed subject who learned to live in the cross fire between the Turkish military and the PKK. Neyzi and Darıcı provide a multilayered analysis that reveals the conditions and limits within which agency among the younger generation has been constituted. That agency is neither fully fearful nor fully resistant; rather, the agent is open, cautious, and politically conscious of his or her own and others' expectations, hopes, and fears.

9. For critical analyses of the peace process, see Nazan Üstündağ's essays, available on boun.academia.edu/NazanÜstündağ "Gendering Negotiations: Some Notes on the Peace Process Between the Turkish State and the PKK," "Barış Sürecinin Sorunları ve Çözum Yolları I (Problems of the Peace Process and Resolutions I)," and "Barış Sürecinin Sorunları ve Çözum Yolları II (Problems of the Peace Process and Resolutions II)." See O'Connor and Başer (2018) for an analysis of violence in the aftermath of the 2015 elections. See Ertür and Martel (2016) for a thought-provoking essay on the breakdown of the peace process and acceleration of violence.

10. See Hakyemez (2017b) for analysis of the reasons for the breakdown of the peace process. Hakyemez also locates the sources of the breakdown in the absence of legal frameworks, despite the presence of popular support stimulated by the AKP government.

11. For the most thoughtful and critical interpretations of the effects of the struggle of the YPG and YPJ on the armed movement of the Kurdish youngsters on the Turkish side, see Üstündağ (2015) and Darıcı (2015).

12. See the report of the Office of the United Nations High Commissioner for Human Rights (2017).

13. In her sensitive work on the conflict in Sri Lanka, Sharika Thiranagama (2011) carries out a suggestive analysis of war as violence on a continuum. With reference to Stephen Lubkemann's (2007) well-known work on war, she discusses how lives lived in protracted conflicts must be understood not only in terms of spectacular violence but also through other processes, including the transformation of political cultures and kinship relations. At the same time, Thiranagama highlights the importance of differentiating war from other processes, viewing war not as existing "along a continuum with other forms of social life, but as a powerful and distinct force, period, and subjectivity, a making on a site of unmaking" (10). I agree with Thiranagama about the need to pay attention to how people differentiate various forms of violence and their impact, between insurrections, state violence, and internal violence directed within a resistance movement.

14. See especially Scalbert-Yücel and Le Ray (2006) and the introduction of Güneş (2012) for comprehensive analyses of scholarship on the Kurdish resistance movement.

15. See also Taussig (1984, 1992) for similar analysis of the mirroring relationship between the state and the subject-citizens.

16. These are known as the Ergenekon and Balyoz trials. Colonel Cemal Temizöz's case, the most important in the Balyoz trials, is emblematic of the pursuit of accountability and justice for the atrocities and human rights violations carried out in the region. For a historical and political overview and analysis of these trials, see hakikatadalethafiza.org/en/new-state -policy-aims-to-cover-up-atrocities-in-1990s/.

Chapter 1

1. There is abundant literature on the political, social, and legal effects of the Gezi Park protests. For an insightful analysis of the protests, see Bakıner (2013), Tugal (2013), the essays in *Cultural Anthropology Online*, 31 October 2013, Ertür (2016a).

2. For acute and intense analysis on the relationship on different aspects of AKP authoritarianism and Gezi Park protests, see the essays in "Fieldsights—Hot Spots," *Cultural Anthropology Online*, 31 October 2013.

3. See www.dw.com/en/erdogan-restarts-controversial-gezi-park-development/a-19340656.

4. For a significant analysis of the Kurdish involvement in the Gezi events, see Bozcalı and Yoltar (2013).

5. For significant analysis on the gentrification, urbanization, and construction projects during the AKP government, see Bartu and Kirlioglu (2008), Kuyucu and Ünsal (2010), Yüksel (2011), and Karaman (2013).

6. Sarkis Lole has been regarded as the most prominent Armenian architect in the city of Mardin, who constructed the architectural landmarks between the end of the nineteenth century and the beginning of the twentieth.

7. For information and visual images from the activities related to the Historical Transformation Project, see www.facebook.com/Mardin-Tarihi-D%C3%B6n%C3%BC%C5%9F%C3%BCm-Projesi-338732252816025/.

8. Interview with an officer from the Ministry of Urban Planning and the Environment.

9. Interviews with the engineers appointed to work on this project for the state.

10. For significant ethnographic studies on different uses of heritage, see Breglia (2006) and Herzfeld (2006, 2010). For examples of ethnographic studies that critically analyze the process of making heritage out of ruins, see Abu El-Haj (2001), Collins (2008, 2015), Dumper and Larkin (2012), and Kavuri-Bauer (2011). For examples of studies of the politics of cultural heritage in Turkey, see Bartu (2001), Atakuman (2010), Zencirci (2014), Çaylı (2016), Girard (2014), Girard et al. (2018), and Boucly (2018). For examples of ethnographic studies on the (in)tangible heritage and politics of the past, culture, and ethnicity in southeast Turkey, see Biner (2007), Aykan (2015), Torne (2015), and Schafers (2015).

11. There are many castles in the vicinity of the city of Mardin such as Mardin Castle, Kala'tul Al-Mara, Erdemest, Anir Castle, Dara, Rabbat, and Dermedinan. Mardin Castle and Kala'tul Al-Mara are the most well-known and cited ones in the historical narratives of the city.

12. See Özcoşar and Günes (2006), cited in Alkan Reis (2012:12).

13. Basing his calculation on missionary accounts from the nineteenth century, Michael Abdalla (2013) estimates the population in 1838 and 1850; Southgate reports that "there are 3000 families living in the city. 500 families were Armenian Catholics, 400 families were Syrian Orthodox, 250 families were Syriac Catholics, 100 families were Caldeans and 10 families were Jewish" (cited in Abdalla 2013:134). Abdalla notes that during this period, the Christians represented 48 percent of the population. The Muslim population was counted as the total number of Arabs, Kurds, and Turks without paying any attention to their ethnic differences (Abdalla 2013:135). See also Göyünç (1991) for the changing numbers of the non-Muslim population between 1834 and 1914. The Muslim community gradually came to outnumber the rest of the population.

14. David Gaunt argues that the city of Mardin was one distinctive place where the atrocities toward Armenians and Syriacs were documented and narrated on a daily basis (2013:15). Gaunt further asserts that Armenian and Syriac Mardinites did not expect this hostile attitude from the local Muslim community as it did not fall into the historical rules and ethics of coexistence in the city. During the 1895 pogroms, it was the local Muslim tribal families who protected the local Armenians and Syriacs from the attacks of the Kurds from outside (Gaunt 2013:16; Abdalla 2013:136). Uğur Üngör (2011) interprets the interethic and interreligious relations differently, arguing that relations were already fragile due to the political and economic crisis in the empire. Furthermore, Üngör argues, thousands of refugees (Circassians and Chechens from the Caucasus) were resettled in the eastern provinces and their sudden presence added to tensions between Muslims and Christians (19).

15. It is difficult to estimate the Christian and Muslim population in the district of Mardin before and after 1915. According to sources that Michael Abdalla (2013:138) references,

only 36 percent of the Christian population survived the massacres in 1915. David Gaunt (2013:19) mentions similar numbers on the basis of his archival resources. For detailed information about the population of the ethnic and religious communities in the province of Diyarbakır, which also includes the numbers in the district of Mardin, see Üngör (2011: 16–17).

16. See Ternon (2013) for a detailed description of 1915 in the city of Mardin, the surrounding areas, and the region. Üngör (2011:65, 67–69) offers a detailed description of the detainment and imprisonment of six hundred Armenian notables artisans in Mardin (see also Kieser et al. 2015:309–329).

17. See Çetinoğlu (2013:43–46, 47–48, 51–52) for court verdicts on the transfer of abandoned properties to individuals; a list of the abandoned properties, their original Armenian owners, and their new function; and a list of Syriac occupiers of Armenian properties.

18. The independence tribunals were special courts established during the Turkish War of Independence to punish and prosecute the people who were opposed to the new republican regime in the aftermath of the dissolution of the Ottoman Empire. They operated until 1927.

19. See Abdalla (2013) for the list of Armenian and Syriac properties confiscated by the Turkish state in the first decade of the republic.

20. See Çetinoğlu (2013:52–68) for a detailed description of the different means and legal procedures used to appropriate the abandoned properties.

21. The word *Mhallami* (Arabic meaning "coming from a thousand neighborhoods") refers locally to an Arabic-speaking community that migrated from the villages of Midyat, which as noted earlier was close to Mardin. For detailed information about the history of Mhallamis, see Aslan (2013).

22. Since 1999, the city has been represented and documented through different kinds of academic, visual, and literary publications, hence turned into an artistic and academic object. As early publications and representations of the genre, Murathan Mungan's books (1992a, b, c, 1999) were particularly influential in the construction of the public imaginary of Mardin as part of the orientalized geography, with its forms and rules of life in Mesopotamia. Published by the prestigious Yapi Kredi publication house, Filiz Özdem's edited book (2005) has been another significant example of the interdisciplinary and visual documentation of the city. İbrahim Özcoşar's edited volumes (2007a, b, c, d) were early examples of the local academic productions on the city of Mardin that collected a wide range of information from different disciplines, without much attention to current politics. The cultural and architectural heritage that supported the prevalent official and public discourse of tolerance and multiculturalism became the dominant focus of the academic publications. For a review of the general focus and a list of the academic works about Mardin, see Küçük and Günes (2009). For a few exceptional examples of academic work that focuses on the current politics of everyday life, see Küçük (2012), on the meaning of Arabic identity, and Costa (2013), on the effects of social media in the city.

23. See also Iğsız (2014) and Potuoğlu-Cook (2011), Silverstein (2010) for further critical analysis on the relationship between cultural and neoliberal policies in Turkey. For discussions of heritage and contemporary cultural politics of the state, see Atakuman (2010) and Girard (2014).

24. In 2013, two thousand Turkish liras amounted to U.S. $1,054.

25. For comparisons of estate prices in the region, see Yüksel (2011).

Chapter 3

1. This amounted to approximately U.S. $12,500 in 2013.

2. The terminology of the spiritual beings is complicated because there are so many similarities between different spiritual beings that exist in different cosmologies. The same applies to the analysis of their constructive and destructive effects. See the introductory chapter by Levy et al. (1996:17) for a significant and comprehensive discussion of these overlaps. In their discussion of possession, they note that the full possession they describe as the spirit entering the body should be distinguished from other experiences (visual or auditory) related to possession. Here I suggest that this distinction applies to haunting and possession.

3. Spirit possessions have common explanations, but they differ from place to place. For instance, based on his observation in Morocco, Crapanzano asserts that "men and women who are angry or frightened or associated with a change in social status are particularly liable to attack" (1992:158). Levy et al. (1996:15) argue that people who are often perceived of as weak, without power or status, may experience possessions, or "they may be experienced by stronger people in marginal places or states (in the forest or bush, in the twilight or dark, entering or waking up from sleep) and notably more often by women." In their view, the jinn do not only bother the weak. In some cases, they also help them.

Chapter 4

1. As mentioned in the preface, due to İsa Acer's request, his name and the name of his home village, Zaz, and the Perbume hill have not been changed. They have been mentioned with their original names throughout the book. Yet, the names of all other locations and interlocutors have been changed for reasons of confidentiality. Zaz is a village located in the region of Tur Abdin, which is known as the heartland of Syriacs in Turkey. Tur Abdin is translated from Aramaic as "the mountain of servants of God" and is assumed to refer to the monks and ascetics who spread Christianity in the region from the second to fourth centuries (Armbruster 2013:25). Heidi Armbruster notes that the source of the Aramaic name is uncertain and that scholars cannot date its first emergence in the literature. The translation might be more recent (241). Tur Abdin is a mountainous area that expands westward toward the city of Mardin and the Mesopotamian Plain and continues to the Turkish-Syrian border in the south. The main town in Tur Abdin is Midyat, and the rest of the area is full of churches, monasteries, and villages, some of which have a mixed population of Syriacs and Kurds, though a few (known as Isla villages) are populated only by Syriacs.

2. Throughout the 1980s and 1990s, Syriac diasporic communities revitalized the memory of the Sayfo and initiated a political struggle for its international recognition as the genocide of the Assyrians, Syriacs, and Chaldeans. The details of the struggle and its reverberations in the political lives of the families and communities are discussed in sections of the next two chapters.

3. To summarize exclusion from official status meant that the Syriacs were neither provided protection for their religious establishment nor awarded the right to establish any religious or social institutions for education or instruction. See Hurst (2012) and Önder (2012) for detailed explanations of the provisions of the Lausanne Treaty and the political situation of the Syriacs in Turkey. The legal aspect of the discussion has no purpose here, but it is important to note that the exclusion from the official status of minority prompted the discourse and imagination about being the unrecognized minority, a political signifier that the Syriac activists and intellectuals reiterated in the discussions that particularly flourished in the postemergency period.

4. The wealth income tax (*varlık vergisi*) was a form of tax imposed by the Turkish state on citizens of Turkey in 1942, with the declared aim of raising funds for the country's defense in case of an entry into the Second World War. Yet the main reason was to move the assets of the non-Muslim minorities to the Muslim bourgeoisie. Many people sold their properties or borrowed money to pay the tax. The ones who could not pay were sent to labor camps in eastern Anatolia. For detailed historical analysis of the wealth tax, see Aktar (2014).

5. In his classic study *State, Tribe and Society*, Martin van Bruinessen (1992) explains the historical transformation of the Kurdish tribal system from the imperial to the republican regime and highlights the fact that despite the attacks on the Kurdish tribal system and its claims to autonomy, neither the tribal structures nor the ağas as the local sovereigns disappeared. With reference to the formation of two confederations, Van Bruinessen mentions that the Haverkis appeared in 1860 under the leadership of Haco Agha. The Haverkis consolidated themselves as a confederation of twenty-four *aşirets* (tribes) that also involved Syriac and Yazidi communities (126–131). In her ethnographic study of the political life of the Kurdish tribal structure, Lale Yalçın-Heckmann (1991, 2000) writes against the grain of associating the Kurdish tribal structure with the qualities of nonmodern traditional society. She discusses the ways in which these tribal structures persisted and endured, taking different forms against the background of political and military conflicts and their consequences of displacement that produced transnational networks. Rather than viewing them as fixed and homogenous political entities, Yalçın-Heckmann (2000) emphasizes the political fact that these tribal structures would not disappear as long as they adjusted to the needs and demands of the Kurdish political movement. Along these same lines, Neşe Özgen (2007) offers an ethnographic study of the political and social conditions that underpin the formation and transformation of a tribal structure. Following the life trajectories of two nomadic Kurdish tribes, Özgen demonstrates the political and economic logic of the transformation of the tribal structures from nomadic to settled life and the change of their political alliance especially in the context of the military conflict between the PKK and the Turkish Armed Forces. Haverki also appears in her narrative as a historical and political signifier of belonging and loyalty. She observes that she has not encountered Yazidis or Assyrians among Dekşuris. Most of the Arabs and all of the Mhallamis that she met during her long-term sociological work belong to the Dekşuris. However, she refers to an Assyrian villager who returned from Europe and claimed to have recently changed sides from Haverkis to Dekşuris. Nevertheless, Özgen warns that those are not easy decisions to take. Those shifts do not occur simply, due to the personal choices of the people (ibid., 249). Özgen's detailed ethnographic account provides fruitful

ground for making further comparisons with İsa Bey's narratives about the ways of coexistence with Kurds.

6. For information on this call and the Syriacs' immediate responses to the idea of return, see www.suryaniler.com/haberler.asp?id=232.

7. The Bilge Köyü event that occurred in 2010 ended with the killing of forty people from one family by members of another branch of the same family. It was a key incident that signaled the potential dangers and explosiveness of the village guard system. Even though it was portrayed as an honor crime, the massacre of forty people turned out to be an effect of long-term hostility between two korucu families that were competing over access to economic resources in the vicinity of their villages. The killing of so many people in a single house at an engagement party underscored the legitimacy of violence and absence of legal consequences.

Chapter 5

1. The dispute over the land at the Mor Gabriel Monastery is the most widely publicized case involving the property rights of Syriacs in Turkey. Since the outset, it has been covered by the media, national and international NGOs, Syriac activists, and academics who have published reports and books to support the cause of the monastery. One of the first reports was published under the name of Turabdin, the bishop of Mor Gabriel Monastery in 2008 (see Aktaş 2008; also the reports by Gusten 2015 and 2016 on the return of the Syriac diasporic communities and property rights). For a detailed interdisciplinary analysis of the monastery case, see Omtzigt et al. (2012) and Atta (2013).

2. For a recent important example of this, see the essays in the book edited by Omtzigt et al. (2012). For a significant critical analysis of ethnicized interpretations of violence, space, and ethnic and religious identity, see Herscher (2010), particularly the introduction. Gambetti and Jongerden (2015) also provide important analyses of the Kurdish issue that are critical of noncontextualized temporal interpretations.

3. For detailed historical information about Mor Gabriel Monastery, see Dolapönü (1971), Palmer (2011), Bilge (2012), and Brock (2012). For a significant ethnographic work on Mor Gabriel, see Armbruster (2013). Her multisited work includes the life of the nuns within the monastery and discusses the effect of the symbolic sources from Aramaic language and religion on the Syriac-Assyrian identity. Armbruster's work is also the only ethnographic study about the internal life of the Mor Gabriel Monastery.

4. Interviews with the representative of the Mor Gabriel Monastery Foundation.

5. See also the essays by Eckert, Kirsch, and Ander in the same volume (Eckert, Donahoe, et al. 2012).

Chapter 6

1. If the deeds were not available, the commission would refer to statements provided by older villagers as witnesses. The legacy of the internal conflict within the village would sometimes affect these statements.

2. In 2009, 14,000 Turkish liras amounted to $94,136 U.S.; 2,000 Turkish liras amounted to $1,344 U.S.; 1,000 Turkish liras amounted to $14,120 U.S.

3. In August 1992, fifty-three people who were protesting the killings and injuries that occurred during the Newroz celebration were shot to death by members of the Armed Forces in downtown Sirnak, a city on the Iraqi border. Newroz is originated from Zoroastrian religious traditions before Islam and is celebrated as the beginning of the new year by Central Asian and Middle Eastern countries. Particularly in the 1980s, Newroz has become a crucial symbol of Kurdish identity in Turkey (Aykan 2014).

4. For an insightful analysis of rumors in the daily struggle for rights, see Eckert (2012).

5. The two procedures are not dependent on each other. People were not required to return to the villages in order to apply for compensation. There are some exceptional decisions on this matter that I do not discuss in this chapter.

6. The human rights lawyers I interviewed mentioned a few cases in which the judges made decisions that disclaimed the families' responsibilities for the criminal deeds of their children or other cases in which the Supreme Court did not support the decision of the civil court on the ground that there was not sufficient evidence to prove the responsibility of the dead militant for the alleged crime.

Epilogue

1. See https://www.aljazeera.com/news/2015/07/kurdish-group-claims-revenge-murder-turkish-police-150722132945249.html, accessed 1 January 2018.

2. In thinking about the procedures dealing with the mismatch between DNA samples and human remains, I cannot avoid the comparison between the mix-up of owners' names and parcels of land on the cadastral map in Midyat. As noted earlier, İsa Bey had spent months to amend the error.

3. The acts of insurance companies in their nonreimbursement of damages were covered both by the conventional newspapers as part of their economic sections (e.g., www.sozcu.com.tr/2016/ekonomi/guneydogu-sigorta-pazarinda-son-durum-1415769/ and www.hurriyet.com.tr/konutlarin-yuzde-90i-sigortalanmis-en-az-5-milyar-lira-istiyorlar-40233276, accessed 1 June 2018) and in the pro-Kurdish newspaper as part of the section concerning material damage inflicted during the curfews in Kurdish towns (www.yeniozgurpolitika.org/index/ek/index.php?rupel=lezgin&id=3114, accessed 15 June 2018).

REFERENCES

Abdalla, Michael. "19. Yüzyılın Ortaları Ile I. Dünya Savaşı Arasında Mardin Ve Halkı: Yabancı Misyonerlerin Ve Eski Sakinlerin İzahları." In *Mardin Tebliğleri: Mardin Ve Çevresi Toplumsal Ve Ekonomik Tarihi Konferansı*, 131–143. Istanbul: Hrant Dink Foundation, 2013.

Abourahme, Nasser. "Assembling and Spilling Over: Towards an 'Ethnography of Cement' in a Palestinian Refugee Camp." *International Journal of Urban and Regional Research* 39, no. 2 (2014): 200–217.

Abu-El Haj, Nadia. *Facts on the Ground: Archaeological Practice and Territorial Self-Fashioning in Israeli Society*. Chicago: University of Chicago Press, 2001.

Açıksöz, Salih Can. "Sacrificial Limbs of Sovereignty: Disabled Veterans, Masculinity and Nationalist Politics in Turkey." *Medical Anthropology Quarterly* 26, no. 1 (2012): 4–25.

Açıkyıldız-Şengül, Birgül. "Architecture of Mardin in the Ottoman Period." Turkish Cultural Foundation. 2012, http://www.turkishculture.org/architecture/houses/architecture-of -mardin-in-the-ottoman-period-1088.htm?type=1. Accessed 1 April 2017.

Agamben, Giorgio. *Homo Sacer: Sovereign Power and Bare Life*. Stanford: Stanford University Press, 1998.

———. *State of Exception*. Translated by Kevin Attell. Chicago: University of Chicago Press, 2005.

Akçam, Taner, and Ümit Kurt. *The Spirit of the Laws: The Plunder of Wealth in the Armenian Genocide*. Translated by Aram Arkun. London: Berghahn, 2015.

Akkaya, Ahmet Hamdi, and Joost Jongerden. "Confederalism and Autonomy in Turkey: The Kurdistan Workers' Party and the Reinvention of Democracy." In *The Kurdish Question in Turkey: New Perspectives on Violence, Representation and Reconciliation*, edited by Cengiz Güneş and Welat Zeydanlıoğlu, 186–205. London: Routledge, 2013.

Aktar, Ayhan. *Varlık Vergisi Ve Türkleştirme Politikaları*. Istanbul: İletişim, 2014.

Aktaş, Samuel Timotheos. *Report on the Imminent Problems Facing the Syriac Monastery of St. Gabriel in Midyad*. Midyat, Turkey: Mor Gabriel Monastery, 2008.

Akyüz, Gabriel. *Mardin İli'nin Merkezinde, Civar Köylerinde, İlçelerinde Bulunan Kiliselerin Ve Manastırların Tarihi*. Mardin: Mardin Kırklar Kilisesi, 1998.

Al-Rustom, Hakem. "Re-thinking the Post-Ottoman: Anatolian Armeniance as an Ethnographic Experience" in A Companion to the Anthropology of the Middle East, edited by Soraya Altorki, 452–479. London: Wiley-Blackwell, 2015.

Alexander, Catherine. *Personal States: Making Connections Between People and Bureacracy in Turkey.* Oxford: Oxford University Press, 2002.

Alkan Reis, Amine Seyhun. "Mardin Kentinin Korunmasi Kapsaminda 'Surp Kevork Ermeni Kilisesi' Restorasyon Onerisi (The Conservation and Restoration Project of the 'Surp Kevork Armenian Church' in Mardin)." MA diss., Yıldız Technical University, 2012.

Allen, Lori. *The Rise and Fall of Human Rights: Cynicism and Politics in Occupied Palestine.* Stanford, CA: Stanford University Press, 2013.

Altuğ, Seda. "Sectarianism in the Syrian Jazira: Community, Land and Violence in the Memories of World War I and the French Mandate (1915–1939)." PhD diss., Utrecht University, 2013.

Amnesty International. "Displaced and Dispossessed: Sur Residents' Right to Return." 2016a, https://www.amnesty.org/en/documents/eur44/5213/2016/en/. Accessed 15 May 2017.

Aras, Ramazan. *Formation of Kurdishness in Turkey: Political Violence, Fear and Pain.* London: Routledge, 2013.

Aretxaga, Begonia. "Maddening States." *Annual Review of Anthropology* 32 (2003): 393–410.

Arıkan, Burçak. "Assyrian Transnational Politics: Activism from Europe Towards Homeland." MA diss., Middle East Technical University, 2011.

Armbruster, Heidi. *Keeping the Faith: Syriac Christian Diasporas.* Canon Pyon: Kingston, 2013.

Aslan, Mehmet Ali. "Tur Abdin Tarihinin Gizemi: Mıhallemiler." In *Mardin Tebliğleri: Mardin Ve Çevresi Toplumsal Ve Ekonomik Tarihi Konferansı,* 73–89. Istanbul: Hrant Dink Foundation, 2013.

Aslan, Senem. "Incoherent State: The Controversy over Kurdish Naming in Turkey." *European Journal of Turkish Studies* (online), 10, (2009), https://journals.openedition.org/ejts/4142.

Atakuman, Cigdem. "Value of Heritage in Turkey: History and Politics of Turkey's World Heritage Nominations." *Journal of Mediterranean Archaeology* 23, no. 1 (2010): 107–131.

Atta, Hanna. "The Legal Battle over the Monastery of Mor Gabriel in South-East Turkey." MA diss., University of Amsterdam, 2013.

Atto, Naures. *Hostages in the Homeland, Orphans in the Diaspora: Identity Discourses Among the Assyrian/Syriac Elites in the European Diaspora.* Leiden: Leiden University Press, 2012a.

———. "United for the Sake of the Mor Gabriel Monastery." In *The Slow Disappearance of the Syriacs from Turkey and of the Grounds of the Mor Gabriel Monastery,* edited by Pieter Omtzigt, Markus Tozman, and Andrea Tyndall, 231–243. Munster: LIT, 2012b.

Ayata, Bilgin. "The Politics of Displacement: A Transnational Analysis of the Forced Migration of Kurds in Turkey and Europe." PhD diss., Johns Hopkins University, 2011.

Ayata, Bilgin, and Deniz Yükseker. "A Belated Awakening: National and International Responses to the Internal Displacement of Kurds in Turkey." *New Perspectives on Turkey* 32 (2005): 5–42.

Aydın, Suavi. "Tanzimat'tan Sonra Tur Abdin'de Aşiretler Ve Hristiyanlar: Bir Ortak Yaşam, Rekabet Ve Baskı Tarihi." In *Mardin Tebliğleri: Mardin Ve Çevresi Toplumsal Ve Ekonomik Tarihi Konferansı,* 143–157. Istanbul: Hrant Dink Vakfı, 2013.

Aydın, Suavi, Kudret Emiroğlu, Oktay Özel, and Suha Ünsal. *Mardin: Aşiret- Cemaat-Devlet.* Istanbul: Tarih Vakfı Yayınları, 2000.

Aykan, Bahar. "Whose Tradition, Whose Identity? The Politics of Constructing 'Nevruz' as Intangible Heritage in Turkey." *European Journal of Turkish Studies* (online) 19 (2015), https://journals.openedition.org/ejts/5000.

Babül, Elif. "The Paradox of Protection: Human Rights, the Masculinist State, the Moral Economy of Gratitude in Turkey." *American Ethnologist* 42, no. 1 (2015): 116–130.

Bakıner, Onur. "Can the Spirit of Gezi Transform Progressive Politics in Turkey?" *Jadaliyya*, 3 July 2013. Accessed 1 April 2015.

Bali, Rıfat. *Yirmi Kur'a Nafia Askerleri*. Istanbul: Kitapevi, 2008.

Balta Paker, Evren, and İsmet Akça. "Askerler, Köylüler, Paramiliter Güçler: Türkiye'de Köy Koruculuğu Sistemi." *Toplum ve Bilim* 126 (2013): 7–34.

Barry, Andrew. *Material Politics: Disputes Along the Pipeline*. Oxford: Wiley-Blackwell, 2013.

Bartu, Ayfer. "Rethinking Heritage Politics in a Global Context: A View from Istanbul." In *the Hybrid Urbanism: On Identity Discourse and the Built Envoirenment*, edited by Nezar Al Sayyad, 131–156. London: Praeger, 2001.

Bartu-Candan, Ayfer, and Biray Kirlioglu. "Emerging Spaces of Neoliberalism: A Gated Town and a Public Housing Project in Istanbul." *New Perspectives in Turkey no. 39* (2008): 53–61.

Başer, Bahar. "Intricacies of Engaging Diasporas in Conflict Resolution and Transitional Justice: The Kurdish Diaspora and Peace Process in Turkey." *Civil Wars* 19, no. 4 (2018): 470–494.

Bayır, Derya. "Representation of the Kurds by the Turkish Judiciary." *Human Rights Quarterly* 35 (2013a): 116–142.

———. "The Role of the Judicial System in the Politicide of the Kurdish Opposition." In *The Kurdish Question in Turkey: New Perspectives on Violence, Representation and Reconciliation*, edited by Cengiz Güneş and Welat Zeydanlıoğlu, 21–47. London: Routledge, 2013b.

Beller-Hann, Ildiko, and Chris Hann. *Turkish Region: State, Market and Social Identities on the East Black Sea Coast*. Oxford: School of American Research Press, 2001.

Benda-Beckmann, Franz von, Keebet von Benda-Beckmann, and Julia Eckert, eds. *Rules of Law and Laws of Ruling: On the Governance of Law*. London: Routledge, 2009.

Benda-Beckmann, Franz von, Keebet von Benda-Beckmann, and Anne Griffts, eds. *Mobile People, Mobile Law: Expanding Legal Relations in a Contracting World*. Aldershot: Ashgate, 2005.

Benda-Beckmann, Franz von, Keebet von Benda-Beckmann, and Melanie G. Wiber. "The Properties of Property." In *Changing Properties of Property*, edited by Franz von Benda-Beckmann, Keebet von Benda-Beckmann, and Melanie G. Wiber, 1–40. London: Berghahn, 2009.

Bennett, Jane. *Vibrant Matter: A Political Ecology of Things*. Durham: Duke University Press, 2010.

Berlant, Lauren. *Cruel Optimism*. Durham, NC: Duke University Press, 2011.

———. "Cruel Optimism." In *The Affect Theory Reader*, edited by Melissa Gregg and Gregory J. Seigworth. 93–118. Durham, NC: Duke University Press, 2010.

———. *The Queen of America Goes to Washington City: Essays on Sex and Citizenship*. Durham, NC: Duke University Press, 1997.

Bieberstein, Alice von. "Treasure/Fetish/Gift: Hunting for 'Armenian Gold' in Post-Genocide Turkish Kurdistan." *Subjectivity* 10, no. 2 (2017): 170–189.

Bieberstein, Alice von, and Nora Tataryan. "The What of Occupation: 'You Took Our Cemetery, You Won't Have Our Park!' Hot Spots, *Cultural Anthropology* (online), 2013, https://culanth.org/fieldsights/394-the-what-of-occupation-you-took-our-cemetery-you-won-t-have-our-park.

Bilge, Yakup. *Geçmişten Günümüze Süryaniler.* Istanbul: Zvi-Geyik, 2001.

———. "The Saint Gabriel Monastery Trust." In *The Slow Disappearance of the Syriacs from Turkey and of the Grounds of the Mor Gabriel Monastery,* edited by Pieter Omtzigt, Markus Tozman, and Andrea Tyndall, 209–219. Munster: LIT, 2012.

Biner, Zerrin Özlem. "Retrieving the Dignity of a Cosmopolitan City: Contested Perspectives on Rights, Ethnicity and Culture." *New Perspectives on Turkey* 37 (2007): 31–58.

———. "Acts of Defacement, Memory of Loss: Ghostly Effects of the Armenian Crisis in Mardin, Southeastern Turkey." *History and Memory* 22, no. 2 (2010): 68–94.

———. "Multiple Imaginations of the State: Understanding a Mobile Conflict of Justice and Accountability from the Perspective of Assyrian-Syriac Christians." *Citizenship Studies* 15, no. 3 (2011): 367–379.

———. "Documenting Truth in the Margins of the Turkish State." In *Law Against the State: Ethnographic Forays into Law's Transformations,* edited by Julia Eckert, Brian Donahoe, Christian Strumpell, and Zerrin Özlem Biner, 228–245. Cambridge: Cambridge University Press, 2012.

———. "The Logic of Compensation: Between the Right to Compensation and the Right to Justice in Turkey." *Humanity* 4, no. 1 (2013): 73–91.

———. "Ethnographic Explorations on Past Legacies of Violence and Present Legal Struggles in Midyat, Southeastern Turkey." In *The Spatial (Re)Production of the Kurdish Issue: Multiple and Contradicting Trajectories,* edited by Zeynep Gambetti and Joost Jongerden. London: Routledge, 2015.

———. "Haunted by Debt: Calculating the Cost of Loss and Violence in Turkey." *Theory and Event* 19, no. 1 supplement (2016).

Boucly, Julien. "World Heritage Manufacture in Turkey and the Introduction of a New Public Policy System." In *Turkish Cultural Policies in a Global World,* edited by Muriel Girard, Jean-François Polo, and Clémence Scalbert Yücel, 233–257. London: Palgrave Macmillan, 2018.

Bozarslan, Hamit. *From Political Struggle to Self Sacrifice: Violence in the Middle East.* Princeton, NJ: Markus Wiener, 2005.

———. "The Kurds and the Middle Eastern State of Violence: 1980s and 2010s." *Kurdish Studies* 2, no. 1 (2014): 4–13.

Bozcalı, Fırat, and Çağrı Yoltar. "A Look at Gezi Park from Turkey's Kurdistan." Hot Spots, *Cultural Anthropology* (online), 2013, https://culanth.org/fieldsights/396-a-look-at-gezi-park-from-turkey-s-kurdistan.

Breglia, Lisa. *Monumental Ambivalence: The Politics of Heritage.* Austin: University of Texas Press, 2006.

Brock, Sebastian. "The Monastery of Mor Gabriel: A Historical Overview and Its Wider Significance Today." In *The Slow Disappearance of the Syriacs from Turkey and of the Grounds of the Mor Gabriel Monastery*, edited by Pieter Omtzigt, Markus Tozman, and Andrea Tyndall, 181–201. Munster: LIT, 2012.

Brock, Sebastian, Aaron M, Butts, George Kiraz and Lucas Van Rompay, eds. *The Gorgias Encyclopedic Dictionary of the Syriac Heritage*. Piscataway, NJ: Gorgias Press, 2011.

Brumann, Christoph. "Outside the Glass Case: The Social Life of Urban Heritage in Kyoto." *American Ethnologist* 36, no. 2 (2009): 276–299.

Bunten, Alexis C. "Sharing Culture or Selling Out? Developing the Commodified Persona in the Heritage Industry." *American Ethnologist* 35, no. 3 (2008): 380–395.

Busse, Mark, and Veronica Strang. "Introduction: Ownership and Appropriation." In *Ownership and Appropriation*, edited by Veronica Strang and Mark Busse. Oxford: Berg, 2011.

Butler, Judith. *Frames of War: When Is Life Grievable?* London: Verso, 2010.

———. *Precarious Life: The Powers of Mourning and Violence*. London: Verso, 2004.

Butler, Judith, and Athena Athanasiou. *Dispossession: The Performative in the Political*. London: Polity Press, 2013.

Çağlar, Ayşe. "Rescaling Cities, Cultural Diversity and Transnationalism: Migrants of Mardin and Essen." *Ethnic and Racial Studies* 30, no. 6 (2007): 1070–1095.

Çapatay, Soner. "Kim Türk, Kim Vatandas? Erken Cumhuriyet Dönemi Vatandaslık Rejimi Üzerine Bir Çalisma." *Toplum Bilim* 98 (2003): 166–185.

Casier, Marlies. "Contesting the 'Truth' of Turkey's Human Rights Situation: State-Association Interactions in and Outside the Southeast." *European Journal of Turkish Studies* (online), 10 (2009), https://journals.openedition.org/ejts/4190.

Casier, Marlies, Joost Jongerden, and Nic Walker. "Fruitless Attempts? The Kurdish Initiative and Containment of the Kurdish Movement in Turkey." *New Perspectives on Turkey* 44 (2011): 103–127.

Çaylı, Eray. "Inheriting Dispossession, Mobilizing Vulnerability:Heritage amid Protest in Contemporary Turkey." *International Journal of Islamic Architecture* 5, no. 2 (2016): 359–379.

Çelik, Ayşe Betül. "Non-Governmental and International Organisations in the Possible Peace Process in Turkey's Conflict-Induced Displacement." *Journal of Refugee Studies* 26, no. 1 (2013): 1–25.

Çerme, Tomas. "Taşçılık Zanaati Ve Mimarisiyle Mardin Şehri." *Tarih ve Toplum* 200 (2000): 79–82.

Cesari, Chiara de. "Creative Heritage: Palestinian Heritage NGOs and Defiant Arts of Government." *American Anthropologist* 112, no. 4 (2010): 625–637.

Çetinoğlu, Sait. "Soykırımı Laboratuarında İncelemek: Mardin 1915." In *Mardin 1915: Bir Yıkımın Patolojik Anatomisi*, edited by Yves Ternon, 9–77. Istanbul: Belge, 2013.

Çetrez, Önver A., Sargon G. Donabed, and Aryo Makko, eds. *The Assyrian Heritage: Threads of Continuity and Influence*. Uppsala: Uppsala University Press, 2012.

Collins, John F. "'But What If I Should Need to Defecate in Your Neighborhood, Madame?': Empire, Redemption and the 'Tradition of the Oppressed' in a Brazilian Historical Center." *Cultural Anthropology* 23, no. 2 (2008): 279–328.

———. *Revolt of the Saints: Memory and Redemption in the Twilight of Brazilian Racial Democracy*. Durham, NC: Duke University Press, 2015.

———. "Ruins, Redemption, and Brazil's Imperial Exception." In *Imperial Debris: On Ruins and Reflection*, edited by Ann L. Stoler, 162–194. Durham, NC: Duke University Press, 2013.

Comaroff, John L., and Jean Comaroff. "Law and Disorder in the Postcolony: An Introduction." In *Law and Disorder in the Postcolony*, edited by Jean Comaroff and John L. Comaroff, 1–57. Chicago: University of Chicago Press, 2006.

Coole, Diana, and Samantha Frost. "Introducing the New Materialisms." In *New Materialisms: Ontology, Agency and Politics*, edited by Diana Coole and Samantha Frost, 1–47. Durham, NC: Duke University Press, 2010.

Costa, Elisabeth. *Social Media in Southeast Turkey*. London: UCL Press, 2013.

Crapanzano, Vincent. *Hermes' Dilemma and Hamlet's Desire: On the Epistemology of Interpretation*. Cambridge, MA: Harvard University Press, 1992.

———. *Tuhami: Portrait of a Moroccan*. Chicago: University of Chicago Press, 1980.

Darıcı, Haydar. "Adults See Politics as a Game: Politics of Kurdish Children in Urban Turkey." *International Journal of Middle Eastern Studies* 45 (2013): 775–790.

———. "The Kurdish Self-Governance Movement in Turkey's South-East: An Interview with Haydar Darıcı." LEFTEAST, 2015, http://www.criticatac.ro/lefteast/kurdish-self-governance/.

———. "Of Kurdish Youth and Ditches." *Theory and Event* 19, no. 1 supplement (2016).

Das, Veena. *Critical Events: An Anthropological Perspective on Contemporary India*. Oxford: Oxford University Press, 1997.

———. "The Act of Witnessing, Violence, Poisonous Knowledge and Subjectivity." In *Violence and Subjectivity*, edited by Veena Das, Arthur Kleinman, Mamphela Ramphele, and Pamela Reynolds, 205–226. Berkeley: University of California Press, 2000.

———. *Life and Words: Violence and Descent into the Ordinary*. Berkeley: University of California Press, 2006.

———. "The Life of Humans and the Life of Roaming Spirits." In *Rethinking the Human*, edited by J. Michelle Molina and Donald K. Swearer, 31–51. Cambridge, MA: Harvard University Press, 2010.

Das, Veena, and Arthur Kleinman. Introduction. In *Violence and Subjectivity*, edited by Veena Das, Arthur Kleinman, Mamphela Ramphele, and Pamela Reynolds, 1–19. Berkeley: University of California Press, 2000.

Das, Veena, and Deborah Poole. "State and Its Margins: Comparative Ethnographies." *Anthropology in the Margins of the State*, edited by Veena Das and Deborah Poole, 3–35. Santa Fe, NM: School of American Research Press, 2004.

Dawdy, Shanon. "Clockpunk Anthropology and the Ruins of Modernity." *Current Anthropology* 51, no. 6 (2010): 761–793.

Dolapönü, Hanna. *Tarihte Mardin*. Istanbul: Hilal Matbaacılık, 1971.

Douglas, Mary. "Foreword: No Free Gifts." In *The Gift*, by Marcel Mauss, edited by Mary Douglas, ix–xxiii. London: Routledge, 2002.

Dumper, Michael, and Craig Larkin. "The Politics of Heritage and the Limitations of International Agency in Contested Cities: A Study of the Role of UNESCO in Jerusalem's Old City." *Review of International Studies* 38, no. 1 (2012): 25–52.

Dündar, Fuat. *İttihat Ve Terakki'nin Müslümanları İskan Politikasi (1913–1918).* Istanbul: Iletişim, 2001.

———. *Modern Türkiye'nin Şifresi: İttihat Ve Terakki'nin Ethnisite Mühendisliği, 1913–1918.* Istanbul: İletişim Yayınları, 2008.

Düzel, Esin. "Fragile Goddesses: Moral Subjectivity and Militarized Agencies in Female Guerrilla Diaries and Memoirs." *International Feminist Journal of Politics* 20, no. 2 (2018): 1–16.

Eckert, Julia. "Rumours of Rights." In *Law Against the State: Ethnographic Forays into Law's Transformations*, edited by Julia Eckert, Brian Donahoe, Christian Strumpell, and Zerrin Özlem Biner, 147–171. Cambridge: Cambridge University Press, 2012.

Eckert, Julia, Zerrin Özlem Biner, Brian Donahoe, and Christian Strumpell. "Introduction: Law's Travels and Transformations." In *Law Against the State: Ethnographic Forays into Law's Transformations*, edited by Julia Eckert, Brian Donahoe, Christian Strumpell, and Zerrin Özlem Biner, 1–23. Cambridge: Cambridge University Press, 2012.

Eckert, Julia, Brian Donahoe, Christian Strumpell, and Zerrin Özlem Biner, eds. *Law Against the State: Ethnographic Forays into Law's Transformations.* Cambridge: Cambridge University Press, 2012.

Edensor, Tim. *Industrial Ruins: Aesthetics, Ruins and Materiality.* London: Berg, 2005.

Ekmekçioglu, Lerna. *Recovering Armenia: The Limits of Belonging in Post-Genocide Turkey.* Stanford: Standford University Press, 2016.

Eng, David L. and David Kazanjian, eds. *Loss: The Politics of Mourning.* Berkeley: University of California Press, 2003.

Erol, Su. *Mazlum Ve Makul: İstanbul Süryanilerinde Ethno-Dinsel Kimlik İnşası Ve Kimlik Stratejileri.* Istanbul: İletisim, 2016.

Ertür, Başak. "Barricades: Resources and Residues of Resistance." In *Vulnerability and Resistance*, edited by Judith Butler, Leticia Sabsay, and Zeynep Gambetti, 97–121. Durham, NC: Duke University Press, 2016a.

Ertür, Başak, and James Martel. "Introduction: Something Is Rotten in the State." *Theory and Event* 19, no. 1 (2016b).

Fehervary, Krisztina. "Goods and States: The Political Logic of State-Socialist Material Culture." *Comparative Studies in Society and History* 51, no. 2 (2009): 426–459.

Ferry, Elisabeth Emma. *Not Ours Alone: Patrimony, Value and Collectivity in Contemporary Mexico.* New York: Columbia University Press, 2005.

Franquesa, Jaume. "On Keeping and Selling: The Political Economy of Heritage Making in Contemporary Spain." *Cultural Anthropology* 54, no. 3 (2013): 346–369.

Gambetti, Zeynep. "The Conflictual (Trans)Formation of the Public Sphere in Urban Space: The Case of Diyarbakır." *New Perspectives on Turkey* 32 (2005): 43–71.

Gambetti, Zeynep, and Joost Jongerden, eds. *The Kurdish Issue in Turkey: A Spatial Perspective.* London: Routledge, 2015.

Gaunt, David. "Mardin'in Çatılarının Manzarası: Kılıç Yılında Herkes Ne Gördü?" In *Mardin Tebliğleri: Mardin Ve Çevresi Toplumsal Ve Ekonomik Tarihi Konferansı*, 14–27. Istanbul: Hrant Dink Foundation, 2013.

———. *Massacres, Resistance, Protectors: Muslim- Christian Relations in Eastern Anatolia During World War 1*. Piscataway, NJ: Gorgias Press, 2006.

Gaunt, David, Naures Atto, and Soner O. Barthroma. *Let Them Not Return: Sayfo—the Genocide Against the Assyrian, Syriac, and Chaldean Christians in the Ottoman Empire*. London: I. B. Tauris, 2017.

Girard, Muriel. "What Heritage Tells Us About the Turkish State and Turkish Society." *European Journal of Turkish Studies* (online), 19 (2014), https://journals.openedition.org/ejts/5227.

Girard, Muriel, Jean-François Polo, and Clémence Scalbert-Yücel. "Introduction: Turkish Cultural Policies in a Global World—Circulations, Territories, and Actors." In *Turkish Cultural Policies in a Global World*, edited by Muriel Girard, Jean-François Polo, and Clémence Scalbert-Yücel, 1–22. London: Palgrave Macmillan, 2018.

Göcek, Fatma Müge. *Denial of Violence: Ottoman Past, Turkish Present, and Collective Violence against the Armenians, 1789–2009*. Oxford: Oxford University Press, 2014.

Göyünç, Nejat. XVI. *Yüzyılda Mardin Sancağı*. Ankara: Türk Tarih Kurumu, 1991.

Gordillo, Gaston R. *Rubble: The Afterlife of Destruction*. Durham, NC: Duke University Press, 2014.

Graeber, David. *Debt: The First 5,000 Years*. London: Melville House, 2011.

Gündoğan, Azat. "Space, State-Making and Contentious Kurdish Politics in Turkey." In *The Kurdish Issue in Turkey: A Spatial Perspective*, edited by Zeynep Gambetti and Joost Jongerden, 27–62. London: Routledge, 2015.

Güneş, Cengiz. *The Kurdish National Movement in Turkey: From Protest to Resistance*. London: Routledge, 2012.

Güneş, Cengiz, and Welat Zeydanlıoğlu. "Introduction: Turkey and the Kurds." In *The Kurdish Question in Turkey: New Perspectives on Violence, Representation and Reconciliation*, edited by Cengiz Güneş and Welat Zeydanlıoğlu. 1–20. London: Routledge, 2013.

Gusten, Susan. *A Farewell to Turabdin*. Istanbul: Istanbul Policy Centre, 2016.

———. *The Syriac Property Issue in Turabdin*. Istanbul: Istanbul Policy Centre, 2015.

Hakyemez, Serra Makbule. "Margins of the Archive: Torture, Heroism and the Ordinary in Prison No 5. Turkey." *Anthropological Quarterly* 90 (2017a): 107–138.

———. *Turkey's Failed Peace Process with the Kurds: A Different Explanation*. Waltham, MA: Crown Center for Middle East Studies, Brandeis University, 2017b.

Hale, Charles R. "Neoliberal Multiculturalism: The Re-making of Cultural Rights and Racial Dominance in Central America." *Political and Legal Anthropology Review (POLAR)* 28, no. 1 (2005): 10–19.

Hann, Chris, ed. *Property Relations: Renewing the Anthropological Tradition*. Cambridge: Cambridge University Press, 1998.

Hansen, Blom Thomas, and Finn Stepputat, eds. *Sovereign Bodies: Citizens, Migrants and States in the Postcolonial World*. Princeton, NJ: Princeton University Press, 2005.

Harris, Leila M. "States at the Limit: Tracing Contemporary State-Society Relations in the Borderlands of Southeastern Turkey." *European Journal of Turkish Studies* (online), 10 (2009). https://journals.openedition.org/ejts/4122.

Harvey, David. "The 'New' Imperialism: Accumulation by Dispossession." *Socialist Register* 40 (2004): 63–87.

Harvey, Penelope. "Cementing Relations: The Materiality of Roads and Public Spaces in Provincial Peru." *Social Analysis* 54, no. 2 (2010): 28–46.

Hermez, Sami. "The War Is Going to Ignite: On the Anticipation of Violence in Lebanon." *Political and Legal Anthropology Review (POLAR)* 35, no. 2 (2012): 327–344.

Hernández, Marie Theresa. *Delirio: The Fantastic, the Demonic and the Réel; The Buried History of Nuevo Leon.* Austin: University of Texas Press, 2002.

Herscher, Andrew. *Violence Taking Place: The Architecture of the Kosova Conflict.* Stanford, CA: Stanford University Press, 2010.

Herzfeld, Michael. "Engagement, Gentrification, and the Neoliberal Hijacking of History." *Current Anthropology* 51, no. 2 (2010): 259–267.

———. "Spatial Cleansing: Monumental Vacuity and the Idea of the West." *Journal of Material Culture* 11, no. 1–2 (2006): 127–149.

Hirsch, Eric, and Marilyn Strathern, eds. *Transactions and Creations: Property Debates and the Stimulus of Melanesia.* London: Berghahn, 2004.

Housing and Land Rights Network. "Expropriation, Evictions and Demolitions in Suriçi, Diyarbakır, Turkey." Housing and Land Rights Network, Habitat International Coalition, 2016. https://www.hlrn.org/violation.php?id=pW1pZq0=.

Humphrey, Caroline. "Sovereignty." In *A Companion to the Anthropology of Politics*, edited by David Nugent and Joan Vincent. London: Blackwell, 2008.

Humphrey, Caroline, and Katherine Verdery. "Introduction: Raising Questions About Property." In *Property in Question: Value Transformation in the Global Economy*, edited by Katherine Verdery and Caroline Humphrey, 1–25. Oxford: Berg, 2004.

Hurst, Alan. "The Lausanne Treaty: High Aspirations, Highly Neglected." In *The Slow Disappearance of the Syriacs from Turkey and of the Grounds of the Mor Gabriel Monastery*, edited by Peter Omtzigt, Markuz Tozman, and Andrea Tyndall, 25–47. Berlin: LIT, 2012.

Iğsız, Aslı. "From Alliance of Civilisations to Branding the Nation: Turkish Studies, Image Wars and Politics of Comparison in an Age of Neoliberalism." *Turkish Studies* 15, no. 4 (2014): 689–704.

———. "Palimpsests of Multiculturalism and Museumization of Culture: Greco-Turkish Population Exchange Museum as an Istanbul 2010 European Capital of Culture Project." *Comparative Studies of South Asia, Africa and the Middle East* 35, no. 2 (2015): 324–345.

Ismail, Salwa. *Encountering the Everyday State: Political Life in Cairo's New Quarters.* Minneapolis: University of Minnesota Press, 2006.

Jansen, Stef. "Hope for/Against the State: Gridding in a Besieged Sarajevo Suburb." *Ethnos Journal of Anthropology* 79, no. 2 (2014): 238–260.

———. "People and Things in the Ethnography of Borders: Materialising the Division of Sarajevo." *Social Anthropology* 21, no. 1 (2013): 23–37.

Jansen, Stef, and Staffan Löfving. "Introduction: Violence, Movement and the Making of Home." *Focaal: European Journal of Anthropology* 49 (2007): 3–14.

Jongerden, Joost. *The Settlement Issue in Turkey and the Kurds: An Analysis of Spatial Policies, Modernity and the War.* Leiden: Brill, 2007.

———. "Crafting Space, Making People: The Spatial Design of Nation in Modern Turkey." *Special Issue: State and Society Relations in the Southeast. European Journal of Turkish Studies* (online), 10 (2009), https://journals.openedition.org/ejts/4014

———. "Looking Beyond the State: Transitional Justice and the Kurdish Issue in Turkey." *Ethnic and Racial Studies* 41, no. 4 (2018): 721–738.

Jongerden, Joost, and Ahmet Hamdi Akkaya. "Democratic Confederalism as a Kurdish Spring: The PKK and the Quest for Radical Democracy." In *The Kurdish Spring: Geopolitical Changes and the Kurds*, edited by Mohammed M. A. Ahmed and Michael M. Gunter, 163–185. Mazda: Costa Mesa, 2013.

———. "The Kurdistan Workers' Party and a New Left in Turkey: Analysis of the Revolutionary Movement in Turkey Through the PKK's Memorial Text on Haki Karer." *European Journal of Turkish Studies* (online), 14 (2012), https://journals.openedition.org/ejts/4613.

———. "Kurds and the PKK." In *The Wiley Blackwell Encyclopedia of Race, Ethnicity, and Nationalism*, edited by John Stone, Rutledge M. Dennis, Polly Rizova, Anthony D. Smith, and Xiaoshuo Hou, 1–5. London: Wiley-Blackwell, 2016.

Jongerden, Joost, and Jelle Verheij, eds. *Social Relations in Ottoman Diyarbekir.* Leiden: Brill, 2012.

Karaca, Banu. "Governance of or through Culture? Cultural Policy and the Politics of Culture in Europe." *Focaal—European Journal of Anthropology* 55 (2009): 27–40.

———. "Images Delegitimized and Discouraged: Explicitly Political Art and the Arbitrariness of the Unspeakable." *New Perspectives on Turkey* 45 (2011): 155–184.

Karaman, Ozan. "Urban Renewal in Istanbul: Reconfigured Spaces, Robotic Lives." *International Journal of Urban and Regional Research* 37, no. 2 (2013): 715–733.

Kavuri-Bauer, Santhi. *Monumental Matters: The Power, Subjectivity, and Space of India's Mughal Architecture.* Durham, NC: Duke University Press, 2011.

Kelly, Tobias. "The Attractions of Accountancy: Living an Ordinary Life During the Second Palestinian Intifada." *Ethnography* 9, no. 3 (2008): 351–376.

Kelly, Tobias, and Alpa Shah. "Introduction—a Double Edged Sword: Protection and State Violence." *Critique of Anthropology* 26 (2006): 251–257.

Kieser, Hans-Lukas, Kerem Öktem, and Maurus Reinkowski, eds. *World War I and the End of the Ottomans: From the Balkan Wars to the Armenian Genocide.* London: I. B. Tauris, 2015.

Kirişci, Kemal, and Gareth M. Winrow. *The Kurdish Question and Turkey: An Example of a Trans-state Ethnic Conflict.* London: Psychology Press, 1997.

Koğacıoğlu, Dicle. "Conduct, Meaning and Inequality in an Istanbul Court-House." *New Perspectives on Turkey* 39 (2008): 97–127.

Kohn, Eduardo. "Anthropology of Ontologies." *Annual Review of Anthropology* 44 (2015): 311–327.

Küçük, Bülent, and Ceren Özselçuk. "The Rojava Experience: Possibilities and Challanges of Building a Democratic Life." *South Atlantic Quarterly* 115, no. 1 (2016): 184–196.

Küçük, Murat. "Aidiyetin Mekanı: Mardin'de Kimlik Ve Mekanin Değişimi." *İdealkent* 9 (2013): 114–137.

———. "Intersecting Identities: Context and Change in the Case of Mardinian Arabs." MA Diss.,Middle East Technical University, 2012.

Küçük, Murat, and Nurdan Z. Atalay Güneş. "Sosyal Bilimlerde Mardin Üzerine Araştırmalar Ve Tezler Hakkında Bir İnceleme Denemesi." In *VI. Ulusal Sosyoloji Kongresi: Toplumsal Dönüşümler ve Sosyolojik Yaklaşımlar*. Aydın: Adnan Menderes Üniversitesi, 2009.

Kurban, Dilek. "Human Rights Watch, Kurdish Human Rights Project, and the European Court of Human Rights on Internal Displacement in Turkey." In *Coming to Terms with Forced Migration: Post-displacement Restitution of Citizenship Rights in Turkey*, edited by Dilek Kurban, Deniz Yükseker, Ayşe Betül Çelik, Turgay Ünalan, and Tamer A. Aker, 119–145. Istanbul: TESEV, 2007.

Kurban, Dilek, and Kezban Hatemi. *The Story of an Alien(Ation): Real Estate Ownership Problems of Non-Muslim Foundations and Communities in Turkey*. Istanbul: TESEV, 2009.

Kurban, Dilek, Deniz Yükseker, Ayşe Betül Çelik, Turgay Ünalan, and Tamer A. Aker, eds. *Coming to Terms with Forced Migration: Post-Displacement Restitution of Citizenship Rights in Turkey*. Istanbul: TESEV, 2007.

Kuyucu, Tuna, and Özlem Ünsal. "'Urban Transformation' as State-Led Property Transfer: An Analysis of Two Cases of Urban Renewal in Istanbul." *Urban Studies* 47, no. 7 (2010): 1479–1499.

Lambek, Michael. *Knowledge and Practice in Mayotte: Local Discourses of Islam, Sorcery and Spirit Possession*. Toronto: University of Toronto Press, 1993.

———. *Ordinary Ethics: Anthropology, Language and Action*. New York: Fordham University Press, 2010.

Laszczkowski, Mateusz. "'Demo Version of a City': Buildings, Affects, and the State in Astana." *Journal of the Royal Anthropological Institute* 22, no. 1 (2015): 148–165.

Latour, Bruno. "From Realpolitik to Dingpolitik or How to Make Things Public." In *Making Things Public: Atmospheres of Democracy*, edited by Bruno Latour and Peter Wiebel. 4–31. Cambridge, MA: MIT Press, 2005.

Lazzarato, Maurizio. *Governing by Debt*. Cambridge, MA: MIT Press, 2015.

Lebling, Robert. *Legends of the Fire Spirits: Jinn and Genies from Arabia to Zanzibar*. London: I. B. Tauris, 2011.

Leezenberg, Michiel. "The Ambiguities of Democratic Autonomy: The Kurdish Movement in Turkey and Rojava." *Southeast European and Black Sea Studies* 16, no. 4 (2016): 671–690.

Levi, Primo. *The Drowned and the Saved*. London: Abacus, 1989.

Levy, Robert I., Jeannette Marie Mageo, and Alan Howard. "Gods, Spirits and History: A Theoretical Perspective." In *Spirits in Culture, History and Mind*, edited by Jeannette Marie Mageo and Alan Howard, 11–29. London: Routledge, 1996.

Lorey, Isabell. *State of Insecurity: Government of the Precarious*. London: Verso, 2015.

Lubkemann, Stephen C. *Culture in Chaos: An Anthropology of the Social Condition in War*. Chicago: University of Chicago Press, 2007.

Macar, Elçin. "Mardin'deki Amerikalı Protestan Misyonerler Ve Kurumları." In *Mardin Tebliğleri: Mardin Ve Çevresi Toplumsal Ve Ekonomik Tarihi Konferansı*, 113–126. Istanbul: Hrant Dink Foundation, 2012..

Macdonald, Sharon. "Reassembling Nuremberg, Reassembling Heritage." *Journal of Cultural Economy* 2, no. 1 (2009): 117–134.

Mandıracı, Berkay. "Turkey's PKK Conflict: The Death Toll." https://www.crisisgroup.org /europe-central-asia/western-europemediterranean/turkey/turkey-s-pkk-conflict-death -toll. Accessed 10 July 2017.

Massumi, Brian. *Parables for the Virtual: Movement, Affect and Sensation*. Durham, NC: Duke University Press, 2002.

Maurer, Bill, and Gabriele Schwab. "Introduction: The Political and Psychic Economies of Accelerating Possession." In *Accelerating Possession: Gobal Futures of Property and Personhood*, edited by Bill Maurer and Gabriele Schwab, 1–17. New York: Columbia University Press, 2006.

Mauss, Marcel. *The Gift*. London: Routledge, 2001.

Minow, Martha. *Between Vengeance and Forgiveness: Facing History After Genocide and Mass Violence*. Boston: Beacon Press, 1998.

Mitchell, Timothy. "The 'Limits' of the State." *American Political Science Review* 85 (1991): 77–96.

Mittermaier, Amira. "Dreams from Elsewhere: Muslim Subjectivities Beyond the Trope of Self-Cultivation." *Journal of the Royal Anthropological Institute* no. 18 (2012): 247–265.

Mungan, Murathan. *Geyikler Ve Lanetler: Mezopotamya Üçlemesi*. Vol. 3. Istanbul: Metis, 1992a.

——. *Mahmud Ile Yezida: Mezopotamya Üçlemesi*. Vol. 1. Istanbul: Metis, 1992b.

——. *Paranın Cinleri*. Istanbul: Metis, 1999.

——. *Taziye: Mezopotamya Üçlemesi*. Vol. 2. Istanbul: Metis, 1992c.

Naby, Eden. "Mardin'de Kadın Misyonerler, Süryaniler Ve Ermeniler." In *Mardin Tebliğleri: Mardin Ve Çevresi Toplumsal Ve Ekonomik Tarihi Konferansı*, 126–131. Istanbul: Hrant Dink Foundation, 2013.

Navaro-Yashin, Yael. "Editorial—Breaking Memory, Spoiling Memorization: The Taksim Protests in Istanbul." Hot Spots, *Cultural Anthropology* (online), 2013, https://culanth.org /fieldsights/411-editorial-breaking-memory-spoiling-memorization-the-taksim -protests-in-istanbul.

——. *Faces of the State: Secularism and Public Life in Turkey*. Princeton, NJ: Princeton University Press, 2002.

——. *The Make-Believe Space: Affective Geography in a Postwar Polity*. Durham, NC: Duke University Press, 2012.

Naveeda, Khan. "Of Children and Jinn: An Inquiry into an Unexpected Friendship During Uncertain Times." *Cultural Anthropology* 21, no. 2 (2006): 234–264.

Neyzi, Leyla, and Haydar Darıcı. "Generation in Debt: Family, Politics and Youth Subjectivities in Diyarbakır." *New Perspectives on Turkey* 52 (2015): 55–75.

O'Connor, Francis, and Bahar Başer. "Communal Violence and Ethnic Polarization Before and After the 2015 Elections in Turkey: Attacks Against the HDP and the Kurdish Population." *Southeast European and Black Sea Studies* 18, no. 1 (2018): 53–72.

Office of the United Nations High Commissioner for Human Rights. "Report on the Human Rights Situation in South-east Turkey: July 2015 to December 2016." UN High Commissioner for Human Rights, 1–25, 2017, https://www.ohchr.org/Documents/Countries/TR/OHCHR_South-East_TurkeyReport_10March2017.pdf.

Öktem, Kerem. *Angry Nation: Turkey Since 1989.* London: Zed Books, 2011.

———. "Incorporating the Time and Space of the Ethnic 'Other': Nationalism and Space in Southeast Turkey in the Nineteenth and Twentieth Centuries." *Nations and Nationalism* 10, no. 4 (2004): 559–578.

Olson, Robert. *The Emergence of Kurdish Nationalism and the Sheikh Said Rebellion, 1880–1925.* Austin: University of Texas Press, 1989.

Omtzigt, Pieter, Markuz Tozman, and Andrea Tyndall, eds. *The Slow Disappearance of the Syriacs from Turkey and of the Grounds of the Mor Gabriel Monastery.* Munster: LIT, 2012.

Onaran, Nevzat. *Emval-I Metruke Olayı: Osmanlı'da Ve Cumhuriyette Ermeni Ve Rum Mallarının Türkleştirilmesi.* Istanbul: Belge, 2010.

Önder, Soner. "Minority Rights in Turkey: Quo Vadis, Assyrians?" In *The Slow Disappearance of the Syriacs from Turkey; and of the Grounds of the Mor Gabriel Monastery,* edited by Pieter Omtzigt, Markus Tozman, and Andrea Tyndall, 99–121. Munster: LIT, 2012.

Oran, Baskın. "Reconciled by Mor Gabriel." In *The Slow Disappearance of the Syriacs from Turkey and of the Grounds of the Mor Gabriel Monastery,* edited by Pieter Omtzigt, Markus Tozman, and Andrea Tyndall, 201–209. Munster: LIT, 2012.

Özcan, Kemal Ali. *Turkey's Kurds: A Theoretical Analysis of the PKK and Abdullah Ocalan.* London: Routledge, 2006.

Özcoşar, İbrahim. "19. Yüzyılda ABD Misyonerlerinin Mardin Süryanilerine Yönelik Faaliyetleri." *Elektronik Journal of Social Sciences* 18, no. 5 (2006): 142–154.

———, ed. *Makalelerle Mardin: Önemli Simalar-Dini Topluluklar.* Vol. 4. Istanbul: Imak Ofset, 2007a.

———, ed. *Makalelerle Mardin: Tarih-Coğrafya.* Vol. 1. Istanbul: Imak Ofset, 2007b.

———, ed. *Makalelerle Mardin: Eğitim-Kültür-Edebiyat.* Vol. 3. Istanbul: Imak Ofset, 2007c.

———, ed. *Makalelerle Mardin: Ekonomi-Nüfus-Kentsel Yapı.* Vol. 2. Istanbul: Imak Ofset, 2007d.

Özcoşar, İbrahim, and Hüseyin H. Güneş. *252 Nolu Mardin Şeriye Sicili Belge Özetleri Ve Mardin.* Mardin: Mardin Tarihi İhtisas Kütüphanesi, 2006.

Özdem, Filiz, ed. *Taşın Belleği Mardin.* Istanbul: Yapı Kredi Yayınları, 2005.

Özgen, H. Neşe. "Devlet, Sınır, Aşiret: Aşiretin Etnik Bir Kimlik Olarak Yeniden İnşası." *Toplum ve Bilim* 108 (2007): 239–261.

———. *Toplumsal Hafızanın Hatırlama Ve Unutma Biçimleri: Van-Özalp Ve 33 Kurşun Olayı.* Istanbul: TÜSTAV, 2003.

Özgül, Ceren. "Legally Armenian: Tolerance, Conversion, and Name Change in Turkish Courts." *Comparative Studies in Society and History* 56, no. 3 (2014): 622–649.

Özkahraman, Cemal. "Failure of Peace Talks Between Turkey and the PKK: Victim of Traditional Turkish Policy or of Geopolitical Shifts in the Middle East?" *Contemporary Review of the Middle East* 4, no. 1 (2017): 50–66.

Özmen, Abdurrahim. "Hafıza Ve Hayat: Tur Abdin Süryanileri Sözlü Tarihinden Örnekler." In *Mardin Tebliğleri: Mardin Ve Çevresi Toplumsal Ve Ekonomik Tarihi Konferansi*, 99–113. Istanbul: Hrant Dink Foundation, 2013.

Özoğlu, Hakan. *Kurdish Notables and the Ottoman State: Evolving Identities, Competing Loyalties and Shifting Boundaries*. Binghamton: SUNY Press, 2004.

Özselçuk, Ceren, and Bülent Küçük. "Mesafeli Devletten Hizmetkar Devlete: Akp'nin Kısmi Tanıma Siyaseti." *Toplum ve Bilim* 132 (2015): 162–190.

Özsoy, Hişyar. "Between Gift and Taboo: Death and the Negotiation of National Identity and Sovereignty in the Kurdish Conflict in Turkey." PhD diss., University of Texas, 2010.

———. "The Missing Grave of Sheikh Said: Kurdish Formations of Memory, Place, and Sovereignty in Turkey." In *Everyday Occupations: Experiencing Militarism in South Asia and the Middle East*, edited by Kamala Visweswaran, 191–220. Philadelphia: University of Pennsylvania Press, 2013.

Palmer, Andrew. "Saints, Scribes and Survival: The Renovation and Replacement of the Manuscripts and Monasteries in Midyat." In *International Midyat Symposium*, edited by İbrahim Özcoşar, 597–624. Mardin: Artuklu Üniversitesi Yayınları, 2011.

Pandey, Gyanendra. *Routine Violence: Nations, Fragments, Histories*. Stanford, CA: Stanford University Press, 2006.

Pandolfo, Stefania. "The Thin Line of Modernity: Some Moroccan Debates on Subjectivity." In *Questions of Modernity*, edited by Timothy Mitchell, 115–147. Minneapolis: University of Minnesota Press, 2000.

Parla, Ayşe, and Ceren Özgül. "Property, Dispossession, and Citizenship in Turkey; or, the History of the Gezi Uprising Starts in the Surp Hagop Armenian Cemetery." *Public Culture* 28, no. 3 (2016): 617–653.

Potuoğlu-Cook, Öykü. "The Uneasy Vernacular: Choreographing Multiculturalism and Dancing Difference Away in Globalised Turkey." *Anthropological Notebooks* 26, no. 3 (2011): 93–105.

Povinelli, Elisabeth. *Economies of Abandonment*. Durham, NC: Duke University Press, 2011.

Rojas Pérez, Isaias. "Writing the Aftermath: Anthropology and 'Post-conflict.'" In *A Companion to Latin American Anthropology*, edited by Deborah Poole, 254–276. Oxford: Wiley-Blackwell, 2008.

Rothenberg, Celia Ealine. *Spirits of Palestine: Gender, Society and the Stories of the Jinn*. New York: Lexington Press, 2004.

Rubaii, Kali. "Concrete and Livability in Occupied Palestine." In *Engagement*: American Anthropological Association, 2016 https://aesengagement.wordpress.com/2016/09/20/concrete-and-livability-in-occupied-palestine/

Salemink, Oscar, and Mattias Borg Ramussen. "After Dispossession: Ethnographic Approaches to Neo-liberalisation." *Focaal—Journal of Global and Historical Anthropology* 74 (2016): 3–12.

Scalbert-Yücel, Clemence, and Marie Le Ray. "Knowledge, Ideology and Power. Deconstruct-
    ing Kurdish Studies." *European Journal of Turkish Studies* (online), 5 (2006), (Online),
    https://journals.openedition.org/ejts/777.

Scarry, Elaine. *The Body in Pain: The Making and Unmaking of the World.* New York: Oxford
    University Press, 1987.

Schafers, Marlene. "Being Sick of Politics: The Production of Dengbeji as Kurdish Cultural Her-
    itage in Contemporary Turkey." *European Journal of Turkish Studies* (online), 20 (2015),
    https://journals.openedition.org/ejts/5200.

———. "Writing Against Loss: Kurdish Women, Subaltern Authorship, and the Politics of
    Voice in Contemporary Turkey." *Journal of the Royal Anthropological Institute* 23, no. 3
    (2017): 1–19.

Scheper-Hughes, Nancy, and Philippe Bourgois. "Introduction: Making Sense of Violence."
    In *Violence in War and Peace: An Anthology,* edited by Nancy Scheper-Hughes and
    Philippe Bourgois, 1–27. London: Wiley-Blackwell, 2003.

Schmitt, Carl. *Political Theology: Four Chapters on the Concept of Sovereignty.* Translated by
    George D. Schwab. 1922. Chicago: University of Chicago Press, 1985.

Şengül, Serap Ruken. "Qirix: An 'Inverted Rhapsody' on Kurdish National Struggle, Gender,
    and Everyday Life in Diyarbakır." In *Everyday Occupations: Experiencing Militarism in
    South Asia and the Middle East,* edited by Kamala Visweswaran, 29–59. Philadelphia: Uni-
    versity of Pennsylvania Press, 2013.

Sert, Deniz. "Turkey's Position on IDP Properties: Lessons (Not) Learned." *International Mi-
    gration* 55, no. 5 (2017): 150–163.

Shah, Alpa. *In the Shadows of the State: Indigenous Politics, Environmentalism, and Insurgency
    in Jharkhand, India.* Durham, NC: Duke University Press, 2010.

Silverstein, Brian. "Reform in Turkey: Liberalisation as Government and Critique." *Anthro-
    pology Today* 26, no. 4 (2010): 22–25.

Slyomovics, Susan. "Financial Reparations, Blood Money, and Human Rights Witness Testi-
    mony: Morocco and Algeria." In *Humanitarianism and Suffering: The Mobilisation of Em-
    pathy,* edited by Richard A. Wilson and Richard D. Brown, 3–22. Cambridge: Cambridge
    University Press, 2009.

Söylemez, Ayça. "Şırnak Morgundaki Cenazeler Kimsesizler Mezarlığına Mı Defnedilecek?"
    Bianet, 2016. https://m.bianet.org/bianet/insan-haklari/170870-sirnak-morgundaki
    -cenazeler-kimsesizler-mezarligina-mi-defnedilecek. Accessed 10 June 2017.

Stewart, Kathleen C. *Ordinary Affects.* Durham, NC: Duke University Press, 2007.

Stoler, Ann Laura. "Affective States." In *A Companion to the Anthropology of Politics,* edited
    by David Nugent and Joan Vincent. 4–21. Oxford: Blackwell, 2007.

———, ed. *Imperial Debris: On Ruins and Ruination.* Durham, NC: Duke University Press, 2013a.

———. "Introduction: 'The Rot Remains': From Ruins to Ruination." In *Imperial Debris: On
    Ruins and Ruination,* edited by Ann L. Stoler, 1–39. Durham, NC: Duke University Press,
    2013b.

Strang, Veronica, and Mark Busse, eds. *Ownership and Appropriation.* London: Berg, 2011.

Strathern, Marilyn. *Property, Substance and Effect: Anthropological Essays on Persons and
    Things; Collected Essays, 1992–98.* London: Athlone Press, 1999.

Strathern, Marilyn, and Edward Hirsch. Introduction. In *Transactions and Creations: Property Debates and the Stimulus of Melanasia*, edited by Edward Hirsch and Marilyn Strathern, 1–18. New York: Berghahn, 2004.

Tambar, Kabir. "Brotherhood in Dispossession: State Violence and Ethics of Expectation in Turkey." *Cultural Anthropology* 31, no. 1 (2016): 30–55.

———. "Historical Critique and Political Voice after the Ottoman Empire." *History of the Present: A Journal of Critical History* 3, no. 2 (2013): 119–139.

Taneja, Anand Vivek. "Jinnealogy: Everyday Life and Islamic Theology in Post-partition Delhi." *HAU: Journal of Ethnographic Theory* 3, no. 3 (2013): 139–165.

———. "Saintly Visions: Other Histories and History's Others in the Medieval Ruins of Delhi." *Indian Economic and Social History Review* 49, no. 4 (2012): 557–590.

Taşğın, Ahmet, Canan Seyfeli, and Eyüp Tanriverdi, eds. *Süryaniler Ve Süryanilik*. 4 vols. Istanbul: Orient, 2005.

Taussig, Michael. "Culture of Terror-Space of Death." *Comparative Studies in Society and History* 26, no. 3 (1984): 467–497.

———. *Defacement: Public Secrecy and the Labor of Negative*. Stanford, CA: Stanford University Press, 1999.

———. *The Magic of the State*. London: Routledge, 1997.

———. *The Nervous System*. London: Routledge, 1992.

Ternon, Yves. *Mardin 1915: Bir Yıkımın Anatomisi*. Istanbul: Belge, 2013.

Tezcür, Güneş Murat. "Violence and Nationalist Mobilisation: The Onset of the Kurdish Insurgency in Turkey." *Journal of Nationalism and Ethnicity* 43, no. 2 (2014): 248–266.

Tezcür, Güneş Murat, and Mehmet Gürses. "Ethnic Exclusion and Mobilization: The Kurdish Conflict in Turkey." *Comparative Politics* 49, no. 2 (2017): 213–234.

Thiranagama, Sharika. *In My Mother's House: Civil War in Sri Lanka*. Philadelphia: University of Pennsylvania Press, 2011.

———. "A New Morning? Re-occupying Home in the Aftermath of Violence in Sri Lanka." *Focaal: European Journal of Anthropology* 49, no. 1 (2007): 45–61.

Thrift, Nigel. "Intensities of Feeling: Towards a Spatial Politics of Affect." *Geografiska Annaler: Series B; Human Geography* 86, no. 1 (2004): 57–78.

———. *Non-representational Theory: Space/Politics/Affect*. London: Routledge, 2008.

Tőrne, Annika. "On the Grounds Where They Will Walk in a Hundred Years' Time:Struggling with the Heritage of Violent Past in Post-genocidal Tunceli." *European Journal of Turkish Studies* (online), 20 (2015), https://journals.openedition.org/ejts/5099.

Tozman, Markus. "Cadastral Registration of Lands and Preservation Orders in Turkey's Southeast: Subtle Forms of Discrimination?" In *The Slow Disappearance of the Syriacs from Turkey and of the Grounds of the Mor Gabriel Monastery*, edited by Pieter Omtzig, Markus Tozman, and Andrea Tyndall, 139–157. Munster: LIT, 2012.

Travis, Hannibal, ed. *The Assyrian Genocide: Cultural and Political Legacies*. London: Routledge, 2017.

Tugal, Cihan. "Resistance Everywhere: The Gezi Revolt in Global Perspective." *New Perspectives on Turkey* 49 (2013): 147–162.

Ünalan, Turgay. "Internal Displacement: Current Global Conditions and Trends." In *Coming to Terms with Forced Migration: Post-Displacement Restitution of Citizenship Rights in Turkey*, edited by Dilek Kurban, Deniz Yükseker, Ayşe Betül Çelik, Turgay Ünalan, and Tamer A. Aker, 33–43. Istanbul: TESEV, 2007.

Ünalan, Turgay, Ayşe Betül Çelik, and Dilek Kurban. "Internal Displacement in Turkey: The Issue, Politics and Implementation." In *Coming to Terms with Forced Migration: Post-displacement Restitution of Citizenship Rights in Turkey*, edited by Dilek Kurban, Deniz Yükseker, Ayşe Betül Çelik, Turgay Ünalan, and Tamer A. Aker, 77–107. Istanbul: TESEV, 2007.

Üngör, Uğur Ümit. *The Making of Modern Turkey: Nation and State in Eastern Anatolia, 1913–1950*. Oxford: Oxford University Press, 2011.

Üngör, Uğur Ümit, and Mehmet Polatel. *Confiscation and Destruction: The Young Turk Seizure of Armenian Property*. London: Bloomsbury, 2013.

Üstündağ, Nazan. "New Wars and Autonomous Self Defense." *Jadaliyya*, 18 November 2015 (online), http://www.jadaliyya.com/Details/32715/New-Wars-and-Autonomous-Self-Defense.

———. "Pornografik Devlet-Erotik Direniş: Kürt Erkek Bedenlerinin Genel Ekonomisi." In *Erkek Millet Asker Millet—Türkiye'de Militarizm, Milliyetçilik, Erkek(Lik)Ler*, edited by Nurseli Yeşim Sünbüloğlu, 513–537. Istanbul: İletişim, 2013.

———. "Self-Defense as a Revolutionary Practice in Rojava or How to Unmake the State." *South Atlantic Quarterly* 115, no. 1 (2016): 197–210.

Van Bruinessen, Martin. *Agha, Shaikh and the State: The Social and Political Structures of Kurdistan*. London: Zed Books, 1992.

———. *Kurds and Identity Politics*. London: I. B. Tauris, 2010.

Verdery, Katherine. *The Vanishing Hectare: Property and Value in Postsocialist Transylvania*. Ithaca: Cornell University Press, 2004.

Verdery, Katherine, and Caroline Humphrey, eds. *Property in Question: Value Transformation in the Global Economy*. Oxford: Berg, 2004.

Visweswaran, Kamala. "Introduction: Everyday Occupations." In *Everyday Occupations: Experiencing Militarism in South Asia and the Middle East*, edited by Kamala Visweswaran, 1–28. Philadelphia: University of Pennsylvania Press, 2013.

Watts, Nicole. *Activists in Office: Kurdish Politics and Protest in Turkey*. Washington DC: Washington University Press, 2010.

———. "Re-considering State-Society Dynamics in Turkey's Kurdish South-East." *European Journal of Turkish Studies* (online), 10 (2009), https://journals.openedition.org/ejts/4196

Weizman, Eyal. *Hollow Land: Israel's Architecture of Occupation*. London: Verso, 2007.

Wilson, Richard A. "Anthropological Studies of National Reconciliation Processes." *Anthropological Theory* 3, no. 3 (2003): 367–387.

Yadırgı, Veli. *Politucal Economy of Kurds of Turkey: From the Otoman Empire to the Turkish Republic*. Cambridge: Cambridge University Press, 2016.

Yalçın-Heckmann, Lale. *Tribe and Kinship Among the Kurds*. Frankfurt am Main: Peter Lang, 1991.

———. "Kürt Aşiretleri, Aşiret Liderleri Ve Global Süreçler: Hakkari'de Oramari Örnegi." *Toplum ve Bilim* 84 (2000): 172–188.

Yeğen, Mesut. "The Kurdish Peace Process in Turkey: Genesis, Evolution and Prospects." In *Global Turkey in Europe*, edited by Senem Aydın-Düzgit, Daniela Huber, Meltem Müftüler-Baç, E. Fuat Keyman, Nathalie Tocci, 1–15. Istanbul: Stiftung Mercator, Institut Affari International, Istanbul Policy Center, 2015.

———. "The Kurdish Question in Turkey: Denial to Recognition." In *Nationalism and Politics in Turkey: Political Islam, Kemalism and the Kurdish Issue*, edited by Marlies Casier and Joost Jongerden, 65–85. London: Routledge, 2010.

———. *Son Kürt İsyanı*. Istanbul: İletisim, 2016.

———. "Turkish Nationalism and the Kurdish Question." *Ethnic and Racial Studies* 30, no. 1 (2007): 119–151.

Yıldırım, Umut. "Editorial—an Uprising on the Verge of Comparison." Hot Spots, *Cultural Anthropology* (online), 2013, https://culanth.org/fieldsights/410-editorial-an-uprising-on-the-verge-of-comparison.

———. "Militant Experts: A Study of the Transformation of the Revolutionary Self in Diyarbakır, Turkey." PhD diss., Cambridge University, 2010.

Yörük, Erdem, and Hişyar Özsoy. "Shifting Forms of Turkish State Paternalism Toward the Kurds: Social Assistance as 'Benevolent' Control." *Dialectical Anthropology* 37, no. 1 (2013): 153–158.

Yüksel, Ayşe Seda. "Rescaled Localities and Redefined Class Relations: Neoliberal Experience in South-east Turkey." *Journal of Balkan and Near Eastern Studies* 13, no. 4 (2011): 433–455.

Zencirci, Gizem. "Civil Society's History: New Constructions of Ottoman Heritage by the Justice and Development Party in Turkey." *European Journal of Turkish Studies* (online), 19 (2014), https://journals.openedition.org/ejts/5076.

Zengin, Aslı. "Cemile Çağırga: A Girl Is Freezing Under State Fire." *Jadaliyya*, 17 September 2015 (online), http://www.jadaliyya.com/Details/32470.

INDEX

Acar, İsa, 101–102, *103*, 104–105; cadastral survey and, 120, 202n2 (Epilogue); citizenship economy and, 122–123; daily struggle against gift-debt economy, 127–130; in Germany (Hamburg), 118, 181; on indebtedness and Syriac–Kurd relationship, 120–121; petitions to the Turkish state, 125–127; Sayfo and family of, 109–111, 130; in Scotland and Australia, 113–114, 130; as student at Mor Gabriel Monastery, 112; village guard (*korucubaşı*) and, 124–127, 147

actor-network theory, 26

Agamben, Giorgio, 20

agency, 15, 26, 29, 195n8; limits of, 100; property and, 24–25; of ruined stone buildings, 67–68

aghas [ağas] (Kurdish tribal leaders), 102, 108, 124, 128–129; cash gifts as protection fees to, 120, 121; extended families of, 125; Mor Gabriel land dispute and, 134, 148; sovereignty and, 116. *See also* Çelebi Agha

AKP [Adalet ve Kalkınma Partisi] (Justice and Development Party), 10–13, 108, 180, 182; Compensation Law and, 151; diasporic Syriacs' property/cultural rights and, 122; electoral losses (2015), 171; Gezi Park protests and, 33–34; heritage-construction-tourism business and, 53–58, *56*; Mor Gabriel land dispute and, 138, 144; "neoliberal multiculturalism" and, 39–40, 43; urban renewal projects of, 36, 39; Erdoğan, Recep Tayyip, 10, 12, 34, 131–132

Anti-Terror Law (1991), 151, 155, 157, 165

Apocu Fedailer (Apoist Team of Self-Sacrifice), 172

appropriation, 5, 15, 42, 48, 71; as dispossession, 6; diverse acts of, 24; heritage-making ventures and, 54; re-appropriation, 31, 41; as state-engineered fantasy, 18

Arabic language, xiii, xxii

Arabs, ix, xiii, 78, 191, 197n13; AKP supporters, 190; Compensation Law and, 153; departure of Arab families from Mardin, 175; in early history of Mardin, 44; Haverki–Dekşuri division and, 200n5; local elites/notables, xv, 62; in Mardin city, xii, 4; "neoliberal multiculturalism" and, 39–40; participation in massacres (1915), 48; PKK-Turkish Armed Forces conflict and, 3, 179–180; state discourse of multiculturalism and, 52; votes for pro-Kurdish party (HDP), 171

Aramaic language, xiv, xxii, 43, 46, 114; Surayt (neo-Aramaic) language, xxii

archaeological excavations, xi, 85, 181

architecture/architects, xii, 4, 45, 55, 80, 100; diggers and, 73, 93, 95, 100; heritage and, 51, 79, 80; historical architecture of Old City, 44; Jewish and Christian architectural styles, 93, 95; neo-Syriac, 117, 118; restoration and, 64, 77; Sarkis Lole, 37, 177, 197n6; valis (provincial governors) and, 59. *See also* stone buildings/houses, of Old City

Aretxaga, Begoña, 18, 19

Armbruster, Heidi, 108
Armenian Catholic Foundation, 69, 77,
    79–81
Armenian churches, 45, 69; Surp Hosep,
    48; Surp Kevork (Red Church), 49,
    77–81
Armenian genocide (1915), xiv, xv, xviii, 8,
    172, 194n4; abandoned properties and,
    46–47; centenary of, 39, 81; diggers and,
    98, 100; life in aftermath of, 35; transit of
    deportees through Mardin, 45
Armenians: absence of, xviii, 52, 60, 80;
    Catholic community, 46, 69, 197n13;
    confiscated properties of, 47–49; in early
    history of Mardin, 43, 44; forced converts
    to Islam, xxi; official recognition as
    minority, 134; pre-1915 residence in
    Mardin, 35, 37, 38; Shemsis and, 194n1;
    stone houses formerly owned by, 63, 64,
    95–96; Armenian Secret Army for the
    Liberation of Armenia, 134
Artuqid, principality of, 44, 53
Assyrians, 14, 200n5; nationalist activism
    and, 113, 117, 133, 194n3; Sayfo and
    identity of, 106. See also Syriacs

Balkan Wars (1912), 45
Balyoz trials, 196n16
Batti, Alike, 110
Benjamin, Walter, 169
Bennett, Jane, 25
Berlant, Lauren, 28–29, 68–69
Bieberstein, Alice von, 98
Bilge Köyü event (2010), 201n7
blood feuds, xv, 10, 48, 52, 82, 182
Bourgois, Philippe, 14
Bruinessen, Martin van, 200n5
built environment, xi, 25, 27, 62; belief in
    jinn and, 7; concretization of, 50; heritage-
    making ventures and, 41; Historical
    Transformation Project and, 59; of Old
    City, 57; ruination and, 42. See also stone
    buildings/houses, of Old City

Butler, Judith, 21–22
Byzantine Empire, 43, 44, 107

cadastral courts, 31, 131, 137, 138, 143
cadastral surveys, 6–7, 24, 31, 117–119,
    129, 189; cadastral registration, 109; cash
    gifts as protection fees and, 121; Mor
    Gabriel land dispute and, 138, 144,
    145, 148
Çelebi, Süleyman, 144
Çelebi Agha, 110, 136–138, 141, 144
cemeteries, 70, 173–174; Armenian and
    Syriac, 49; jinn in, 85, 93, 99; for PKK
    guerrillas, 171
Chaldean Church Foundation, 37
Chaldeans, 44, 46, 114, 197n13
Chechens, 48, 197n14
Christianity, 43, 44, 194n1; Armenian
    churches, 45, 48, 49, 69, 77; Catholic
    Capuchin mission, 45; Protestant mission,
    45; Syriac Christian Church, 107, 189;
    Syriac churches, 45, 48, 49
Christians, 66, 128; architectural style and,
    95; cooperation with Muslims in digging,
    75–76; jinn as, 89, 99; lack of ethnic
    signifier for, 78; Nestorian, 44, 107;
    population figures for Mardin, 197n13,
    198n15; Reform Edict (1856) and, 45.
    See also Armenians; Syriacs
Circassians, 197n14
citizenship, Turkish, 47, 104; limits of, 5;
    Syriacs in diaspora and, 117, 118, 121–123;
    wealth income tax and, 200n4
Collins, John, 40
Committee of Union and Progress (İttihat
    ve Terakki Partisi), 47
Committee of Wise Persons (Akil İnsanlar
    Heyeti), 12
Compensation Law (2004), 32, 149–153;
    access to state resources without justice,
    158–164; compensation recovery cases,
    32, 164–170; damage assessment
    commissions and, 153–157

complicity, 18, 23, 52; fetishization of the state and, 19; "gray zone" and, 15–16; treasure hunting/digging and, 98; village guards and, 2

Court of Cassation, 131, 145, 146

"Cruel Optimism" (Berlant, 2010), 68–69

cultural assets (kültürel varlık), 50, 56, 63, 77

curfews, 13, 174, 175, 180, 184, 187, 188

Darıcı, Haydar, 187

Das, Veena, 20, 23

debt/indebtedness, xi, 24, 127–130; bribery and, 120; cash transactions and, 120–122, 188; diggers and, 71, 87; dispossession and, 6; "generation in debt," 187; jinn and generation of, 24; law as exercise of state power and, 21; property confiscation and, 48; reparative justice transformed into, 150, 166–170; Syriac–Kurd relationship and, 32, 120–121, 127–130; Syriacs in position of perennial debtors, 31, 104

delirio, xvi–xviii, xx–xxii

democratic autonomy, 172–173, 183, 188

democratization package (demokrasi paketi), ix, xi, 131, 146

Deyrulzafaran Monastery, 53, 108

Directorate of National Real Estate (Milli Emlak Müdürlüğü), 92

displacement, xiv, 14, 31, 104; of Armenians, 45; context of, 105–107; forced evacuation of villages, 116; of Kurdish villagers, 6; persistent traces of, 42, 95; PKK–Turkish Armed Forces conflict and, 8; as state-engineered project, 5, 9; of Syriacs, 102, 107

dispossession, 5–8, 25, 104, 147, 190; category of minority and, 6; digging as act of, 68; fragmented history of, 42; state violence and, 150; valis (provincial governors) as agents of, 71

Diyarbakır, city of, xx, xxi, 43, 96, 177; Elçi killed in, 175; Sur neighborhood, 54

dreams/dreaming: diggers and, 68, 76, 90, 91; dream narratives and history, 84

Elçi, Tahir, 175

Erdoğan, Recep Tayyip, 10, 12, 34, 131–132; AKP electoral losses (2015) and, 171; Mor Gabriel land dispute and, 146

Ergenekon trials, 196n16

ethnicity, 96, 190; culture and, 52, 53; multiethnic character of Mardin, 98; nationalism and, 17, 133; social class and, 62

Europa Nostra, 80, 81

European Court of Human Rights (ECHR): Compensation Law and, 150–152, 155, 158, 161, 163, 164, 168; Mor Gabriel land dispute and, 131, 146

European Investment Fund Institute, 80

European Union (EU), 56, 160; "cultural diversity turn" and, 54; endangered landmarks in, 80; funding for heritage and tourism projects, 38–39, 57, 58; Mor Gabriel land dispute and, 132; Turkish state's accession process to, 1, 10, 39, 135, 151

everyday life, 11, 15, 18, 178; formation of the self and, 23; haunted by transgenerational memory of violence, 31; heritage and, 62; structured around conflict, 152, 154

exception, state of, 20–22

Federation of Socialist Youth Association, 172

Franquesa, Jaume, 40

Gaunt, David, 197n14, 198n15

general amnesty (1928), 47

Germany, ix, xviii, 102, 118, 185, 186

Gezi Park protests (Istanbul, 2013), 33–34

Graeber, David, 168

Greeks, 107, 112, 134

Gülen Movement (Gülen Hareketi), 14

haunting, 18, 36, 99, 107; possession distinguished from, 85; temporalities and, 19 heritage, xi, xx, 10, 74, 75, 148, 190; AKP government and, 53–58; cultural heritage experts, 7; destruction and dispossession after 1915 massacres, 46; diggers and, 100; "heritage assemblage," 67; multiculturalism and, 39; states of exception and, 40–41

Hernández, Marie Theresa, xvi

Historical Transformation Project (Tarihi Dönüşüm Projesi), 37, 38, 40, 58–61; houses registered as cultural assets, 63; restoration of stone houses and, 64; vali (provincial governor) and, 81

hodjas (intermediaries for jinn), 86, 88–89, 92

honor crimes, 52, 157, 201n7

human rights activists, 1, 135, 164

Human Rights Association (İnsan Hakları Derneği), 163

Humphrey, Caroline, 20

identity, xxi, 75, 117, 194n2; cruel optimism and, 29; ethnic, xx, 74, 132, 133, 201n2; identity politics, 15, 33, 190; Muslim, 85; religious, 132, 133, 201n2; separate Kurdish identity, 9; Syriac-Assyrian, 106, 108, 113, 133, 148, 194n3; Turkification of, 6; Turkish national identity, 9

inheritance, renunciation of (reddi miras), 167

inheritance law (miras hukuku), 166

Iraq, xii, 47, 107

ISIS (Islamic State of Iraq and Syria), xii, 13, 172

Islam, 43, 45–47, 83, 94

Islamist Free Cause Party (Hür Dava Partisi), xii

Jansen, Stef, 26, 105

Jews, 4, 44, 107, 197n13; architectural style and, 93, 95; jinn as, 99; official recognition as minority, 134; old Jewish neighborhood, 82

jinn [Turkish: cinler] (spirits), xx, 7, 26, 83, 190; as guardians of treasure in stone houses, xviii, 66, 70, 91–100; materiality of the everyday and, 23–24; mentioned in the Quran, 84, 94; narratives of encounters with, 85–86; possession by, 85–86, 199n3; pre-Islamic origins of, 84, 85; treasure hunters and, 86–87, 91–98

Kafarbe, village of, 137–139, 194n5; departure of Syriacs from, 133; map, x; Syriac-Kurdish relations in, 140

Kasımıye Maadrasa, 53

Kleinman, Arthur, 23

Kobane, Syria, xii, 13, 172, 179, 183

Kohn, Eduardo, 25–26

Kurdish conflict, xv, xvii, 6; democratization packages, 131; history of, 8–14; Kurdish uprisings in early years of Turkish Republic, 8, 15, 47, 108; literature on causes and effects of, 194n2; Kurdish opening (Kürt açılımı), 11, 56. See also PKK–Turkish Armed Forces conflict

Kurdish language, xiii, xxii, 114, 175; banned by Turkish state, 9; mixed with Turkish, 1; Zaza dialect, 176

Kurds, ix, xiii, 6, 78, 191, 197n13; blood feuds among villagers, xv, 10; Compensation Law and, 153, 158–164; as diggers/treasure hunters, 82–83; elected representatives, 13, 14; elites, 62; Gezi Park protests and, 34; Haverkis and Dekşuris, 110–112, 114, 136, 200n5; integration into urban consumer lifestyle, xvii; living in formerly Armenian-owned houses, 95–96; in Mardin city, xiii, 4; "neoliberal multiculturalism" and, 40; Newroz celebration and Kurdish identity, 202n3 (chap. 6); participation in massacres (1915), 8, 48; PKK guerrillas sheltered by, 3; state of emergency and, xv; state discourse of multiculturalism and, 52; support for mainstream Turkish or Islamic parties, 17; in Syria, xii; tribal system and leaders, 44, 45, 110, 200n5; in village guards, 2, 3; votes for pro-Kurdish party (HDP), 171. *See also* aghas [ağas]; Syriac–Kurdish relations

Lambek, Michael, 7
land confiscation, 14, 21, 41, 102
Land Registry and Cadastre Directorates, 135
Latour, Bruno, 25
Lausanne Treaty (1923), xv, 46, 107, 134, 200n3
Law of Obligations (Borçlar Hukuku), 165
lawyers, xii, 7, 123; cash transactions and, 120; Compensation Law and, 150–161; economy of reparation and, 164; from EU countries, 132; human rights lawyers, 151, 163, 166, 202n6; Kurdish, 144; land registration and, 108; petitions submitted to, 102, 104
Lazzarato, Maurizio, 168–169
Lebanon, 107
Lebling, Robert, 84
Levi, Primo, 15–16
Löfving, Stefffan, 105
Lole, Sarkis, 37, 177, 197n6

Mardin, city of, xi, 4; architectural heritage, 4; Armenian population (before 1915), 35, 37, 38; bid for UNESCO World Heritage Site status, 4, 38–39, 51–53, 60, 71, 79, 189; Bienal art exhibition, xii, xx, 53, 172; branding of, 53; as "city of spies," xv; cosmopolitan makeup of, xv, xvi; experience of delirio in, xvi–xviii, xx–xxii; general elections (2015) in, 171; half of Christian population forcefully disappeared (1915), 45–46; history and ruination in, 42–51; location on maps, *x*, *xix*; as multilingual city, xxii; Muslim and Christian population figures, 44, 45–46, 197–198n15, 197n13; original (*orijinal*) inhabitants, xiv; remaining five Armenian families, 48; Savurkapı neighborhood, 194n1; as sole ethnolinguistically mixed city in region, xiii, xv; spatial transforma-

tion of, 30; state of emergency after coup attempt (2016), 178; stone architecture of, 51–52; urban lifestyle in post-emergency period, xii; as wartime headquarters, 175. *See also* New City; Old City
Mardin province, Turkey, ix, 31; Kurdish towns and villages, 47; maps, *x*, *xix*; place-names in, 193n2
materiality, 24, 188; affective, 67; "nonhuman actants" and, 25; spirituality and, 7, 23; subjectivity and, 24
MAYA-DER association, 171
memory, xx, 61; of the Armenian genocide, xv; jinn and, 84; of the Sayfo, 32; spaces of death and, 16; of violence, xiv, 23, 31, 102
Mhallamis, 48–51; Haverki–Dekşuri division and, 200n5; as migrants from villages of Midyat, 198n21
Midyat, town of, xviii, 104, 112, 199n1 (chap. 4); cadastral surveys/court and, 118, 120, 135–136, 144, 145, 202n2 (Epilogue); Çelebi Agha's power base in, 136; map, *x*, *xix*; Mor Gabriel Monastery land dispute and, 131; Syriac Association, 108
militarism, 5, 16, 24, 29, 188, 190
Ministry of Culture, Turkish, 39, 51, 63, 81
Mittermaier, Amira, 84
Monuments Council (Anıtlar Kurulu), 59
Mor Gabriel Monastery, land dispute around, 5, 31, 112, 131–133, 135–138, 194n5, 201n1 (chap. 5); cadastral survey and, 131, 137–139, 143; history of, 139–141; monastery location (map), *x*; social and political life of Mor Gabriel, 133–135; wall of monastery and, 143–148
muhtar (village head), 1, 3–4, 124, 137, 138, 142, 143
multiculturalism, 5, 16, 135; neoliberal, 39–40, 61, 190; as reinvented tradition, 53; state discourse of, 52, 74
Muslims, xiii, xiv, 45; Armenians protected and hidden by, 95, 96; atrocities against Christian neighbors, xv; cooperation

Muslims (continued)
with Christians in digging, 75–76;
immigrant populations, 48; jinn as, 89,
94, 99; legend about origin of Mardin
and, 43; as majority population, 9,
197n13; state repressive measures against,
47; tribal families, 95, 197n14. *See also*
Arabs; Kurds; Mhallamis; Turks

National Intelligence Organization, 12
Nationalist Movement Party (Miliyetçi
Hareket Partisi), xii
Navaro-Yashin, Yael, 18, 26, 67
neoliberalism, 5, 11, 16, 50; accumulation
logic of, 168; AKP government and, 33,
34, 39, 53; materiality and, 25
New City [Mardin] (Yenişehir), 35, 51, 71,
79, 193n2; concretization of, 55;
construction of, 50; housing market in,
63; Mardin Houses project, 55
Neyzi, Leyla, 187
nostalgia, 41, 95

Öcalan, Abdullah, 1, 10, 11, 13, 172, 183–184
Old City [Old Mardin] (Eski Mardin), 30,
35, 57–58, 66, 193n2; geography of, 43;
historical architecture of, 44; images from
1920s, 38; Mardin castle, 44, 49, 53, 70,
197n11; New Road (Yeni Yol) and, 50;
Republican Street restoration project,
35–36, 36, 38, 49; ruined and abandoned
spaces of, 50–51; tunnel system, 70,
73–74. *See also* stone buildings, of
Old City
optimism, cruel, 27–30, 68–69, 98–100, 189
Oslo process, 11
Ottoman Empire, xv, 42, 84; dissolution of,
5, 8; Mardin taken over by, 44; Reform
Edict (1856), 45; sovereign violence of,
107; Tanzimat reforms, 44–45
Özcoşar, İbrahim, 198n22
Özdem, Filiz, 198n22
Özgen, Neşe, 200n5

Pandey, Gyanendra, 105, 132
Patriotic Revolutionary Youth Movement
(Yurtsever Devrimci Gençlik Hareketi), 173
Peace and Democracy Party (Barış ve
Demokrasi Partisi), 144
peace process/peace talks, ix, 11–13, 131;
breakdown in, 13; collapse of, 189; elections
and, 171; political mobilization and, 182
People's Democracy Party (HDP), 171, 173,
178, 179, 182–184. *See also* pro-Kurdish
party
PKK [Partiya Karkeren Kurdistane]
(Kurdistan Workers' Party), xi, xviii, 14,
50, 123, 159; burial of dead militants, 169,
171; Compensation Law and, 155, 165;
democratic autonomy and, 183;
formation of, 113; as leading party for
Kurdish resistance movement, 158;
martyrs of, 182; as Marxist-Leninist
national liberation organization, 9;
militants killed in fighting, xii; political
and social authority in Kurdish areas, 10;
Repentance Law and, xi; sovereignty and,
188–189; state of emergency and, ix,
193n1; Syriac villagers and, 114–115;
unilateral cease-fire declared by, 1, 10;
village evacuations and, 160, 162; village
guard system and, 110; violence of, 187;
withdrawal from cities (2016), 174
PKK–Turkish Armed Forces conflict, xx,
31, 32, 121, 149, 151; cease-fires, 11;
dispossession and, 6; duration of, 8;
suspension of, 30; village guards and, 2;
villages evacuated during, 36; Kurdish
tribal system and, 200n5; Mor Gabriel
land dispute and, 134; Syriac–Kurdish
relations and, 140; Syriac villagers
displaced by (1993), 102, 108, 109; revival
of the conflict, 178
Polatel, Mehmet, 46, 47
Poole, Deborah, 20
post-emergency period, xvii, 1, 188, 200n3;
call for return of Syriacs in diaspora,

116–118; complexity of life in, xi; end of, 32; spatial transformation of Mardin in, 30

poverty, 7, 52, 113, 130, 134, 140; development projects and, 10; state policies to alleviate, 22; treasure hunting/digging and, 69

precariousness, 21–22

pro-Kurdish party, xii, 7, 57, 125–126, 159, 175, 187; Compensation Law and, 161, 165; Mor Gabriel land dispute and, 144; municipalities run by, 11; sovereignty and, 188–189. *See also* People's Democracy Party (HDP)

property rights, 100, 137, 148

Reconciliation Committee, 59

Repentance Law, xi

restoration, xi, 7, 10, 60

Rojas-Pérez, Isaias, 189

Rojava, in Kurdish region of Syria, 13, 171, 187

Routine Violence (Pandey, 2006), 105

ruination, 41–42, 67, 190; cruel optimism and, 99; digging as ongoing form of, 65, 68; Historical Transformation Project and, 60; multiple layers of, 43–51; personal narratives of, 70

rumors about buried treasure in houses, 30, 66, 86, 87, 90; about evacuation of villages, 160, 161; about land disputes, 136–137; about property values, 59; about responsibility for village evacuations, 160; about sale prices of stone houses, 63; Historical Transformation Project and, 57

Sayfo (massacres of Syriacs, 1915), xiv, xvii, 8, 15, 31, 128; dispossession in aftermath of, 46; memory of, 32; Mor Gabriel monks and priests killed, 140, 142; movement to gain official recognition for, 116, 117; narratives of survivors and witnesses, 114; outmigration of Syriacs and, 133; Syriac diaspora and memory of, 199n2 (chap. 4); in Tur Abdin villages, 109–110

Scheper-Hughes, Nancy, 14

Schmitt, Carl, 20

secrecy, public, xv–xvi, xvii, 19, 71, 98, 125

sheikhs, as intermediaries for jinn, 86, 87

Shemsis, 4, 44, 194n1

smuggling, 1–3, 87, 101

sovereignty, 20–22, 44, 181

state of emergency, Agamben's notion of, 40

state of emergency [*olağanüstü hal*] (OHAL), ix, 4, 193n1; atrocities and disappearances during, 21, 196n16; end of, 1, 10; human rights violations during, 151; sudden house searches and arrests during, xv; Turkish state strategies of, 9

Stewart, Kathleen, 68

Stoler, Ann, 41–42

stone buildings/houses, of Old City, 55, 58, 60, 61, 66, 180; as abandoned sites, 56; absent Armenians and, 62; as backdrop for films and TV series, 52; Bienal art exhibitions in, xii, xx; concrete extensions built onto, 72; demolition of, 49; diggers' knowledge of, 70–71; haunted treasure in, 29; history of Mardin and, 44; jinn as guardians of treasure in, xviii, 66, 91–98; Kurdish and Mhallami migrants in, 49; as nonhuman actants, 27; qualities of stone, 62–63; registered as cultural assets, 50, 68, 75; restoration of, 62, 63, 72–73; as ruins, 37, 42, 53; rumors/fantasies of buried treasure in, 30, 66, 86, 87, 90; sold at high prices, 63; spatial/social segregation and, 51; as symbolic emblems of heritage, 30, 63; walls covered with cement, 64, *65*, 75

subjectivity, 105, 191; encounters with jinn and, 84, 100; propertied, 24–27; violence and, 67, 194n2

Suruç bombing (2015), 172, 173

Sweden, ix, xvii, xviii, xxi, 102

Syria, 43, 45, 47; Armenians' flight to, 96; flight of Kurds accused by tribunals to, 47; Kurdish region of, xii, 13; Sayfo survivors in, 107, 109–110; smuggling of goods across border with, 1; war in, 179

Syriac–Kurdish relations, 31, 109, 111, 116–117, 119; coexistence, xvii, 117, 125, 126, 128, 134, 150; Syriacs' indebtedness to Kurds, 32, 120–121, 127–130. *See also* Mor Gabriel Monastery, land dispute around

Syriacs, ix, xiii–xv, 4, 44, 191; Catholic community, 46, 51; in Mardin city, xii; Mardinites exempted from deportation (1915), 46, 107; "neoliberal multicultural-ism" and, 39–40; Orthodox community, 46, 51; participation in massacres (1915), 48; returns from diasporic exile, 107–108; self-designation terms used by, 193–194n3; Shemsis and, 194n1; state discourse of multiculturalism and, 52; villagers displaced by armed conflict, *103*; votes for pro-Kurdish party (HDP), 171. *See also* Assyrians; Sayfo (massacres of Syriacs, 1915)

Syriacs, in diaspora, xviii, xxii, 7, 106, 114; forced hospitality to cadastral officers, 121; in Germany (Hamburg), 109, 118, 123, 127; memory of Sayfo and, 199n2 (chap. 4); Mor Gabriel land dispute and, 132, 133; political lobbies of, 126; returnees in post-emergency period, 116–118; in Sweden, xvii, 127; in Switzerland, 117

Syrian refugees, 34, 55, 180

Taussig, Michael, ix, xv, 16, 18

Temizöz, Colonel Cemal, 196n16

terror events (*terör olayları*), xii

"terrorism," 3, 155, 164

terror's talk, ix, xii, 4, 32, 182

Thiranagama, Sharika, 106, 196n13

Thrift, Nigel, 68

TOKI [Toplu Konut İdaresi] (Housing Development Association), 37, 54, 174

tourism, xi, xii, xx, 11, 179; in Old City of Mardin, 35, 80; stone buildings restored by the state for, 63

treasure hunters/diggers, 6, 24, 71, 76, 87, 180–181, 190; frequency and visibility of, 65; hodjas and, 88–92; jinn and, xviii, 86–87, 91–98; limits of optimism for, 98–100; motives, 70, 90; Muslims and Christians working together, 75–76; "ordinary affects" and, 68; public activity of, 65–66

tribal families/leaders, 7, 31, 32, 44, 49, 188–189

tribunals of independence (istiklal makhemeleri), 47, 198n18

Tur Abdin region, 106, 107, 193n2, 199n1 (chap. 4); history of Sayfo in, 109, 142; isolation and remoteness of, 112; map, *x*

Turkey Council of KCK [Koma Ciwaken Kurdistan] (Union of Communities in Kurdistan), 11, 12

Turkish Armed Forces, xi, 2; Compensation Law and, 164–166; evacuation of villages and, 160; PKK-affiliated urban militias in conflict with, 13; Syriac and Armenian churches appropriated by, 48. *See also* PKK–Turkish Armed Forces conflict

Turkish Intelligence Service, 11

Turkish language, xiii, xxi–xxii, 1, 114, 185, 186

Turkish leftist movement, 9

Turkishness, xxi, 9

Turkish state, ix, 22, 49, 53, 117; abandoned Armenian properties liquidated by, 47–48; ambivalence toward recognizing losses of 1915 massacres, 80; Arab notable families empowered by, 47; assimilation policies, 8, 9, 17; Council of State (Danıştay), 123, 156, 167; courts, 131–132, 144, 145, 150, 155, 165, 167, 202n6; cultural heritage of Mardin and, 4; debt-producing mechanisms and, 150, 188; Deed and Cadastral Department, 109; "double edge sword of protection and violence," 152, 160; ethnography of, 18; European Union accession process of, 1, 10, 39, 135, 151; Forest Department, 144;

formation and consolidation of, 5, 6; Kurdish society permeated by, 158–159; military coup (1980), 50, 108; military coup attempt (2016), 14, 177, 178, 190; NATO membership of, 49; as omnipresent entity in Kurdish region, 16–17; response to democratic autonomy, 173; sovereign violence of, 107, 179; Treasury Department, 145, 147, 165, 167; War of Independence, 8, 198n18. *See also* Turkish Armed Forces

Turks, 4, 44, 113, 197n13

Turoyo (neo-Aramaic) language, xxii

UNESCO, 52, 56, 79–81

Üngör, Uğur Ümit, 46, 47, 197n14

United Nations: Development Program, 4; High Commissioner for Human Rights, 151

Upper Mardin (Yukarı Mardin). *See* Old City

urban renewal (*kentsel dönüşüm*), 36–38

vali [pl. *valiler*] (provincial governor), 3, 4, 6, 69; Compensation Law and, 150, 153, 156; Historical Transformation Project and, 57, 59; international capital and, 71; treasure hunters/diggers and, 92

village guards (korucubaşılar), xi, xii, 2, 7, 162, 181; collaboration with Çelebi Agha, 136, 141; Compensation Law and, 155; haunted by subversive power of Kurdish rebels, 19; introduction of system, 9; Kurdish tribal system and, 110; as landlords and warlords, 115–116, 124; return of Syriacs in diaspora and, 118; as targets of the PKK, 140–141; in Zaz village, 102, 109, 123–125

violence, 8, 14, 26, 65, 131–132, 168; Compensation Law and, 169; context of, 105–107; continuum of, 14–16, 31, 106, 196n13; dispossession and, 5, 6; endless cycles of, 191; experience of, 26, 154, 156;

158, 159; "gray zone" of, 15–16, 22; historical legacy of, 31; human rights violations and, 151; law established through, 20–21; "lawfare" and, 146; legal and nonlegal means of, 178; material ghost of, 167; materiality of destruction, 188; means and ends of, 181–182; memory of, 23, 31; the ordinary and, 22–24; of the PKK, 187; in postconflict settings, 189; repressive legal policies and, 11; resources provided in compensation for, 159; resumption of (July 2015), ix; ruination and, 42; in shared sacred and daily spaces, 133; shift of war theater from mountains to towns/cities, 172; state sovereignty and, 107, 179; subjectivity and, 67, 194n2; Turkish state's "double edge sword of protection and violence," 152; by village guards, 123, 201n7

violent peace, xi–xiii, 14, 21–22, 29, 40, 147

Watts, Nicole, 17

wealth income tax, 108, 200n4

Weizman, Eyal, 105

World War I, 37, 45

Yalçın-Heckmann, Lale, 200n5

Yazidis, xii, 4, 111, 200n5

YPG [Yekîneyên Parastina Gel] (People's Protection Forces), 13

YPJ [Yekîneyên Parastina Jin] (Women's Protection Forces), 13

Yüksel, Ayşe Seda, 54

Zaz, village of, 31, 101, *103*, 194n5, 199n1 (chap. 4); Compensation Law and, 122; Haverki–Dekşuri division in, 111–112; map, *x*; PKK–Turkish Armed Forces conflict in, 114–116; Syriac diaspora from, 104, 109, 118; Syriac villagers displaced from (1993), 109

ACKNOWLEDGEMENTS

This book has taken many years to write and I have many people to thank. I am indebted most to my friends from Mardin and Sweden. They opened up their intimate spaces—rooms, homes, and villages—for over a decade and shared their views, memories, and experiences about life and death with doubt, patience, affection, and care. I was given the courage to return to their places whenever I got lost in their narratives, whenever I got lost with my own life. They taught me the art of patience, how to listen to words and silence, and how to deal with the deep sense of loss and injustice. The times I spent in Mardin and Sweden have been the most inspiring, explosive, uneasy, thoughtful moments of my life; they have followed me in my journey between different countries and continents.

In Mardin, Baranlar became a family for me. On each visit, they shared new sources of hope, connections, and threads to understand life in and beyond Mardin. The friendship of Cansel and Mehmet Baran has been invaluable at each and every step of my life. Türkan Elik, İsmail Elik, and Nilüfer Elik Yılmaz shared their experiences, times, and spaces for over a decade. They interpreted with me all the delicate edges of tragedies of life in the region. They helped me to make sense of whatever had frozen my mind and heart. Our connection in words and silence has always been an anchor for me. From the very first day we met, my friend Özlem believed in what I had set out to achieve. She never gave up thinking with me about the future possibilities of life. Eser, Safiye, and Ceren opened up my horizons in our short but intense encounters. Selahattin Bilirer taught me how to talk about the most irreconcilable differences in the most genuine way. İsa Acar—as is clear in the book—shared with me all the predicaments he faced in attempting to return to the region to make a home. He taught me how to relearn to live with the ghosts from the past. Yakup Gabriel showed me the most remote corners of the Tur Abdin region. İskender de Boso shared his reflections and memories of the complicated histories. Fırat Ulaş Tur always greeted me with enthusiasm to restart from where we had left our previous conversations; he also opened up space for our endless talks about past memories. Yektanurşin Duyan carried her unique patience, deep curiosity, precious labor, and thoughtful knowledge of the place first to our joint projects and then to what became a deeply rooted friendship. At the most unexpected times, she brought Mardin back to my life despite the temporal and spatial distances. In Sweden, Nuran, İskender, and Ayfer Önder taught me the most creative ways of making a home despite lurid memories. Their unique affection and wisdom allowed me to find ways for a deep engagement with the experience of the Syriac community in diaspora. Jan Beth-Sawoce and Feyyoz Kerimo patiently shared me the histories about the complicated processes to create a personal and collective archive for the endless search for the recognition of the loss. I am eternally grateful to all. Without their friendship, support, and faith, this book would not have been possible.

Many people in Turkey, Germany, the United Kingdom, and elsewhere have over the years inspired and supported my work. I had the unique privilege to learn my foundations in sociology and anthropology from the most dedicated scholars and teachers. Aysegül Baykan, Ferhunde Özbay, Leyla Neyzi, Dicle Koğacıoğlu have inspired me to start searching for my path in academia. Their passionate engagement with knowledge has my first source of guidance. Another crucial moment in this long journey has been my encounter with Neşe Özgen. Her friendship allowed me to make my first visits to the region and develop a long-term emotional and intellectual commitment to the place. With Neşe, I had the chance to witness pushing the limits of the visible and speakable, and to learn the acute significance of returning to places. I had the privilege to write my dissertation at the Department of Anthropology, University of Cambridge, where Yael Navaro became an immense source of inspiration for my imagination and thinking. Her mentorship and friendship had a significant impact on different stages of this work and has continued at many crucial times of our lives, leading to new ends and new beginnings. At the Max Planck Institute, in Germany, I was unconditionally looked after by Julia Eckert and Lale Yalçın-Heckmann. Julia Eckert not only shared her knowledge and critical mind when it came to thinking anthropologically through the law. She also always extended her support beyond discussion and made my life hopeful, first in Berlin and then in other places where we have walked together and talked. Lale Yalçın-Heckmann always believed in me, even when I did not. Her diligence and genuine engagement with research and training has been another source of inspiration. I am also indebted to Esra Özyurek for her guidance and friendship. Without her continuous support and her affectionate wisdom, this project would not have been completed and others would not have been started.

I am blessed with solid friendships. In Cambridge, Nolwazi Mkhwanazi, Marta Magalhães, Hadas Yaron, Umut Yıldırım, Alice von Bieberstein, and Eirini Avramopolu filled my life with joy and enthusiasm. Their critical input has always been the source of long-lasting wisdom. Our thoughtful exchanges always helped me to rethink my own existential dilemmas and my insistence in working about violence. I particularly would like to thank Umut Yıldırım for our intense conversations during the dullest winters of Cambridge; Hadas Yaron for her sisterhood; Alice von Bieberstein for her powerful words at the most significant junctions of life. I also want to thank Dina Gusejnova, Lucy Delap, and Clive Delap for turning Cambridge into one of my homes. In Germany, I would like to thank Miro Kaygalak for his unique friendship and Agnieska Pasieka, whose precious presence made my years in Halle enjoyable. My friendship with Diren Yeşil started in Istanbul, continued in Germany, and has since developed over many long phone calls. I am indebted to Diren for her insights, reflections, and thoughts, which accompanied me like a compass during my journey in the Kurdish region.

Reading groups were the most crucial components of this writing project. The first reading group that I established with Alice von Bieberstein, Eirini Avramopolu, and Erdem Evren, connecting us between Berlin, Athens, London, and Toronto, set the stage for the most illuminating times and allowed me to digest many complicated thoughts. In parallel to this virtual reading practice, we established another reading group in London, where Başak Ertür, Eray Çaylı, and Mayur Suresh provided exciting and enthusiastic exchanges. Their presence as friends and colleagues were lifesavers against the isolation that writing imposes. They reminded me of the real joy of thinking together and gave me strength to continue. I am truly grateful to them. I would also like to thank Cengiz Güneş, Naif Bezwan, Meltem Ahıska, Haydar Darıcı Nazan Üstündag, Bülent Küçük, and Hakem Al-Rustom for sharing their reflections, thoughts and visions about the long term effects of violence on our present and future. I am also thankful to Ahmet Taşğın for the intense conversations as we were witnessing the legal battles around the Mor Gabriel monastery. I have learned immensely from those genuine exchanges.

Yael Navaro, Julia Eckert, Brian Donahoe, Christian Strumpell, Esra Özyürek, Alice von Bieberstein, Seda Altuğ, Zeynep Gambetti, Joost Jongerden,

Füsun Üstel, Sharika Thrinagama, and Hakem Al-Rustom read earlier versions of the chapters in this book and contributed to their final shape with their valuable comments. Ann Laura Stoler, Elisabeth Dunn, Rosalind Morris, Valentina Napolitano, Serap Ruken Şengül, Aslı Iğsız, Caroline Osalla, Sabine Strasser, Magda Schmukalla, and Gill Anidjar shared their comments and suggestions on different sections of chapters that I presented in the form of seminars and conferences during the writing of this book. Özge Biner, Başak Ertür, and Esin Düzel read the latest versions of the chapters with patience and shared their stimulating thoughts at the most critical stages of the project. Without their gentle reminders and encouraging pushes, I would have not convinced myself that I had completed the book. I am thankful to all. I am grateful to Miro Kaygalak for his delicate work on the design of the cover and the maps as well as Seda Altuğ and İsa Acan for extending their genuine support and knowledge to complete the production of maps with accuracy. I owe a special debt to Tobias Kelly and Peter Agree for their extraordinary patience and faith for this project. I will be eternally grateful for their support.

This project would not have been possible without the support of many institutions: the Zentrum Moderne Orient, the Max Planck Institute for Social Anthropology, University of Bern, the European Research Council, and the European Institute at the London School of Economics and Political Science. A section of Chapter 5 was published in an earlier version as "Ethnographic Explorations on Past Legacies of Violence and Present Legal Struggles in Midyat, Southeastern Turkey," in *The Spatial (Re)Production of the Kurdish Issue: Multiple and Contradicting Trajectories*, edited by Zeyenep Gambetti and Joost Jongerden (London: Routledge, 2015); part of Chapter 6 was published as "The Logic of Compensation:Between the Right to Compensation and the Right to Justice in Turkey," *Humanity* 4, no. 1 (2013); part of Chapter 6 was published as "Haunted by Debt: Calculating the Cost of Loss and Violence in Turkey," *Theory and Event*, 19, no. 1 (2016).

It has always been a challenge to write in another language. I owe special thanks to Jane Tienne for her wonderful friendship, patience, care, and faith in me and my writing; to Kate Goldman for her continuous support; and to Theresa Truax-Gischler for her incredibly thoughtful, encouraging, and sensitive contribution to the completion of this project. I would also like to thank Candie Furber for her precious support during the last phase of research and writing of this book.

I owe so much to my friends and family members for all they have given and taught me. Jean and Amelie Derdoy always believed in what I did. Sevil

Serbes has been the closest witness, friend, and family for all the years that have I spent researching and writing this book. She listened to all my stories with wisdom. Cavit and Akgül Baylar, Ayşe Bircan, and Gonül Ekmekçi provided me with musical care and thoughts during my first years in London. My friends in Walthamstow have turned the busy and cloudy life of London into an amazingly enjoyable time. I would like to thank Daniel Edelstyn and Hilary Powell, as well as Tanja Pfittzner, Api Ascaso, and Magda Schmukalla for their wonderful friendship and patience with my disappearances during the writing of this book. I am also grateful to the citizens of Krashnakrovia: we never spoke in the same language and I did not have a chance to explain to them in depth about this project. But I always knew that they recognized my struggles through their own. I have always felt surrounded by their thoughts and I am thankful to them.

I am blessed for having the immense love and support of my parents, Şahin and Güler Biner, and my sister, Özge Biner. My parents were the first ones who taught us how to care for people, as well as how to trust and engage difference without fear. Without my father's encouragement, I would have never dared to start such a long intellectual journey. I am eternally grateful to him for teaching me how to run after what I want to follow in life. Without the unconditional support of my mother, I would not have been able to finish writing this book. I am indebted for her precious love and care. My sister, Özge Biner, has accompanied me through this journey as my best friend and colleague. In this long process, we went through the painful loss of our father. Her presence has been a unique source of support and inspiration in navigating life in the middle of these mysterious times of book writing. I am grateful to her for reminding me how to look after myself. I am also grateful to my parents-in-law, Manuel Arroyo Castellanos and Mary Therese Kalin, for the wonderful way in which they extend their care and love from the other side of the ocean and mountains.

I decided to write this book after my eldest daughter, Ruya Luanda, was born and wanted to finish it before the arrival of Irene Mara. Their presence made me think even harder about the value of life and gave me strength to confront with my internal reasons to follow the lives of others. Their calls to play taught me how to keep my eyes, mind, and heart wide open at all times. And Manuel. Fifteen years ago, we bumped into each other for the first time in front of the Haddon Library, Cambridge. He was on his way to the Brazilian Amazon and I was about to start my first trip in the Kurdish region. He told me that he knew about the place where I would be travelling to. He had seen the well-known film *Yol* (Road), by Yılmaz Güney, in his home city, Santiago de Chile. *Yol* has become the keyword of our life while we have continued to travel after and due to our connections with our existential homes in different continents, while we have made ours in Cambridge, Berlin, and London.

Y, gracias Manuel por todo; for inspiring me in and outside music, for showing me different paces of movement, for helping me to sharpen my thoughts, for reading over and over again different versions of this book; for encouraging me to see and push my limits, and for being such a courageous and loving compañero.